# TEN MILE INN

The Pantheon Asia Library

New Approaches to the New Asia

# TEN MILE INN

## Mass Movement in a Chinese Village

by Isabel and David Crook

Pantheon Books, New York

Library of Congress Cataloging in Publication Data

Crook, Isabel.
  Ten Mile Inn.

  (The Pantheon Asia Library)
  1. Communes (China)—Case studies.  I. Crook,
David, joint author.  II. Title.
JS7365.T45C76     334'.683'0951     78–20414
ISBN 0–394–41178–1
ISBN 0–394–73328–2 pbk.

Manufactured in the United States of America

First Edition

# Contents

## Acknowledgments

Our first debt is to the people of Ten Mile Inn, who "opened their hearts" to us; to the work team and to the group of Border Region cadres who served not only as interpreters but as fellow researchers. We also owe thanks to the Border Region Government and Party leaders who granted us the facilities needed for our work; to the Chinese and Western friends who read all or part of the original draft and gave us many helpful suggestions for correcting and improving it; and to students of the Foreign Languages Institute of Peking, who helped with the translation of documents. Finally we express special appreciation to Mary Barnett, Jeffrey Faude, and James Peck for their constant encouragement, editorial expertise, and inexhaustible energy in whipping our unwieldy manuscript into shape. Without this collective effort, the book could not have been written.

# A Note on Romanization

The system used in this book for rendering Chinese words, including names, is Hanyu Pinyin, the official Chinese system of spelling. It has the advantage of helping people who do not know Chinese to pronounce it more accurately than do other systems, most of which are misleading to the ordinary person. In Hanyu Pinyin most letters are pronounced roughly as in English or other languages using the Latin alphabet. The following are some exceptions: c is pronounced ts (as in its); o before ng rhymes with oo (as in look); q is pronounced ch (as in cheese); x as sh (as in sheep); zh as j (as in Jack); e as in her. The diphthong ao rhymes with ow (as in now). Thus Mao Tse-tung in Hanyu Pinyin is written Mao Ze-dong.

# TEN MILE INN

# —1—

# Arrival at
# Ten Mile Inn

In the middle of the civil war between the Chinese Communists and the Guomindang, we floated on a barge down the Grand Canal through no man's land and into the Liberated Areas. As we passed into these vast, scattered patches of North China, we entered a world of over 140 million people engaged in the final stages of the struggle against Jiang Jie-shi. The year was 1947, the turning point in the demise of Jiang's twenty years of corrupt and reactionary rule. Feudalism in China was collapsing, even in the smallest villages.

We quickly found that the people in the Liberated Areas had coined new words to express the ideas and circumstances of this revolutionary society. Few of them more powerfully symbolize the heart of the revolutionary process than the word "fanshen."

Literally, fanshen means "to turn the body." Freely translated, it means to get up on one's feet, stand up for one's rights, and come into one's own. For the peasant the heart of this individual and social transformation was land reform. When the Communists set out to change the traditional land relationships in China, they literally began an effort to reform all of Chinese society. To China's hundreds of millions of landless and land-poor peasants, this meant the overthrow of the omnipresent landlord yoke. It meant the acquisition for the first time of animals and houses. It was a struggle in which the peasants were urged to overcome their ancient feeling of deference and dependence and to assert themselves against those who had long oppressed them.

The Chinese speak of "dissecting a sparrow"—making a careful and thorough examination of a particular situation in order to discover the general processes at work. This is what we sought to do in one Chinese village—Ten Mile Inn. Though unique in many ways, it also served us as a microcosm for what was taking place in countless villages throughout the Liberated Areas.

3

Farmland outside Ten Mile Inn, showing terraced hillsides coated with snow.

Behind the fields are the foothills of the mountains. The least valuable farm plots were on their stony slopes.

In November 1947 we arrived at Ten Mile Inn, one of a cluster of villages forming the capital of one of the border regions which constituted the Liberated Areas. This particular region was called Jin-Ji-Lu-Yu and comprised vast borderlands of four adjoining provinces, Shanxi, Hebei, Shandong, and Hanan. It covered an area of some 80,000 square miles with a population of about 30 million. The village itself is about 275 miles southwest of Peking and 600 miles northeast of Shanghai. It straddles the major trade and transport route in the area, which connects the village to the county town of Wu An 20 miles to the east and to the city of Handan, which was a train stop along the Hankow-Peking Railway.

Ten Mile Inn stands beside the Min River. Approaching the village from the east, the old dirt road follows the riverbed, dry nine months of the year. The valley narrows and the hills rise more steeply, their lower slopes laboriously terraced, their tops eroded and bald "as a monk's pate."

From a distance there appear to be two villages rather than one. Down in the valley is the main village, or "the Street," as it is usually called; to the northeast, climbing up the side of the hills, is "the Fort." With its cobbled causeway slanting up to a massive stone gate and the backs of its stone houses rising sheer from the hillside, cut away below

(*left*) Lao Wang, an upper-middle peasant, uses a carrying pole to take compost to his fields. He was wrongly made "a struggle object" but later cleared.

(*below*) Planting millet, with a small boy leading the mule.

to form a cliff, the Fort once was a citadel from which the feudal landlords dominated the peasants in the village below.

We arrived by mule cart passing through the picturesque south gate. In bold white letters above the graceful arch was a line from a popular folk tune set to new words. "Mao Ze-dong is the great savior of the Chinese people." Other slogans lambasted Jiang Jie-shi. And on another wall was chalked up the day's edition of the "Blackboard News" copied from the official Party paper, the *People's Daily*, which always carried a simply written feature especially for this purpose.

Although the village street was part of the highway, it contained only one shop of note—the cooperative. In addition, there were a couple of inns and restaurants catering to passing travelers and peddlers, and a mutton-soup shop known far and wide as a good pull-up for carters.

All these places served as social centers. Groups of men gathered in front of them, while in gateways or other sheltered spots were

(*above*) Double gates at the north end of Ten Mile Inn. The road that ran through the gates and the lower village was called the Street.

(*right*) Three members of the Children's Corps who acted as sentries at the entrance to the village, examined travelers' road passes, and reported suspicious characters to the Ten Mile Inn Security Officer. The inscription above the gate says, "Mao Zedong is the great savior of the Chinese people."

women sitting in their own groups spinning, reeling yarn, or hanging up pieces of newly dyed cloth. Children were everywhere, adding their shrill voices to the other village sounds—the rumble of wooden-wheeled carts on the potholed street; the musical chant of doughnut peddlers; the braying of donkeys; the clang of picks and hoes intermittently striking stones up on the hillsides.

Before arriving at Ten Mile Inn, we had submitted our plan for a study of land reform in one village. While awaiting the official decision on our request, we were invited to stay in the border government guest house in Ten Mile Inn. Actually, the "guest house" was a number of rooms scattered in different villagers' homes. We slept in one, ate in another.

The village leaders and Communist Party members were told that we were foreign friends visiting the Liberated Areas. Consequently we had a free run of the village and were treated in a friendly fashion by the great majority of villagers, who took the time to answer our constant questions.

We had arrived at an eventful moment. The Communist Party of China had called a conference in September 1947 to draft an agrarian law which was to bring about the thoroughgoing reform of the feudal land system; for this, it considered, was the key to rousing the entire peasantry to enthusiasm for production and for bringing the war to a victorious conclusion. The draft law that was drawn up included instructions for carrying out its decisions in three different sets of circumstances: in old Liberated Areas where feudalism had been pretty well smashed, but where land holdings were still not equitable, democracy inadequate, and where, it was believed, many Party branches were impure (that is, leadership had fallen into the hands of landlords, rich peasants, or other "class aliens"); in "semi-old areas" where much more sweeping measures were required*; and in newly liberated areas which were not yet sufficiently consolidated to embark on fullscale land reform. To work out the detailed plans for implementing the law, the Central Committee's Party Bureau for each Border Region held a followup conference.

At the time of our arrival the Jin-Ji-Lu-Yu Border Region agrarian conference was in session. It was a lengthy session which not only worked out the practical details for carrying through the campaign, but also conducted a "self-rectification" for senior Party cadres to prepare them for leading the work of agrarian reform.

When this conference was over, we discussed our plans with the Border Region chairman. He suggested that the most valuable course for us to pursue would be to study the operations of one of the pilot "work teams" which were to be organized to carry out the conference's decisions. One of these teams was soon to start work in Ten Mile Inn, which was a typical old Liberated Areas village. We agreed that this village would be an appropriate location for our work.

There were still six weeks until the work team was due in Ten Mile Inn. So from early December until February 1948, we gathered material for a ten-year history of the village (1937–1947) and of the transformation of the feudal land system which had already been basically completed during the preceding eighteen months. Collecting the materials was the work of a team, the size and composition of which varied at different periods. Out of this collective effort with our Chinese colleagues came *Revolution in a Chinese Village*.†

* For an account of the campaign in such areas, see William Hinton, *Fanshen* (New York: Vintage Books, 1966).

† David and Isabel Crook, *Revolution in a Chinese Village* (London: Routledge and Kegan Paul, 1959).

Then from February 26 to April 15, 1948, a campaign for thorough implementation of the Agrarian Law was launched in Ten Mile Inn. Since the village was in an old liberated area and some of the provisions of the law were already in effect, it was not necessary to start from scratch. The new campaign, therefore, was called the "Adjustment of Landholdings and Educating and Re-organizing the Party Members" or, for short, the Adjustment Campaign. We were given facilities for observing this campaign and investigating what was going on. The only limitation was that of our own ability to understand what we saw and heard. We were permitted to attend meetings of all sorts— of the villagers themselves and of the work team—and to examine a mass of written material: village documents, statistical records, instructions to the work team, and so on. Besides this, we saw much of the ordinary course of daily village life, and attended numerous meetings concerned with routine village matters. This book is a play-by-play account of the seven-week Adjustment Campaign as we saw it with our own eyes.

Ten years of struggle had profoundly changed Ten Mile Inn.* In 1937 before the beginning of the reforms, 70 percent of the people of the village lived in the most dire circumstances. For much of the year they subsisted on husks, wild herbs, and watery gruel "so thin you could see the reflection of the moon in it." In terms of an economically advanced country, there were no wealthy people in Ten Mile Inn. Landlords and peasants alike were pitifully poor. Nevertheless there was a profound difference between them. In time of famine, it was the members of the poor families who died or emigrated, who were forced by poverty to kill or sell children whom they could not feed, who were driven by hunger to join the warlord armies, who were imprisoned for the nonpayment of taxes or lost their meager property by default for nonpayment of debts. But for the landlords and rich peasants, famine was a time for foreclosure on mortgages and for adding to their own landholdings.

In 1937 there were just over 1,400 people in Ten Mile Inn, and just under 700 acres of land. This would have worked out to half an acre a head if it had been evenly divided. But it was not. Eight households of landlords and rich peasants owned 120 acres, and landlords living in other villages owned another 90 or so. There were 40 families of upper-middle peasants who had enough to get along on and could even put aside a little each year. The remaining 373 families had only 218 acres among them.

* What follows is some of the basic facts from *Revolution in a Chinese Village*.

For every ten people in the village there was only one draft animal. But here again, the twenty richest families had two animals each; the remaining families averaged only "one leg each," as the peasants said when four of them shared a donkey. In fact, most of them owned "not even one hair of a donkey."

Poverty drove numerous peasants to leave Ten Mile Inn. There was simply too little land for the poor to make a living. As a result many became itinerant brickmakers during the slack farming season. When they were lucky enough to find work, the brickmakers earned more in a month than a farmhand could make in a year. But the work was too irregular to afford a reliable income. Nonetheless, in 1937 as many as 201 families had men engaged in this craft. Other villagers found work in other areas. Without such secondary occupations, many of the poor-peasant families could not have survived even at their customary miserable level.

Before the Communists came, Ten Mile Inn limped along in this crippled condition. Landholdings had long since become uneconomically small, for according to Chinese inheritance tradition, the land was divided equally among all the sons. Most landlords and rich peasants tried to keep themselves from falling into this pit of land fragmentation by supplementing their income from rents with business or usury. The traditional aim in each generation was to add so much to the family estate by purchase, foreclosure, and other practices, that each son could inherit as much as his father had done before him. Since usury—supported by hired toughs—yielded a much higher profit than productive enterprise, it was by far the most practical method of realizing this aim. Demanding the most extortionate rates of interest might thus be interpreted as an act of loyalty to the family.

This diversion of capital into usury rather than production or construction not only grossly hampered the already retarded development of the economy; it also engendered a dog-eat-dog world within the village, a ruthless competitive struggle for existence that practically destroyed genuine cooperative efforts.

In 1940 the Japanese Imperial troops swept up the valley, bringing with them death and destruction and undercutting the power of the local Guomindang authorities. Elements of Jiang's Nationalist Army had been stationed in Ten Mile Inn on and off until that year, when they fled Wu An County and left behind them villages with bitter memories of brutal conduct by Guomindang soldiers, but no defense against the Japanese invaders. Although the Japanese never occupied Ten Mile Inn, a "mopping up" mission looted the village and killed ten villagers.

Then, as the peasants say, "The sun arose in the West." Units of the Communist-led Eighth Route Army, driving eastward from their bases in the heart of the Taihang Mountains, organized the peasants to defend themselves.

In 1942 and 1943, in the midst of a growing struggle with the enemy, famine struck. For untold generations famine had been a regular feature of Chinese rural life. It had brought death and disease to millions and sent millions more into beggary. It had broken up families, forcing parents to sell, give away, abandon, and even kill their own children rather than see them starve.

The famine of 1942–1943 was exceptionally severe, and in adjoining areas under Guomindang administration the misery of the people was on a scale and of a nature which hardly bear description. The Communists, however, urged the peasants to mobilize against the famine and the enemy. It was in the course of combatting this bitter disaster that the newly formed peasant union established itself as the village's most powerful mass organization. In the first big campaign— that of "Digging out the Landlord's Hidden Grain"—the union succeeded in substantially decreasing hoarding, speculation, and profiteering. The booty was distributed free to those who needed it, and in the process the bonds between the poor peasants and the middle peasants were considerably strengthened. Thus, a unity was being forged which would pave the way for the peasants' first attempts at wielding political power.

Yet these initial steps took place in the cruelest of contexts. They lessened suffering, but they could not prevent it. People still went begging, sold their children, hanged themselves. In 49 of Ten Mile Inn's 400-odd families, 59 people starved to death.

Thoroughgoing social, political, and economic reforms were clearly a matter of survival for the majority of the villagers. Not surprisingly, it was the poor and middle peasants who rallied most closely around the newly formed underground Communist Party. And it was mainly from them that new Communists were recruited during the Party's campaigns for successive reforms. In the early 1940s, after organizing against the famine and the Japanese invaders, the Party introduced a new taxation system. Taxes were now levied proportionately among the richest 30 percent of the families. Thus 70 percent of the villagers were freed from taxation. Never before had the peasants dreamed of such good fortune. For the first time, many villagers found that they had enough seed for sowing. Gone was the need to borrow at seeding time when grain prices were highest and to repay at harvest time when they were lowest. By this simple but sweeping reform, the cycle of peasant debt was frontally assaulted.

As in all the campaigns which followed, the goal was to raise production and support the war first against Japan and later against Jiang by mobilizing all available resources and people. To Western ears, the names of the ensuing campaigns may seem contrived—the Black Lands Campaign, Filling the Holes and Leveling the Tops, Digging Out the Air-Raid Shelters. But they symbolically capture the nature of this great transformation in a colorful blending of the language of old and new China.

In the course of these reforms, the peasants began to see their lives and their society with new eyes. At the heart of this new consciousness was the process of delineating classes or "classification." The theory and practice of classification had been worked out by the Chinese Communist Party as far back as the late 1920s and early 1930s. Minor modifications were made from time to time, but the basic principles which determined whether a man was a landlord, a rich peasant, a middle or poor peasant, or a hired laborer remained the same. Class was based on whether a man depended for his livelihood upon his own labor, exploited the labor of others, or was himself exploited.*

In the old society, the misery of the peasants and their hatred of their oppressors had expressed itself in an often explosive but ultimately sterile sense of personal grievance and hatred against individual landlords and rich peasants. Yet despite the ways in which the clans and other institutions served to obscure class conflict, it tore at the very heart of the Chinese village. The Communists did not introduce class struggle; they made the peasant conscious of it and sought to harness it for the liberation of the country and the building of a new social order.

As a result of the Communist-led reforms, a new class emerged— the "new middle peasants." And when we arrived in Ten Mile Inn, roughly one-third of all the families in the village had moved into it from the ranks of the poor peasants and hired laborers. Poor peasants still made up about one-third of the total number of families in the village, but now they all owned land. Although their holdings were small and they were far below the average in standard of living, their subsistence was at least guaranteed. And the threat of moneylenders', or landlords', bailiffs sweeping down on their homes to seize their few belongings—wooden doors, quilts, cooking pots, or pottery jars—was now at an end. Former landlords and rich peasants held only one-sixth the land they had had in the past. And there was not a single person in Ten Mile Inn who lived by exploiting the labor of others.

* For a definition of the various classes, see pp. 47–8.

Ten years was not a long time for achieving this, especially in the midst of invasion and civil war. The difficulties were enormous; mistakes were unavoidable. But the first great task was accomplished. Feudalism had been dealt a mortal blow.

This was everywhere apparent. Along with changes in land ownership there were deep-going social and political changes. For the first time labor was being effectively utilized through the mutual-aid groups —groups of peasants who were encouraged to get together voluntarily to pool their work, implements, and draft animals. In Ten Mile Inn, mutual aid groups had been organized to promote farm production, to set up a dyeing plant for locally woven cloth, to run a lime kiln located half a mile outside the village, and so forth. Everywhere we witnessed the enthusiasm which such cooperative measures were generating and its favorable effect on other aspects of life—social, political, and educational. The stagnation and widespread unemployment, born of lack of capital, which used to be especially acute during the winter months, were on the way out.

Certain older institutions had either disappeared or greatly changed. Ancestor worship was no longer common village practice. The feudal ideal of a family ruled by the patriarchal head was weakening. The clan organization could no longer make much pretense of serving a useful function, for the village government collected taxes, the village school provided education, the newly formed mutual-aid groups solved problems of those who needed man- or animal-power during rush seasons, or capital for side-occupation in slack seasons. Clan loyalties had begun to give way to class solidarity. This found direct expression not only in the peasants' hatred of the old power structure. It was expressed in their feeling of solidarity with the Communist Party, which led them in the struggle to destroy that structure.

Yet problems, even major ones, remained. Despite the new prosperity of the 125 families who had changed their class from poor to new middle peasant, many new middle peasant bachelors were still unable to find wives in a society that had long practiced female infanticide. Traces of the age-old interclan rivalries also remained. Ninety-five percent of the families in Ten Mile Inn were named Wang, Fu, or Li, and when village leaders did something unpopular, older men named Li or Fu might mumble that most of the cadres were Wangs. Surviving feelings of bonds of clan kinship could still to some extent obscure class conflict within the clans.

A more harmful legacy of the past was the tendency of cadres to be domineering. Most cadres had shown themselves to be brave and hard-working. But quite a number of them took too many responsibilities on their own shoulders instead of "mobilizing the masses," a job requiring infinite patience. Too often they relied only on a few militants to help them carry through the various struggles. From long experience, the Party had learned how diverse and complex the masses were. Only a minority was politically advanced; another minority was backward; the great majority was in between. A successful campaign required that the politically advanced should work closely with the great majority. Without this groundwork necessary for a mass-based campaign, the cadres would find themselves isolated, commanding rather than leading the peasants. And without deep roots among the majority, the activists would veer toward extremes, right or left. This involved the problem of democracy.

However, the most acute problem in the winter of 1947 was the effect of one of the campaigns: The Cutting Off of Feudal Tails. This had been launched a few months earlier in an attempt to deal with the land shortage of the almost one-third of the peasants of Ten Mile Inn who had not completely fanshenned. In the past struggles, fear of reprisal had kept these peasants passive, or clan loyalties had led them to side with the landlords or rich peasants. This sizable number of unfanshenned peasants had still to be roused. But now there were no longer readily available goods or land to distribute to them. Despite the only partial mobilization of the peasants in the past, despite the skillful evasion tactics of the landlords and rich peasants, the latter had been pretty well cleaned out. By now there were no longer any families in Ten Mile Inn whose incomes were derived from exploiting labor or who had conspicuously large holdings of land.

This was the situation in many parts of North China when numerous Communist cadres in subregional or county governments sought to mobilize the unfanshenned for the war effort by assuring them of a fair share of the land. With nothing to be had from the landlords and rich peasants, a new class of "exploiters" was sought from whom land and goods could be taken. And so the new "class" of "feudal tails" was introduced (completely contrary to the Communist Party's principles for delineating classes), and the campaign for Cutting Off Feudal Tails was carried through. A feudal tail was defined as anyone in possession of means of production which had not been earned by the sweat of his brow or that of his father or grandfather. And if he, or his forebears of either of the two previous generations, had been a landlord or rich peasant, then their land or property was considered to have been stolen from the people. Almost 25 percent of the middle peasants in numerous villages thus entered the ranks of "struggle objects" along with the landlords and rich peasants.

This leftish current was later called the "poor-peasant line," and was criticized as a serious mistake that alienated middle peasants from the revolutionary regime. The poor-peasant line never had the approval of the Central Committee of the Chinese Communist Party. Government and Party policy, in fact, had stressed the principle of firm reliance upon the poor-and-hired and unity between them and the middle peasants.

The Ten Mile Inn Communists had never fully followed the ultra-left line; indeed, they had led the struggle against "feudal tails" with such restraint that the struggle objects had suffered little damage economically, though they were discriminated against politically and socially.

Yet the harm of the ultra-left tendency was evident in Ten Mile Inn. Poor peasants who had expected to get land from these wrongly labeled "feudal tails" were disappointed. Some felt they were being betrayed by the new village leaders. The middle peasants, on the other hand, felt that leftish excesses were being committed. And even those middle peasants who emerged unscathed from the Feudal Tails Campaign had qualms, wondering when their turn might come.

The middle peasants began to wear their oldest clothes and took care never to be seen eating wheat flour instead of the coarser millet or maize. One of them, fearing that his donkey might some day be "struggled away" from him, sold it and carried fertilizer to his fields on his shoulders. Other middle peasants scarcely troubled to fertilize their land at all, fearing that it might be taken away from them and given to the poor. Production inevitably declined.

To set things right and bring about an upswing in farm production, the Party Committee in the Taihang subregion sent out three directives in succession. These were followed up by meetings throughout the countryside.

By the middle of January a meeting of cadres and peasant representatives had already been organized in the ninth district of Wu An. Its purpose was to correct the ultra-leftward swing of the poor-peasant line and to allay the middle peasants' fears that their land would be confiscated and given to the poor.

After hearing reports the district cadres, who were directing the meeting, led the delegates in a discussion of the need for poor and middle peasant unity. Finally, plans were laid for putting the minds of the middle peasants at rest.

When the Ten Mile Inn delegates had returned home, a village meeting was called to announce the results of the conference. Then each mutual-aid group held meetings to discuss case by case how those of its members who had slowed down their winter production efforts could make up for lost time.

A new slogan was painted over the arch of Ten Mile Inn's north gate: "Poor and middle peasants are two blossoms on one twig."

How was this poetic slogan to be realized? How were the conditions of the remaining poor peasants to be raised to the level of the middle peasants—without harming the middle peasants' interests?

How was democracy to be developed and the Party organization purified and strengthened? These were the problems in Ten Mile Inn— and elsewhere.

At its Agrarian Conference in the winter of 1947–8, the Jin-Ji-Lu-Yu Bureau of the Chinese Party's Central Committee, laid plans for solving such problems in all those parts of the Region which had been liberated earliest. To gain experience in leading the Adjustment Campaign, the Bureau sent pilot "work teams" into the field. One of these Party Bureau work teams arrived in Ten Mile Inn on February 25, 1948.

# —2—

# The Work Team Comes to Ten Mile Inn

February 25, 26

There had been some talk of sending a scout disguised as a peddler to the village, but the team had decided against it. Instead they dispatched an advance party of three, which arrived in Ten Mile Inn on the afternoon of February 25, 1948. One of this group called on the Party branch secretary, Wang Shao-zhen, to tell him why the work team was coming and ask him what sorts of problems the village had. Another went to the various border-region government offices to find out about local conditions.

The next day the rest of the team arrived and began to visit the poor peasants who had not "stood up"—had not fanshenned. That evening a large meeting was called to introduce the team to the villagers.

Skirting the moon-bathed fields of winter wheat, the men and women of Fort and Street headed for the old village temple. (The Fort, a former landlord citadel, was on a hill overlooking the Street, which made up the main part of the village.) Everyone except the "objects of struggle"—former landlords and their hangers-on—had been invited.

Many of the middle peasants came apprehensively, fearing that the new campaign would be directed against them. Some poor peasants were eagerly expecting that they would be allowed to seize the land and animals of more prosperous neighbors. But other poor peasants approached the temple with their age-old resignation, grumbling, "They didn't give me much in the past. I don't suppose they'll give me much now."

Among the villagers were some who had personal enemies, and one of these said to a neighbor, "Maybe I can pay off the score this time. I don't care what happens to me, as long as he gets what he deserves."

And one old peasant expressed an opinion common among the elderly: "Now there'll be another shakeup. I only hope they don't throw out the village head; he's the best we've ever had."

As well as the work team, the local Party members would be formally introduced to the villagers that evening. All but seven of them had been working underground; their own families did not know they were Communists. Now the whole group of twenty-eight squatted under a huge portrait of Mao, which was lit by a hissing kerosene lamp. One said uneasily, "Everyone admires Chairman Mao's Party. Maybe they'll laugh when they find out that a person like me is a Communist."

The branch secretary, however, felt great confidence. He had already told the others, "Of course there are a handful of politically backward characters who'd like to get us out of office. But we're still the model Party branch in this district. We've been active in the struggles and honest with the fruits of the struggles."

The villagers assembled in the temple courtyard, some sitting on bricks or tiny stools they had brought with them, others squatting on their heels. All eyed the team—twelve men and a woman—who had come to lead them in carrying out the new agrarian law.

The meeting began with the introduction of the team members. The first to rise was the leader, Lou Lin, a tall, big-boned man who came from a peasant home in the southern province of Hunan. Quiet and patient, he seemed imperturbable, but the villagers learned later that he had the famous Hunanese temper and on rare occasions could explode with sudden rage. Lou Lin's accent was difficult for them to understand, and he seldom spoke in public during the work team's stay in Ten Mile Inn.

The other team members followed, each receiving a round of applause. The secretary, He Yan-ling, who worked on foreign news at the *People's Daily*, was a slight man who wore steel-rimmed glasses and looked like the student he had recently been. The team's one woman was Wu Fang, a researcher in the library of the *People's Daily*. Her family, landlords who lived near the Yangzi River, had sent her to study at an American missionary university in Peking. There she joined the student movement and eventually came to the Liberated Areas.

Eight other team members who rose in their turn were also journalists. The remaining two were cadres—Party officials from a neighboring district. Tu Bao-kuo, a farm laborer, had recently learned to read and write. Chang Jing-shou was a former middle peasant who had taught himself to read and write when he was thirty-two. Chang first became active in a village cooperative established by the Communists and then went to work as a district cooperative organizer.

(*left*) Calling villagers to a meeting. Fu Bian-de at the extreme left; next to him, oil-press worker Fu Chan-ting.

(*below*) A village meeting in the old temple courtyard.

One of the last to be introduced was Wu Xiang, twenty-seven years old and a front-line correspondent. This evening he had been chosen as the team's chief spokesman, partly because of his simple language and clear delivery.

"We are a work team sent by the Central Bureau of the Communist Party of this border region," Wu Xiang said, "and we've come to help

Some members of the work team. Left to right: Wu Fang, the team's only woman; He Yan-ling, the secretary; Leng Bing; Lou Lin, the leader.

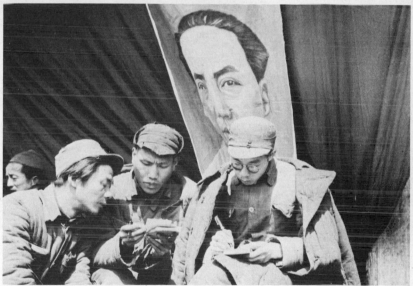

Three of the work team below a picture of Mao. Left to right: Geng Xi, Lou Lin, He Yan-ling.

you carry out the Agrarian Law." In short, plain sentences he explained the main points of the new law:

The land system of feudal and semifeudal exploitation should be abolished; the land should belong to the tillers.

The land that used to belong to the landlords and the public land in the villages should be taken over by the local peasant associations.

This land, together with all the other land in each village, should be equally distributed among the entire rural population, regardless of sex or age.

Peasant associations should take over the draft animals, farm tools, houses, grain, and other property of the landlords and should requisition the surplus property of the rich peasants. The associations should distribute all this property among the peasants and other poor people who are in need of it, and should allot the same share to the landlords.*

Although the team had been in the village for only a short time, Wu Xiang made it clear that they already understood some of the peasants' hopes and fears. He pointed out that the new law would benefit everyone:

"This law was demanded by all the people, and it's designed to be good for all the people.

"It's good for poor peasants and for hired laborers. We know that in your village some have not really 'stood up,' have not fanshenned. We've learned that a certain man has only 1½ mu† of land, that one family of six have only 10 mu between them, and that another couple have only a tiny room for themselves and their old mother. 'Holes' like this must be filled up if we are to have a thorough fanshen.

"The law is good for the middle peasants, too. There are really three kinds of middle peasants: those who can make ends meet, those who can't quite make them meet, and those with a little to spare. According to the new law, those who are short may be given land, those with a balanced budget will not have their holdings changed, and those with a bit more than they need may, if they like, give some land to their poorer brothers. But they will not be asked to give animals, farm tools, or property.

"We know that in the past, some of the middle peasants in the village were struggled against and had property taken from them. This was wrong and must be set right. The middle peasants' right to their land must be clearly established, so that they can do their work with peaceful hearts.

"As for the landlords and rich peasants who were properly struggled against, they must work for a living. That's how we make them into good and useful members of society. Therefore they must be given means of production.

"You can see that this agrarian law designed by Chairman Mao is good for everyone."

---

* "The Present Situation and Our Tasks," *Selected Works of Mao Ze-dong*, vol. IV. Translated directly from the Chinese.

† A *mu* is about ⅙ acre. The village average was approximately 3 *mu* per person.

From the temple steps Wu Xiang looked out over the courtyard packed with villagers. The faces of those at the front of the crowd were lit by the lamp, and even those at the back could be made out, for the moonlight penetrated into every corner. He began to describe the team's plan for putting the law into effect.

"Chairman Mao says we are to rely on the poor peasants and the hired laborers, and unite them with the middle peasants. These groups together will become masters of the house.

"First we'll organize a league of the *laoshi*, the simple and honest poor-and-hired. They may think they aren't good at making speeches and can't handle such a job, but they're wrong. Over in Zhao Village, Jing Fu-you used to be just a farmer who worked hillside land. Now he's become head of his village, and a very good one.

"After the poor-peasant league has been set up, the peasant union will be reorganized, and then we'll hold elections for the village government."

Wu Xiang ended on the note which the work team would sound again and again: that the distribution of land was not an end in itself, but one step in the drive to increase production in order to raise the peasants' standard of living and win the war.

"Now Comrade Leng Bing is going to introduce the village Party members to you," Wu Xiang said.

Excitement filled the courtyard. Leng Bing, a seasoned reporter, was the only person who seemed calm. "The Ten Mile Inn Communist Party branch has twenty-eight members," he said, and began reading the names from the list in his hand. Every man rose as his name was called, and a tremor went through the crowd when each underground member stood up.

"Who ever would have guessed there were so many!" one old man mumbled in his wispy beard.

In a Party branch meeting the day before, Leng Bing had explained that Party members would be given instruction and their ranks reorganized. Now he read the villagers the instructions that all Communists had to obey:

1. Resolutely carry out the Agrarian Law; any words or deeds against it are prohibited.
2. Carry out all the decisions and policies of the Party; no independence from the Party is permissible.
3. Obey all decisions of the poor-peasant league, the peasant union, and the people's congress. No opposition to them is allowed. Be wholehearted members of the masses; there must be no independence from them.

4. When land and property are being distributed, Party members may not demand or accept more than their share.

5. Party members must not show favoritism towards clansmen, relatives, or people with the same surname, nor to the families of soldiers or those who have been killed in action. If Party members commit crimes, they must be handed over to the people's court for trial. Organizations at any level must not cover up for a person because he is a Party member.

6. Set a high value on land, upon the fruits of struggle and upon public property. Damage or extravagant use of them is not permitted.

7. The whole Party must unite! It must unite with the peasants, with the masses. Don't pay off old scores against peasants. Don't undermine the cooperation of the masses, stir up quarrels, or take part in factional conflicts among the peasants.

8. Firmly rely upon the poor peasants and unite solidly with the middle peasants. Consult the masses on everything. Follow the mass line.* Don't be passive or undisciplined. There must be no coercion or authoritarianism, no dictating or taking over other people's tasks.

* "The mass line is the fundamental political and organizational line of our Party," says Liu Shao-qi. He goes on to stress that for the thorough carrying out of this line four concepts must be firmly established in the mind of every Party member.
"Firstly, there is the standpoint that everything is for the masses and for serving the masses wholeheartedly . . . our Party members and those who have joined the revolutionary ranks are serving the people, regardless of whether or not they are aware of it, whether they occupy important, leading positions or are merely privates, cooks or grooms. . . .
"Secondly, there is the standpoint of assuming full responsibility to the masses of the people. . . .
". . . The interests of the people are the very interests of the Party. The Party has no particular interest of its own other than the people's interest.
"Thirdly, there is the standpoint of having faith in the people's self-emancipation . . . that the people alone are the real makers of history . . . that only through their own struggles and efforts can their emancipation be achieved, maintained and consolidated. . . .
"Fourthly, there is the standpoint of learning from the masses of the people. . . . We must have adequate knowledge and must be sufficiently experienced and vigilant before we can successfully raise the people's consciousness, lead their actions and serve them well. . . .
"In all sections of the masses there are generally to be found relatively active elements, intermediate elements and backward elements. In the initial stages the active elements are usually in the minority, while the intermediate and the backward elements make up the broad masses. In accordance with the mass line attention must be paid to the majority, that is, the intermediate and the backward elements, otherwise the advanced sections will become isolated and nothing can be done satisfactorily. The slogans of action and the form of struggle and of organization we put forward before the masses must be acceptable to the intermediate and the backward elements. The development of the consciousness and the self-activity of the masses concerns chiefly these people. A mass movement is possible only when these people are awakened and inspired to action.
"We must pay particular attention to educating, uniting and organizing the active elements so that they may become the nucleus of leadership among the masses. However, it must be clearly understood that we are not organizing the active elements merely for their own sake and that it is absolutely unpermissible to isolate these elements from the intermediate and backward masses. Our sole intention is to attract and set

9. Propagandize for the Agrarian Law. Don't shirk responsibility.

10. Be loyal, honest, and realistic. Don't issue directives or draw up reports which don't conform to the facts. Don't be two-faced and give the appearance of obedience while secretly disobeying.

Members who oppose these ten points will receive severe punishment from both the Party and the people.

Raising his eyes from the paper, Leng Bing spoke directly to the villagers. "Be bold in criticizing the cadres and Party members, and help them reform themselves. But do it through discussion alone; there must be no quarreling or fighting. The Party members must not be maltreated and beaten, as some landlords were in the past. If some cadres have committed crimes, they can be handed over to the people's court. If necessary, a people's court can be organized here in the village.

"Our team has just arrived and doesn't yet know much about Ten Mile Inn. We hope everyone will feel free to come and talk over problems with us at any time."

The work team adjourned the meeting, but the villagers stood about talking in knots even though it was late. The team members joined in their conversations. Gradually the groups broke up, and the peasants drifted home across the fields.

The team members stayed behind. Turning out the lamp to save kerosene, they gathered around the stone porch to evaluate the meeting.

Lou Lin, the leader, began: "The note struck at the end was a little off-key. Of course it's not wrong to invite everyone to come and talk to us about their problems. But the main emphasis should have been on encouraging the poor-and-hired to come. We must get them used to speaking out, so they'll really 'run the house' in cooperation with the middle peasants. It's the poor-and-hired who are most timid and who haven't fanshenned yet. The people who really have 'stood up' don't need any urging; they'll come to us anyway."

Another team member said, "I don't think we should have invited anyone to come to us with problems. We don't want to get bogged down trying to solve every little difficulty in the village. We should

in motion the intermediate and backward elements through the active elements. In other words, it is for rallying the broadest possible masses that the active elements are to be organized. If the intermediate and backward elements are not yet awakened, we must know how to enlighten them as well as how to wait for them. If we are unwilling to wait, but recklessly rush forward with a small number of the active elements following us, we will isolate ourselves from the masses and end in failure." (Quoted from Liu Shao-qi, "Regarding the Mass Line of the Party," *On the Party*, a verbatim report on the Revision of the Party Constitution, delivered by Liu Shao-qi on May 14, 1945, to the Seventh National Congress of the Chinese Communist Party [Peking: Foreign Languages Press, 1950].)

have gone into more detail about forming the poor-peasant league, re-organizing the peasant union, and electing a new village government. It's the new village cadres who'll solve the people's problems, not us."

Du, the young peasant team member, said, "I don't think the people were able to follow the ten points in the Central Bureau's letter, because the language wasn't simple enough. We should have picked out the easiest points, or else rewritten the whole lot in every-day language." Everyone agreed.

Finally Lou Lin said, "Well, we made a start. After the meeting I heard one old peasant say, 'You can't exactly believe everything they say, and yet you can't exactly disbelieve it.' Tomorrow when we call on the poor-and-hired, we'll find out how they took it."

# —3—

# Finding and Awakening
# the Unfanshenned

The team visited the poor-and-hired for several purposes: to learn what their economic situation was and how they were being treated by the Party cadres, to tell them more about the Agrarian Law and Communist policy, and most important, to awaken the unfanshenned. Through the poor-peasant league of a nearby village the team had an introduction to a poor peasant of Ten Mile Inn. He in turn gave the names of two or three unfanshenned peasants in each of the village's nine mutual-aid groups. The team members made house-to-house visits to these peasants and asked the ones who seemed to be genuinely unfanshenned and *laoshi*, or simple and honest, to introduce friends and neighbors like themselves.

One of the team's first discoveries as they visited the peasants was that all the poor-and-hired had about the same amount of land. Thus in terms of size of holdings, hardly anyone in the village had not fanshenned; the fruits of the early struggles had truly been distributed among the poor and landless. In many cases, however, this economic fanshen had simply been bestowed, not earned. Backward peasants who should have been awakened to struggle for their emancipation had passively accepted the distributed land.

However, some peasants grumbled privately that the plots they had been given were hard to cultivate, being stony or too widely scattered, or situated so far from the village that they were hard to fertilize. These drawbacks were all the more important, because people went to and from their fields on foot. They used carrying poles, balanced on the shoulders with loads dangling from each end, to take fertilizer to their plots and to bring back the harvest. Some peasants owned a donkey, or a share in one; a quarter share was called "one leg of a donkey," a half "two legs." Hardly anyone could afford a leg of a mule. Horses were practically unheard-of. The few carts in the village were owned

25

not by individuals but by mutual-aid groups. And carts could be used only on the highways, for land was too precious to make lanes that were any wider than footpaths through the fields.

Housing in the village was generally bad. Peasants of all classes lived in rented or borrowed quarters with cramped rooms and leaking roofs. Because it had been a "beggar" village, with few wealthy families, Ten Mile Inn had hardly any good housing for distribution after the land-reform struggles of 1946–1947. Perhaps the worst building of all was a tiny mud hut thatched with straw. Inside it the old man who lived there, Wang Yi, could not stand upright or stretch out at full length when he slept.

As for the general political situation, the team was prepared to find it unwholesome. They had been warned by certain senior party leaders that there was widespread corruption in the local Party branches and village governments throughout the border region. The team members encouraged the people they called on to talk freely about the cadres, and the peasants soon responded with fierce criticism of the former village heads, Wang Ke-bin and Fu Gao-lin, and the former Party branch secretary. One peasant said, "We killed Li Fa-kui" (a Guomindang collaborator), "and Wang Ke-bin's no better than Li was."

All this criticism, however, was directed at former cadres, not those actually in office. Suspecting that the villagers were afraid to talk about their present government, the team tried to give them confidence. But most of them stubbornly insisted, "Our village has the best cadres," or "Our cadres have very close relations with the masses. They consult us about everything."

"Either the present cadres are really quite good," Lou Lin observed, "or they're so bad that the peasants are afraid of them."

The members of the team who did not ask questions about the cadres were the first to learn the truth. They simply listened as the poor peasants talked about their land and the struggles in which they had received it. The cadres were important figures in their stories, and gradually it became clear that the present cadres had no major vices. That is, they had not murdered people, embezzled large sums, accepted bribes from the landlords, or extracted tribute from the villagers.

Thus, a number of the elderly poor peasants were well satisfied with the reforms and the cadres, for in the old society they had acquired a fatalism which they had yet to overcome. These peasants felt that they were lucky to live in a time when land was given to them, and they wished only to be left in peace to enjoy it. They did not presume to think that they were entitled to more; they had not truly fanshenned.

As one elderly peasant said to Lou Lin, "I didn't have any land before. All my plots were given to me by our cadres. They're good cadres and look after the masses."

Lou Lin replied, "It's not the cadres you should thank for the land, but Chairman Mao. It is he who taught us how to fanshen." But the old man repeated that the cadres were good men.

Some peasants who talked about the struggles, however, did find fault with the cadres and local Communists. For example, in a conversation that a member of the team described to his colleagues, a villager called Wang Lai-xun criticized a cadre for favoritism. He said "that one peasant got between 3 and 4 *mu* of good land during the campaigns, that another got an extra half courtyard of housing, and that a third got three rooms. According to Wang, the reason is that they're all relatives of the peasant-union chairman, Fu Chang-sou. But he maintained that the village head and the public security officer are good men."

A couple of poor peasants from mutual-aid group 8 complained to a team member: "We don't have a single chaser mill in our whole group, and they've got five on the main street between the house of the village head and the south gate. Our group wanted to buy one from the fruits of the struggle, but all we were offered was an old broken-down mill that wasn't any good. So the government milling orders went to other groups. Last winter the village public security officer made a good sum out of milling."

Gradually Lou Lin pieced together a picture of property distribution in the village. He told the team: "The figures on landholdings show that the different classes are now roughly even. But during the movements of the past, the policy of 'filling the holes and leveling the tops' was not consistently carried out. Some of the cadres used their power to get extra or better land, or at least land that was closer to the village than the plots they had had before.

"For example, the militia commander has a family of two. Originally he owned 7 *mu* of land, but last spring he exchanged 3 *mu* of poor land for 7 *mu* of good. Now the estimated yield for each member of his family is 7 *dan** a year—1.3 *dan* more than the average for the village.

"And the year before last, when the fruits of struggle were put on sale during the Black Lands Campaign, the village head, Wang Xi-tang, bought a 6-*mu* plot of good land outside the south gate. A lot of people bid for this land, but in the end he was the one who got it. And when houses were earmarked for those who needed them, but

* A *dan* is about 100 pounds.

were loaned for the time being to the new border-region government, no one was allowed into Wang's new house except the political director.

"Some soldiers' dependents have fanshenned high above the average, but there are quite a few families with 'holes' to be filled up."

The peasants had other criticisms of the struggles and the cadres. Some claimed that the landlords had not been fully struggled against. They said that the peasant-union chairman, Fu Chang-sou, had protected his uncle, a notorious rich-peasant usurer in the old days. The uncle was graded a "second-class struggle object," but although he lost his political rights, he was not "swept out of house and home." Fu Chang-sou saw to it that he suffered socially and politically rather than economically.

One of the biggest complaints was that the cadres had not been thorough enough in carrying out the economic struggles. The mother of a poor peasant said bitterly, "Some of the struggle objects still eat better than we do." Other peasants complained that the landlords were still living in their own houses. During the Feudal Tails Campaign, the leader of mutual-aid group 6 confiscated six or seven donkeys from the group's struggle-object families to distribute among the poor, but then he gave them back. Now he was roundly criticized for it.

At the same time, the work team began to hear about middle and even poor peasants who had been wrongly struggled against. A certain man who had once been a beggar was branded a "feudal tail" (a poor peasant descended from landlords) because his grandfather had exploited villagers. And the sixty-year-old Fu Qin had always worked as a mason, yet he was classified as a "second-class struggle object" because his father had been assistant head of the village in the old days. The father was vividly remembered for his bad temper, his nosiness, and the number of enemies he made during his short term in office. Although some of the villagers had thought it unfair to label Fu Qin a struggle object, they had not mustered the courage to speak out until now. Furthermore, the merit citation given to Fu Qin's son for bravery at the front was taken away from him when the family was put into the struggle-object class. Now his comrades, who had been secretly indignant at the time, openly expressed their disapproval.

As the work team made their visits, they began to encourage the unfanshenned to meet in small groups with the families of friends and neighbors. Informal gatherings sprang up, some composed of the families living around one courtyard, others of all the poor-and-hired in one mutual-aid group or one section of the village. Some meetings were held jointly by the poor-and-hired and the middle peasants; others consisted solely of middle peasants.

The team members working in the various sections of the village

Small-group discussions were the political building blocks for land reform.

were free to use whatever methods seemed to them most suitable for awakening the unfanshenned. But they all made the same points again and again, whether they were speaking in house-to-house visits, small-group meetings, large public meetings, or sessions to educate the Party members. Thus every part of their work reinforced the whole.

On the evening of February 28, team leader Lou Lin arranged a meeting of fourteen poor-and-hired peasants of the south-end section. Everyone crowded into the small room occupied by the poor peasant Wang Wen-sheng and his crippled wife. The crowd sprawled on the *kang*,* squatted on the doorsill, and sat on tiny stools with five-inch legs. The room had never been so full before.

Lou Lin started off with a question. "What is it we're about to do?"

The peasants puffed thoughtfully on their long-stemmed pipes. Finally Wang Wen-sheng replied, "We're going to carry out the Agrarian Law."

"Why is it that we've called men like you together?" Lou Lin asked.

"It's because you want us simple-and-honest poor peasants to be masters of the house," one answered.

"Yes; we haven't fanshenned properly," someone added. "All of us used to be slaves of the landlords."

"Even now we don't have any decent homes or furniture," another said. The talk was drifting away from Lou Lin's question, but he let it go on for a bit to loosen the peasants' tongues.

The speaker continued, "The landlords' houses, furniture, and land weren't given to the poor; people had to buy them. Only those with

---

* A *kang* is a hollow brick platform with a network of heating flues inside. The peasants sit on the *kang* during the day and use it as a bed at night.

money could get good land to farm and good homes to live in. I didn't get so much as a pair of chopsticks. But when it came to rear service* and helping soldiers' families, I did my full share."

Wang Wen-sheng's white-bearded father Wang Yi, who lived in the tiny thatched hut, said, "When they were selling the fruits, I wanted to buy a water crock. But the cadres wouldn't sell it to me even after I'd borrowed the money. Yet they could buy anything they liked. They have money as well as office."

Lou Lin said, "From now on, it's you poor peasants who are going to be masters of the house. Why is it that you still have holes to be filled up?"

"Because of the landlords and—" the speaker hesitated and then said, "because of the cadres."

"And where are we going to get the earth to fill the holes?" Lou Lin asked.

"From the landlords who weren't fully struggled against." The answers were coming more quickly now.

"Yes, that's just it," a peasant said. "The landlords were never properly struggled against. Their houses weren't all taken away from them. And there are still some 'air-raid shelters' to be dug out." Air-raid shelters were people who hid valuables for their relatives or for a landlord during the struggles.

This opinion was shared by nearly everyone. But Lou Lin, afraid that the group might be thinking of taking land from their allies, asked, "What about the middle peasants?"

"It's no good going after the middle peasants," said Wang Wensheng. "If we did, nobody would ever do a good day's work again. But the middle peasants who've got more than they need ought to be asked to give something up. We could talk things over with them."

"And what about the cadres who got all those extra fruits?" asked one old peasant.

"Yes, they should cough some up," said another. "So should the soldiers' families who got too much."

"And there are still some fruits from the last struggle, up in the loft of the granary by the wounded soldiers' staging post. What about distributing them?"

"We don't want to be a lot better off than the others," said one man, "but we do want a fair share."

"Yes, a fair share—that's it! We never got that in the past," a number of others said.

---

* Rear service involved jobs such as carrying supplies to the front and wounded to the rear.

"How was it you never managed to fanshen in the past?" asked Lou Lin.

There was a long silence, broken only by the noise of a peasant striking a flint. A man sitting nearby offered Lou Lin his pipe. Lou took a couple of puffs, handed it back, and repeated the question. Finally Wang Wen-sheng replied, "Well, it was partly the landlords' fault, and partly the cadres'. And it was partly that we ourselves weren't united."

"Well, and now that you are united, who's going to lead the way?"

"I would," said Wang Wen-sheng, "but first you must put power in our hands."

"I'd be willing to give up my life, but I have no ability," said a young man at his side.

"I'd risk my life too," said Wang Wen-sheng, "if I could count on you to stand by me."

"Yes," said another, looking at Lou Lin, "so long as you stay here, we're afraid of nothing. But once you've gone we'll lose our nerve again."

Lou Lin assured them that the work team would not leave until the poor-and-hired had really fanshenned and come into power. He explained that they themselves would safeguard their power by setting up a poor-peasant league, which would unite all the poor-and-hired of the village. The league would take the initiative in reorganizing the peasant union along more democratic lines. Next the league would set up the village people's congress, with one representative for every dozen families. When all this democratic machinery was in good working order, the villagers would elect their new government. By then they could be sure that the voting was fair and that the cadres would serve their interests.

"You can get rid of any bad cadres and elect good ones," Lou Lin went on. "And once you are united, there's no danger that those who were thrown out will seek revenge. First the poor-and-hired must unite; then they must unite with the middle peasants. When you have power, what is there to be afraid of? So the most important thing now is to unite.

"When you go home, think about these things. If any of your poor neighbors haven't fanshenned, call them together and unite with them. But at the same time, explain to the middle peasants that you have no wish to struggle against them. And it's important to keep working your land: take compost out to the fields; build up the terrace walls. Don't let production fall off."

The team soon learned that group meetings had one great advantage over individual visits: they produced the sense of safety that comes from numbers. In groups the peasants gave each other confidence, and what one said stimulated the others. It was not long before they were all criticizing the cadres and Party members.

According to the peasants, the cadres browbeat them during village elections whenever the Party candidates did not have general support. On three occasions in particular, the cadres had used heavy pressure to elect their nominees.

In the election for the village finance secretary, the underground Party branch had proposed the ex-soldier Zhang Zhao-lin, who had just returned to the village after five years with the Eighth Route Army. Many of the villagers, however, favored Li Bao-san, who was skillful with the abacus. "Zhao-lin doesn't know any more about accounting than we do," they said. "What kind of finance secretary will he make?" The village political director sharply criticized this reasoning. "What sort of political stand is that?" he said. "We should elect cadres who have proved loyal in serving the people—not just anyone who happens to be quick-fingered with the abacus." Apparently he convinced the majority, for Zhang Zhao-lin was elected. And in the end, even those who had opposed him admitted that he did the job very well. But some of Li Bao-san's supporters still nursed a grievance about the way the election had gone.

On another occasion the cadres had nominated Fu Zhang-sou for peasant-union chairman. Seeing that their man was not the favorite, they kept postponing the election to campaign all the harder for him. At last the villagers concluded that the process would drag on indefinitely unless they gave in, so they elected Fu Zhang-sou.

On the third occasion that had aroused village resentment, Wang Nan-fang, the Party's candidate for the honorary title of labor hero, lost by a narrow margin to a man from mutual-aid group 8. The local Party members were appalled. The district committee had told them that they must take the lead in this election, which would spur production by honoring those who worked especially hard and efficiently. The cadres took it for granted that a Communist had to win the title. So they immediately annulled the vote, organized an intensive campaign for Wang Nan-fang, and held a new election, which their man did win. This incident provoked the most anger, because it antagonized a solidly united mutual-aid group.

The villagers also began criticizing individual cadres for everything from political defects to personal immorality. Many of them were indignant because the young political director, Wang Shao-zhen, had misappropriated an ancient rifle. Wang had seen it at the front, where he was visiting his brother in the army. By then the troops were capturing modern American equipment from Jiang Jie-shi's forces, and old rifles were no longer needed. So the battalion commander, who knew the importance of weapons for the morale of a village militia, presented the rifle to Wang as a gift for Ten Mile Inn. But when he came home, Wang sold the gun and combined the proceeds with his own savings to buy a house for his family.

Wang Shao-zhen, the peasants said, had also used his position to break off his brother's engagement. The brother was betrothed to a girl in South Yangyi, but he fell in love with a young widow of Ten Mile Inn. To release him so that he could marry the widow, Wang Shao-zhen drew up an official letter revoking the engagement and then stamped it with the village seal. This act offended many people, for in China engagements are almost as legally binding as marriage.

The villagers were equally critical of the public security officer, Wang Lin-yong. According to one peasant, many of them would not travel outside the village because "He gives us three angry looks for every word," and they did not dare ask him for a pass. Even worse, in his zeal for security Wang Lin-yong branded people without proof as secret agents of the Guomindang. When some of the militia's weapons got broken, he denounced two militiamen as enemy agents who had deliberately damaged the equipment. There was no evidence to support his claim, but Wang Shao-zhen and the militia commander had had the two men tied up, beaten, and jailed for three days without allowing anyone to visit them or investigate the matter.

According to one of the victims, the motive had been revenge, not zeal for the militia's safety. The victim had openly criticized the public security officer for committing adultery, thereby publishing what the whole village knew. Wang Lin-yong had fallen in love with a soldier's wife who had had no news of her husband for three years. It was generally assumed in the village that her husband was dead, and in ordinary cases such a long absence would have given her the right to a divorce. But this rule had been suspended for men in the army—and in any case, Wang Lin-yong was already married. The soldier's wife went to the village head and said that she wanted someone to sleep with. Shocked by such brazenness, he scolded her; but she replied, "Then I'll have to see to it myself." After that she and Wang Lin-yong had begun living together.

Another widely criticized cadre was the manager of the cooperative, Fu Pei-yu. "During the Black Lands Campaign, he bought 4 *mu* of land," said a peasant at a meeting of the east-central section, where Fu Pei-yu lived. In that campaign land had been sold far below the market price, and competition for it was intense. The implication was that Fu Pei-yu had obtained it because he was a Party member.

"And last year when he took over the job of managing the cooperative," the peasant continued, "he said he didn't have time to cultivate that land, so he sold it for nearly seven times as much as he paid."

"Yes, he's a regular scrounger," said someone else. "Last year during the recruiting campaign they were trying to persuade his brother to join up. But Pei-yu got him to eat eggs to make his scabies worse, so they didn't want him."

From the back of the room came a woman's indignant voice: "He wouldn't let his wife attend the district meeting, even though she was a delegate. He said that only whores went to meetings, and that if she went she needn't come back."

"He's not the only one," said another woman. "The other cadres are the same; they all look down on women. They don't even take the trouble to tell us about meetings. When the village was struggling against the landlords, we did our share, but we never got so much as a needle or a piece of thread out of it."

"Fu Pei-yu's whole family is backward," said a poor peasant. "Last year I was raising the roof on my house, because it was so low that you bumped your head against it if you stood up on the *kang*. Fu's father said that raising the roof of the house next to his would be unlucky for his family, and that I would have to guarantee their fortunes for three years. If anyone fell sick or died, or if they had any sort of bad luck, it would be my fault. I couldn't take on anything like that, of course, so I had to lower my roof again."

Throughout the village the peasants' tongues wagged in criticism of the cadres and Party members, and in a few days the work team began to get a clear idea of the leadership in Ten Mile Inn. At this point An Gang, the assistant director of the entire Central Bureau team, came to the village on a tour of inspection. The team reported the facts they had learned.

After discussing the details of their work, An Gang concluded, "We must urge the people to speak with complete freedom about the Party members and cadres. But the reason for doing it is to discover problems, not to develop antagonism toward the cadres. We must make it clear that our policy toward the cadres is different from the position we took against the landlords. The Party members, including the cadres, must be given a chance to reform themselves and reorganize their ranks.

"The greatest mistake is to judge people merely according to their 'nature'—to condemn a cadre, for example, simply because he has an abrasive manner or a bad temper, or because he's had relations with prostitutes. Of course, if a cadre has these defects he must correct them. But we must judge cadres from a political viewpoint: How did they behave during the class struggle? What stand did they take against feudalism? Those are the key questions. The people are often confused on this matter," An Gang said, "and we must not let them lead us into the same confusion."

# 4

# Self-Criticism
# by the Party Members

February 26–March 10

> The question of the impure composition and working style of our
> Party's local organizations, especially its primary rural organiza-
> tions, has not been solved. . . . Many landlords, rich peasants, and
> good-for-nothings have taken this opportunity to slip in. . . . They
> bully and oppress the people and distort the Party's policies, causing
> the local organizations to become alienated from the masses and
> preventing the thorough implementation of land reform. . . . The
> most important step is the development of criticism and self-criticism
> within the Party.
>
> —From Mao Ze-dong's speech "The Present Situation and
> Our Tasks," delivered December 25, 1947

While the rest of the team was visiting the poor-and-hired, Leng
Bing began the work of educating the local Party members. The
Agrarian Law could not be put into effect without full democracy in
the village, and democracy could not be achieved unless the Party
members were committed to it. The Party cadres in particular, because
of their key positions in the village government and their moral authority, had a great influence on the people.

Education would proceed in two phases. First, the Party members
would learn what their faults were, how they had developed, and
which fault was important, which trivial. Second, the Party would be
reorganized to carry out the Agrarian Law. The first phase also had
two parts. In step 1, the "closed-door stage," the Party members would
meet with Leng for a period of thirteen days. In step 2, Party branch
meetings would be thrown open to the masses. Communists and non-
Communists would then solve their problems together, teaching and
learning from one another. In fact, this mutual teaching and learning
would pervade the entire process of education, for even during the

closed-door stage the people's criticisms would be relayed to the Party members by the work team.

Leng started the closed-door meetings on February 26, 1948, the day the whole team arrived in the village. He read aloud the Central Bureau's directive to Party members on the Agrarian Law, including the ten points that were to be announced to the entire village that night. Leng's fluency in reading was a rare asset, for even Wang Shao-zhen, the branch secretary, had a hard time working his way through the *People's Daily*, and few of the other local Party members could read as well as Wang. Leng now presented the Central Bureau's directive not as a halting jumble of words but as a series of ideas. He explained the difficult parts and led the Party members in discussing what the ten points meant for them personally.

Wang Shao-zhen, who was the village political director as well as the branch secretary, and Wang Xi-tang, the assistant secretary and village head, listened confidently. They were ready to be examined and reformed, they said, and they hoped that the *laoshi*, the simple and honest peasants, would rise and take power. Some Party cadres in other villages might have stolen the fruits of the struggle, Wang

Leng Bing of the work team, who had responsibility for educating the Party members.

(*left*) Wang Xi-tang, head of the village for more than three years, criticized himself in Party meetings for having been dictatorial.

(*below*) Wang Shao-zhen, secretary of the Party branch and political director of the village, criticized himself for "going through the motions" of democracy while abusing his power.

Xi-tang said, "but here in Ten Mile Inn we have all our accounts in order; you can check them."

"After all, ours is the model village branch of the ninth district," Wang Shao-zhen put in. These assurances gave Leng the impression—actually unfounded—that the Party members were in collusion to hide the facts.

Leng then read and explained Mao Ze-dong's December 25 speech on reorganizing the Party. When he asked the Party members to be honest about their faults, the members replied vaguely that they had been guilty of "commandism" (giving orders instead of democratically persuading and convincing) and "subjectivism" (acting according to their own ideas instead of according to actual conditions). Leng felt that they were not serious, and that Wang Shao-zhen in particular was airy about his shortcomings.

But at the large village meeting that first night, the Party branch saw how seriously the work team and the villagers took the Agrarian Law. When they heard themselves publicly directed to examine their faults and reform themselves, they began to wonder whether they were model Communists after all.

Leng now began to observe some progress in the closed-door meetings. During the next few days Wang Xi-tang, the village head, admitted that he was undemocratic; thinking it over, he saw that he had often forced people to obey orders instead of persuading them to carry out requests. He said that he had bullied the peasants into "volunteering" to carry stretchers and do other rear-service jobs. And during the Feudal Tails Campaign he himself had decided which people were "feudal tails" to be struggled against, instead of letting the masses decide. It was true that in both cases he had done no more than carry out instructions from the higher level. At the time Wang had felt these instructions were not realistic and had protested to his superiors. But since his objections had been ignored, and since he felt the peasants would not willingly do as his superiors required, he had browbeaten them.

Leng listened sympathetically and explained that some of the Party members' shortcomings might well turn out to be the result of unrealistic orders. Extenuating circumstances like these would be carefully studied later, he said; meanwhile the point was to bring matters into the open. Taking heart, Wang Xi-tang criticized himself for having allowed Wang Shao-zhen to abuse his power as political director to break off his brother's engagement.

The fact that the village head was finding fault with himself led the other Party members to describe their failings more concretely. Leng still had the impression, however, that there was some sort of organized opposition in the branch, and he felt that the political director in particular was a slippery type.

Even so, Leng told the work team, he thought the group had made a good start. He felt that the education of the Party members probably wouldn't be too difficult. Lou Lin, the leader, disagreed. "It's not until they start criticizing one another all around that the ground will be cleared for action," Lou said.

The Party cadres knew that the team was encouraging the villagers to evaluate them. This awareness led the cadres to put themselves in the villagers' place—to consider their behavior from the standpoint of the masses. Some of them did not find it easy to reveal their mistakes, but they knew that the team was bound to learn about them sooner or later, perhaps from a personal enemy who would tell a prejudiced tale.

Leng emphasized to the Party members that faults could be overcome only after being honestly exposed, and that the aim of education was to strengthen the Party by improving the quality of its members. Every Communist, he said, was a capital asset to the Party, not something to be carelessly thrown away.

"Moreover, your origins are good," Leng told them. Most of the local Party members were new middle peasants who had suffered from hunger in their poor-peasant days. They had been recruited because they were among the villagers who fought hardest against the Japanese and took the most active part in the land reforms that followed. Leng said, "Obviously men like you, who are experienced in revolutionary struggle, can be reformed if you'll bring your mistakes out into the open."

After five days of closed-door meetings, a picture of the village leadership began to take shape. The most important offices were filled by Party members, who governed by issuing orders and "fixing" things. In village elections they picked their candidates and did all they could to rig the voting. In the words of the branch propaganda secretary, "Elections—they were just something arranged by the branch."

Inside the branch, too, democracy was stunted. Things were run by the five top cadres—the village head, the political director, the peasant-union chairman, the public security officer, and the chairman of the people's defense committee. Meetings were rarely held. The militia commander told Leng, "We had a lot of complaints about the senior members of the branch, but we were afraid to say anything." The leader of a mutual-aid group said that he had once spoken privately to Wang Xi-tang about the highhanded behavior of the political director and the public security officer. Wang had admitted that the complaint was justified, but said that some indirect way would have to be found to express it. Thus the junior members had to curry favor with the influential cadres. They were forced to become "two-sided cakes" —the right way up whichever way you turn them.

In the land-reform campaigns it was the branch which decided who were to be objects of struggle and how the fruits of struggle were to be divided. Some Party members acquired an outsize share, and the cadres had even allowed some landlord and rich-peasant families to buy fruits. Thus the collaborator Wang Ban-yan had purchased mirrors and vases, whereas one poor peasant who needed a carrying pole could not afford it.

"The Party members considered the masses backward, and tried to lay down the law," Leng told the work team. "They felt that teaching them democracy would take too much time and work. Instead, they mobilized a handful of militants to push things through whenever a directive came from the Party. The people say that the Party members and the militants are like fire and gunpowder—when the two get together, watch out!

"Wang Shao-zhen, the branch secretary, finally admitted that they only went through the motions of democracy. If they'd been truly democratic, he says, the village wouldn't have any 'holes.' Wang is remorseful when he thinks of people like that impoverished ex-soldier who lives way up in the hills across the river. He says, 'If I'd had the poor peasants' interests at heart, as a Communist should, I'd never have agreed to sell the struggle fruits instead of giving them away.' And he compares the conditions of the 'hole families' with his own hard life before he fanshenned.

"In fact, by the fifth day," Leng said, "some of them were taking it so seriously that they were beginning to crack. They didn't see how they could repair the damage they had done. At the meeting the day before yesterday, Wang Xi-tang suddenly said, 'Before we leave here tonight we'd better take away everybody's weapons.' He was afraid that some of them might attempt suicide. And then a group who had been sitting dejectedly on the *kung* said, 'We'd better give up this criticism business and just hand ourselves over to the people's court.' The peasant-union chairman, Fu Zhang-sou, even burst into tears."

Leng continued, "When they first mentioned selling the struggle fruits, and said that the landlord traitor Wang Ban-yan had bought the vases and mirrors while a poor peasant couldn't afford a carrying pole, I lost my temper. 'Who do you think you're working for?' I shouted. Then some of them accused me of acting like the landlords and throwing my weight around.

"At that point I didn't know which way to go. I thought that if I let up on the pressure, we wouldn't get to the bottom of things, but that if the pressure were too great, they might not be able to stand it."

Leng took this problem to Lou Lin, and they decided that pressure should be combined with encouragement. Leng visited the Party members in their homes and praised them for their self-criticism. At the same time, he pointed out the political lessons to be learned from their wrongdoing.

In the rest of the thirteen-day closed-door education. Leng eased the emotional strain by raising the proceedings to a higher political level. "We began to discuss things from the standpoint of the branch as a whole instead of focusing on an individual's actions," he said later. "Then, although the discussion was hot, everyone became much less heavyhearted. They concluded that of the six big campaigns of the past, three had defects. The Reduction of Rent and Interest Movement had failed to mobilize the entire mass of poor and middle peasants. And in the Black Lands Campaign, which yielded by far the most wealth for distribution, they had followed the middle-peasant line of selling the fruits of struggle. In the end they realized that the entire branch had some responsibility for these shortcomings.

"They agreed that the most important point about a branch is not its weaknesses but its strengths," Leng said. "After all, it was the branch that led the masses in destroying feudalism in the village. It's true that there are still twenty or thirty 'hole' families, but the average yield of their land is only a little below the village average. So despite its defects, the Party branch really has led the masses to fanshen."

# 5

# Uniting the Poor-and-Hired

March 3, 4

The *People's Daily* of March 12, 1948, published the team's appraisal of their work in mobilizing the poor peasants of Ten Mile Inn. First they described their mistakes:

> After calling together a group of the poor-and-hired and arousing their enthusiasm, we did nothing to organize them. We did not give each group a name, such as Needy Families Group, but simply left them up in the air. This was like pouring cold water on them, for even though the Party cadres were evaluating themselves and learning to reform, the poor-and-hired were still rather afraid of the non-Party cadres.
>
> The period of visiting must not be too long. It is impossible to get to know the poor-and-hired without putting them to the test in some form of activity. We spent six or seven days on visiting, whereas five days would have been long enough. The delay had a bad effect, because the lack of organization and joint action caused disunity in some poor-and-hired groups.
>
> Some visits were too brief and superficial. A few of our comrades were impatient; the work seemed simple to them, and they galloped along as if they were in a horse race. Others, however, were too suspicious; nobody struck them as just right. The peasants seemed either too passive or too active. If a person had the courage to speak out, they considered him too bold and assumed that he was not simple and honest. If a person's floor was swept clean, they suspected that he was not a real hired laborer. They were so afraid of being isolated from the masses that they didn't dare to single out peasants with the capacity to lead.
>
> The fact is that the poor-and-hired are not faultless. The important thing is one's attitude toward them. We must rely upon them open-heartedly and correct their errors patiently.

Though they had made mistakes, the team felt that their methods had been generally sound. They wrote:

> We carried on our work completely in the open. From the outset we came into contact with the majority of the poor-and-hired, so that the small number of undesirables were never able to get the upper hand. In this way the uneasiness and suspicions of the middle peasants were lessened. After the mass meeting, the people went to work in their fields more and more enthusiastically, and it would have been difficult for any bad Party cadres to undermine our work.
>
> The masses soon shed their timidity. When we were visiting the poor-and-hired before the mass meeting, they were afraid to speak up, but a day later they began to come out with their criticisms. At the same time, our work was not confined to paying visits and propagandizing; everything we did was clearly directed toward the democratic movement and the task of classifying the peasants.

By March 3 the team had realized that it was a mistake to postpone organizing the poor peasants and hired laborers. In every section of the village they began to hold small meetings with a few poor-and-hired whom they had come to regard as reliable.

One such meeting was called at noon on that day by the four team members in charge of the south-end and east-central sections of the village. Three of the five poor peasants whom they had invited arrived as the work team secretary was writing up some notes. They were greeted by a second team member, Geng Xi, who chatted with them until two other members of the team came in with the remaining peasants. The conversation became general and gradually focused on four qualifications for joining the poor-peasant league proposed by the team. These were: a peasant should be hardworking, simple and honest, easy to get along with, and enthusiastic about serving the people.

Taking a slip of paper from his pocket, Geng Xi said, "Here are the names of all the poor-and-hired we've spotted in your sections. I'll read them one by one, and you can say how they measure up to the qualifications. First, what about Wang Fu-chen?"

The peasants looked at one another to see who would speak. Their gaze settled on Wang Wen-sheng, who was a member of Fu-chen's mutual-aid group.

Wang Wen-sheng said thoughtfully, "He doesn't keep his promises very well. If he's with good men, he's good; if with bad, he's bad. Whichever way the hill slopes, he falls."

The others nodded; they considered Wang Fu-chen a doubtful candidate.

Geng Xi read the second name—Wang Mi-chuan. All three peasants from the south end spoke: "He's young and rash."

"But he's very direct and outspoken!"

"He's not afraid to say what he thinks about the cadres."

It was generally agreed that the rash Wang Mi-chuan would be an asset to the poor-peasant league.

Geng Xi checked his name on the list. "Now what about these three brothers: Wang Kui-fan, Wang Gui-fan, and Wang Lou-fan?"

"Wang Kui-fan is a carpenter," a peasant said. "He's a funny sort; you can never be sure what he's going to think about things. But he's the best of the three brothers. Gui-fan was with the People's Liberation Army. Though he has a strict sense of duty and public service, he's cold—difficult to get along with. As for Lou-fan, he talks all the time, but he never thinks the same way for more than two minutes. Also, he's touchy."

"That's right," another speaker said. "If he's short-weighted, he never gets over it."

Geng Xi did not check the names of the three brothers. Next he read the name of a villager who had been working as a laborer in the neighboring province of Shanxi. Everyone agreed that he was a good man, though they didn't think much of his mother.

"She's a diviner; she communes with spirits."

"She used to get a lot of gifts from the superstitious women who consulted her about their illnesses. But she hasn't done so well for the last few years."

"Of course, none of the women go to her openly nowadays. So she doesn't think much of the reforms, and she busies herself spreading rumors about this and that."

"She lives in the Fort now, with an old man who used to be a landlord."

But Geng Xi pointed out that the son's suitability for membership was not affected by his mother's relations with spirits or ex-landlords. He checked the villager's name.

"How about Wang Kang-shi?"

All five agreed that he was a good man, suitable for membership in the league—though his mother had her faults, too. As one of them put it, "She has an eye for the men."

The next name was that of Wang Guang-xun.

"He has a dirty mouth; he's always cursing or insulting people."

"And he'd rather have food in his belly than clothes on his back. He even begrudges the money to buy clothes for his kid."

"But his chief fault is that you can't rely on him."

Geng Xi did not check the name, but went on to the next. "What about Wang Kui-nian," he asked.

The peasants conceded that he was an honest man. "But he's as obstinate as a mule, and he's sharp-tongued too."

"He used to be very poor. He's a lot better off now, thanks to the Eighth Route Army. Yet he's always grumbling that he didn't get his share of the fruits, that he's not treated as an equal, that the people in the government offices here eat better food than he does."

"And he's not satisfied to complain privately to a few friends out in the fields; he shoots off his mouth to a big crowd in the street."

The next names were those of two brothers. The peasants quickly agreed that one had all four qualifications, then went on to discuss the other.

"His weakness is that he can't lead people and has to be given pep talks himself. But though he's lazy at the beginning, he sticks to a job once he's started."

"Besides, he's not sly, and he never gives information to the landlords." They decided that both brothers were acceptable.

Next came a clerk who was away from home working in a town shop. He was described as "quick-witted but too cautious."

"He can see so many sides to every question that he can never reach a decision about anything."

The villagers considered Fu Shou-xi, the cooperative miller. Their conclusion was that he was well qualified for the league.

"He's easygoing, and he can get along with anyone. He used to chase after women; in fact, he's living with Chu-zi's wife now, but that's Chu-zi's fault."

The peasants smiled and told the story. Chu-zi, an ardent fan of the local Wu-an opera, idolized its star, who was an actor with the stage name of Three Flags. Chu-zi had struck up an acquaintance with the actor, invited him home, and ended by supporting him and neglecting his own family. The wife then took the two children and went to live with Fu Shou-xi, who had always been too poor to get a wife of his own.

The next name read out was that of a peasant known for his impassiveness.

"He's a good chap, but he's not very active. He's just like an old man; he never gets excited and he never hurries."

"He's not lazy, though. It's like this: if someone needs his help and he's sitting and smoking his pipe, he'll say, 'I'm smoking now.' But when he finishes the pipe, he goes and helps." The peasants agreed that he was suitable.

"Wang Xi-cai?"

"He likes to do things for people, and everyone likes to ask him for favors. It makes him a good middleman."

"When the South Hebei Bank staff put on 'The White-Haired Girl,' he was the one who borrowed the beautiful silk quilts they used for the scenes in the landlord's home. You should have seen them; all colors of the rainbow."

"They were part of the struggle fruits that haven't been distributed yet."

There was a meaningful pause, for the delay in distributing the fruits of a prevous campaign was one of the villagers' grievances.

Another speaker resumed, "He loves visiting people—especially the staff of the government offices here. He's always talking to them about their adventures in the old days of guerrilla fighting."

Thus pondering, gossiping, and analyzing, they went through Geng Xi's list. Similar meetings were held in every section of the village. The poor-and-hired who were approved by these small groups would later be asked to nominate candidates to serve as recruiters for the league. In the meantime nothing more could be done to set up the poor-peasant league, as it was necessary first to know who were the poor peasants and hired laborers. This preliminary stage of finding some activists among the poor-and-hired and explaining policy to them was solely to guarantee that those poor-and-hired who had not yet stood up would have spokesmen during the crucial stage of drawing class lines in the village.

Once this preliminary task was accomplished, the team member embarked on the second stage of the campaign, that of classification. Their first step was to study the principles of classification themselves. They met every day for discussions that were based both on their field work and on a table of definitions originally issued in 1933 and recently revised in a restricted edition for cadres doing land-reform work:

## Definitions of Rural Classes

*Landlords* are those who own land but do not work, or else work at supplementary activities. To live, they exploit the peasants, mainly by exacting rent but also by hiring labor and lending money.

*Rich peasants* own the better means of production and have some floating capital. They themselves work, but as a rule they depend on exploitation for most or a part of their living. This exploitation chiefly takes the form of hiring wage labor (that is, long-term laborers).

*Middle peasants* depend wholly or mainly on their own work for their living. In general they do not exploit others, and many of them suffer exploitation on a small scale in the form of land rent and loan interest. Usually they do not sell their labor.

*Upper-middle peasants** are occasional exploiters on a small scale, but the income from exploitation is not their main support.

*Lower-middle peasants** are self-sufficient on the whole, but they suffer some exploitation in the form of rent or interest.

*Poor peasants* in general have to rent the land they farm. They suffer exploitation in the form of rent and interest, and they must occasionally hire themselves out. The selling of labor for limited periods is the basic feature distinguishing them from lower-middle peasants.

*Workers (including farm laborers)* generally have neither land nor farm tools. They depend wholly or mainly on the sale of their labor.

In their study meetings the team discussed the definitions in terms of particular peasants. Shao Hang, who was assigned to the Fort, said, "There's no problem in classifying someone like Li Xin-hai. He conforms exactly to the definition of a poor peasant. He hasn't much land, and what he has is poor. His family lead a hard life. They couldn't get along at all if he didn't go out to work for other members of his mutual-aid group.

"But what about Fu Shuo-qian? There are eight in his family, and they cultivate 26 *mu* of land. Yet only 18 *mu* is ordinary farmland; the rest is on a stony hillside. He reclaimed the hillside land instead of hiring himself out because, as he says, 'It's better to farm a lot of bad, stony land of your own than to work for someone else.' His family have just as hard a life as Li Xin-hai's, though you might say, 'Li has to sell his labor, while Fu neither buys nor sells it.'

"Then there's Fu Li-ku, whose family have 2.7 *mu* per head. But the land is poor, so he has to work outside with his donkey to make ends meet. He's at home only four months in the year; he takes trade-and-transport jobs for the other eight.

"If a poor peasant by definition has only a small amount of land that doesn't produce all he needs for food, then how should Fu Li-ku be classified? He hasn't enough to be called a middle peasant, but he doesn't work for others; he depends on his donkey. The very fact that he has a donkey makes him seem too rich for a poor peasant. Yet some people with no donkey are better off in terms of their other possessions, though they can still be called poor peasants."

The team worried at this problem until they agreed that a family were poor peasants if their landholdings were too small and poor to

---

* The main difference between these definitions and the current classification in Ten Mile Inn was that the categories of upper-middle and lower-middle peasants would not be used; the term middle peasant was to cover them both. Following the Central Committee's Land Reform Directive of May 4, 1946, middle peasants were divided into two categories, "old" and "new": "old" referring to those who were middle peasants before the land reform, "new" to those who became so following it.

feed them all and if they could make ends meet only by unusually hard labor, which was equivalent to taking work as a farmhand.

It was essential for the team to be clear about classification, but only so that they might teach the peasants to carry it out, not to do the job for them. As a *People's Daily* article of the period said, "The work team has no right to decide anyone's class origin; its members are only 'wick trimmers' who help throw light on matters."

The team members realized that they should be 'wick trimmers' first and foremost for the unfanshenned. If these villagers were to stand up and help shape their own destiny in the current movement, they had to play a leading role in the classification. But they were the most inarticulate. Training and practice was necessary to give them the ability and the confidence to take the lead in broad meetings of all classes.

The team gave the first lesson in classification to five poor peasants in the south-end and east-central sections—the same five who had passed judgment on Geng Xi's list of names. This time their meeting was guided by the team member Pang Qing-chao. After explaining the principles of classification, Pang suggested that one of the peasants at the meeting describe his own economic situation so that the others could use him as a trial case. So Wang Pei-qing began to tell his story.

"There are four of us in my family now," he said. "They are my mother, my younger brother, my young girl cousin, and myself.

"When I was a boy of about ten, our family used to have 10 *mu* of land. But we could hardly scrape along on that, and most of the time we were as poor as beggars. The family hasn't owned an animal for three generations.

"When I was fourteen, I went to Shanxi to make bricks with my father, who had already moved there. But he died in 1935, and I gave up brickmaking. Since I didn't have any experience in farming, I became a shepherd. Though it was no way to get rich, I saved all my wages and came home in 1942, bringing the bones of my father and my uncle, who had also died in Shanxi. (For this I bought two new woollen bags, put one set of bones in each, and slung them on one end of my carrying pole. I tied all my belongings to the other end, and the pole just balanced.)

"When I got home, I found that my mother had had such a hard time during the drought and the famine that she was preparing to leave and wander as a refugee. Instead, we used the money I had saved to redeem 2 *mu* of land that had been mortgaged. My little orphaned cousin was already living with us then, so we decided that somehow we'd have to buy more land. We sold the furniture which was meant for her dowry (she was only six years old) and bought another 2 *mu*. For a little while we were happy, but the drought continued. We reaped no wheat in the spring, and in the autumn we got only one bushel of millet.

"So I went back to Shanxi to make bricks. My mother came with me and got a job cooking for a landlord. While we were away my married sister cultivated the land by herself, and even managed to make enough out of it to buy another 2½ *mu*. So when my mother and I returned, the family had between 6 and 7 *mu*.

"After that I got a job as a laborer and saved enough to buy just over a *mu* and a half outside the south gate. The year before last, I went to North Village and earned a little money making bricks.

"Last spring during the Fill the Holes and Level the Tops Movement, we exchanged part of our poor land in Gravel Gulch for some better land. So now we have 11 *mu* altogether—4 of it good. This is about an average holding, and our normal estimated yield is 10 *dan*. We got between 8 and 9 *dan* of wheat in the last harvest. In the autumn we paid about 1 *dan* of millet in tax to the government and spent another *dan* to hire animals for plowing.

"The grain we have on hand will see us through until the wheat harvest in the fifth month. So if the crop is good, we'll be all right. Last year we raised only enough grain to support us for eight months; for the rest of the time I had to depend on brickmaking. That way, I even earned some extra money that I spent on tools.

"Well, now you know how things are with me. What class do you think I am?"

Wang Pei-qing's long story was followed by an equally long discussion, the peasants finding the tale so absorbing that at first it was difficult for them to see what parts of it were irrelevant. The team members helped them select the details that had a bearing on Wang's classification. The important facts, the peasants decided, were that he did not exploit others but had to sell his own labor, that he owned some land but not enough for his family to live on, that he had no draft animal, and that he had only just begun to acquire farm tools. They concluded—and the team members agreed—that Wang Pei-qing was a poor peasant.

This practice session set the pattern for the 433 people who were to be classified during the coming weeks, including Wang Pei-qing himself. Other selected groups of poor peasants told their stories in similar small meetings and were thus trained by the work team to lead the classification.

Up in the Fort, Shao Hang and other members of the work team spent many hours preparing the poor peasant Fu Bian-de for the classification. In both his strengths and weaknesses Fu Bian-de of the Fort was typical of the best people among the unfanshenned. Thin as a withered millet stalk, he had the look of an elderly man even though he was still in his thirties. He had lost most of his teeth, his cheeks hung loose, and his hair was sparse. But he was not as ineffective as he looked and he had been elected to several minor offices. As a boy, Fu Bian-de had been driven out of his home by his stepmother, who hoped to produce an heir to displace him. He had lived ever since as a farm laborer and brickmaker.

During a week's visiting, investigation, and organizing in the Fort, the team member Shao Hang came to understand why so many of the poor-and-hired were fond of Fu Bian-de. He was the essence of the *laoshi*, the simple and honest peasant, whose timidity was constantly being checked by his sense of justice. With effort and encouragement, this kind of man might take a leading part in mobilizing the poor-and-hired of the Fort.

When Shao Hang first approached him he had quivered like a leaf; but by the night of March 3, after many hours of coaching by team members, he and a handful of others were ready. On the morning of the fourth, classification began.

# 6

# Classification in the Fort

## March 4

The first classification was held in the most spacious and impressive building in the Fort—the house of a former landlord. All the Fort's families except those who had been objects of struggle were entitled to send representatives, and all did so except for five whose men were off transporting coal from the mines at He Village.

Some eighty villagers—about fifty men and thirty women—squatted in the room on little stools, bricks, or straw mats. Many of the women had brought soles to stitch for cloth shoes, and despite the freedom they had gained in recent years, they still sat apart from the men. At a table against the wall two members of the team prepared to take notes. Team members and peasants from the lower village crowded around the doorway, for all were curious to see how classification would go.

The team member Geng Xi, cheerful, down-to-earth, and energetic, began. "Today we are going to do classification. This job is so important that it's worth missing a day's work. Sorting out the classes is going to build unity among us.

"Classification is necessary if we want to organize ourselves. We must classify people according to what they really are, no matter whether they're members of the Fu clan or the Li clan, whether they're men or women, whether they're Party members or not. And there must be no shielding anybody, no face-saving, and no spite. Whatever you are, you are. We'll call a spade a spade: a poor peasant a poor peasant, and a middle peasant a middle peasant.

"What are the standards of classification?" Geng Xi asked, and proceeded to give the Party's definitions of the rural classes. He explained that the process of classification was to be divided into three main stages, and that each stage would have three steps. The first step

52

in each stage would be to arrive at decisions regarding each individual's class, the second would be to post the decisions, and the third would be to discuss the decisions.

In the first stage—the first classification—the peasants were to classify only the members of the basic laboring masses—the villagers who had not been struggled against. They were to sort themselves out into poor peasants, who would form the backbone of the poor-peasant league; new middle peasants, who were to be drawn into the league and might form one-third of the membership; and old middle peasants, who would be drawn into the reorganized peasant union together with the two other classes.

It was only at the second stage—the second classification—that the much more complicated task of sorting out the struggle objects was to be undertaken. The third classification would simply amount to ratification of the results—after amendment, if necessary. The complete classification was scheduled to take about a month. During this time, of course, related projects would also be carried out.

Geng Xi closed his speech with two points:

"The work team has no authority to settle anyone's class. It's here to help you classify yourselves. The team's job is only to trim the wick and make the lamp of the people burn brighter.

"Now, remember: classification is one thing, and filling the holes is another. Of course those classed as poor peasants will have their holes filled up. But if there are some poor peasants who received an unfair share of the fruits, they'll have to hand them back. Some of the middle peasants, on the other hand, may receive some land. So filling the holes is a different process from sorting out classes.

"Now let's ferment."

"Ferment, ferment." Everybody took up the word, which was to become familiar in the course of many meetings during the next few weeks.

There was a shuffling of little stools, a shifting of bricks, a turning of bodies. In a moment the audience was transformed from a crowd focused upon the speaker into a bunch of animated little groups all holding meetings of their own. As a rule friends, neighbors, and members of the same subgroups in the mutual-aid group, the peasant union, or the militia sat near each other at meetings. These now formed natural fermentation groups. Starting with a low buzz, chatter soon filled the room as people discussed what Geng Xi had said, thrashed out points which seemed unclear, registered their opinions, and formulated questions or statements. Even the most timid felt free to talk things over among the people who were their intimate associates in everyday life. Members of the work team who circulated among the groups to answer their questions repeated any that seemed especially significant and answered them loudly for the benefit of all.

Gradually the buzz subsided, and the chairman again called the meeting to order. Spokesmen from each of the informal groupings now reported on the views which had been expressed and the questions which had been raised. Finally Geng Xi announced that if there were no more questions or comments, whoever wanted to begin the classification could make his self-report.

The first to rise was Fu Li-yong, a mild old man who achieved a sinister appearance by knotting the peasant's white towel so far down his forehead that only the lower halves of his eyes were visible. He peered out from under the towel and began:

"I had 8.5 *mu* of land the year before last. And in the spring of last year, the peasant union gave me 1.3 *mu*. So now I have 9.4. I haven't got an animal. I have a hoe, a spade, and a mattock, but none of the big tools like a plow or seeder. I have enough seed, but not enough manure to fertilize more than 3 or 4 *mu*.

"There are three of us in the family, but I'm the only one who counts as a workhand. The yield isn't high enough to see us through, so I have to do short-term labor for others.

"I have four sections of housing." The peasants calculated housing not by the room but by the section, which was the space between two crossbeams.

"The estimated average yield of my land is over 7 *dan*, but the actual crop last year was only a bit over 3 *dan* of unhusked millet and 1 *dan* of corn. In all, that made 4 *dan* and 7 bushels of coarse grain for the year." Wheat and rice were considered fine grain, whereas millet, sorghum, and corn were coarse.

"I wouldn't call myself a poor peasant. You can hardly say I have too little land, for even though it doesn't yield enough to feed the whole family, I can make it up with outside work. My wife can spin and weave, and she and my daughter both make clothes. So there's no difficulty in getting enough food and clothing."

Fu Li-yong paused, then added: "So I think maybe I ought to be considered a middle peasant."

"How do you think he ought to be classified?" asked Geng Xi.

The fermentation groups huddled together and began to whisper. At last the spokesman of one group stood up and said, "We think he's a poor peasant. Although he has plenty of land, its yield is low. And even though he has four sections of housing, they're so small that you can't even turn around inside."

Another speaker rose. "We think he's a poor peasant too, because

Classification: a peasant describes his economic situation as his neighbors listen. Lou Lin, leader of the work team, is seated at the table.

he has to work for others to feed his family. And he has no animal."

Another said, "He fanshenned only recently—less than a year ago."

After a lot of whispering among the women, one of them stood up. "He's a poor peasant, all right. His wife's half crippled, and his daughter's too young to do much. He's the family's only good workhand."

A young man rose. "He wasn't really honest. The conditions he described were those of a poor peasant, weren't they? So why did he classify himself as a middle peasant? He should have said straight out that he was a poor peasant."

At this, Geng Xi asked Fu Li-yong, "Suppose you didn't do outside work. Would you have enough to eat?"

"Certainly not," said Fu.

"Well," said Geng Xi, "everybody here seems to think you're a poor peasant. What's your opinion?"

"I haven't any," Fu replied. Evidently he felt that he really was a poor peasant, but that to say so straight out would have been like asking to have his "hole filled up."

"Has anyone got anything to add?" the chairman asked.

"No, nothing more," came from various parts of the room. "He's a poor peasant."

The second case was that of Li Bao-zhi. "There are three in my family," he said. "I have 11 *mu* of land with an estimated average yield of just over 8 *dan*. I bought a small donkey in the fifth month, but I sold it in the seventh and bought a bigger one. I borrowed 3 *yuan* from the bank and paid it back after making some money by transporting pottery.

"I got a full autumn crop last year, but only half a wheat crop. I have no tools at all; I have to borrow them.

"Still, we don't go hungry. Between my son and me, one or the other is out on trade-and-transport all the time. So although we have to work hard, we can eat.

"Our home's all broken down, though; we haven't got a single decent room.

"As to our land, it's the poorest there is. Its average yield is only half a *dan* per *mu*." This was half the yield of good land.

"Last autumn I got just over 4 *dan*—3 of unhusked millet, 1 of corn.

"Reckoning according to the year before last, I'd be a poor peasant. But judging by the way I lived last year, I'd say I was a new middle peasant."

"Have you lived the life of a new middle peasant for over a year?" asked Geng Xi.

Li Bao-zhi hesitated.

"Have you got enough grain on hand for one year's food?" Geng asked again.

Li and many others in the crowd answered at once: "No; not enough."

"He only got a crop and a half."

"He got the whole autumn crop, but only half the summer crop."

"Well, what class would you say you were?" Geng Xi asked.

This time Li Bao-zhi replied, "Poor peasant."

Once more the meeting broke into fermentation groups, then reunited.

"He has to do outside work, so we think he's a poor peasant," the first group spokesman reported.

"His land isn't so bad," said another. "He suffered in the past, but now he's got land and lives better. And his boy's grown up and can work at trade-and-transport."

"He paid 5 *yuan* for the small donkey and sold it for 7 in the seventh month," another member of the same group cut in. "Then the next one he bought was much bigger; it cost 13 *yuan*.* He's still in debt for

* The *yuan* (commonly mistranslated as "dollar") was and still is the basic money unit in China. At this time there was enormous inflation in the Guomindang areas which inevitably found some reflection in the Liberated Areas, though to nowhere near the same degree. Soon after the setting up of the People's Republic in 1949 inflation was checked by the new People's government, and the currency was reformed,

that. If he didn't go out on trade-and-transport, he and the donkey would both starve to death. When he made the donkey's saddle, he even had to borrow the old cotton for the padding. I think he's a poor peasant, all right."

"It's true," said someone else. "He only got a crop and a half last year. And he has to borrow his tools, so he has a tough time. He's a poor peasant."

"He didn't have a thing to his name in the old days. It was only after the Communists came that he began to fanshen. Last year he began to be a bit better off."

"His land's a long way from the village, and it's on the hilltop. I say he's a poor peasant."

"When he was very poor," one of the women added, "his wife had to take in sewing to earn a little money. She hardly had time to make clothes for her own family."

Usually the men spoke first, then the women. But though they came last, the women generally said something to the point. For a while Wang Xiang, head of the women's association for the Fort and vice-head of the association for the whole village, seemed to be acting as the self-appointed speaker for all the women. As a result the other women showed signs of becoming passive. When he realized what was happening, Geng Xi explained with his genial smile that the women could speak for themselves, without having anyone to represent them.

The conclusion of the entire crowd was that for the time being, Li Bao-zhi was a poor peasant, though after the summer harvest he would doubtless become a middle peasant.

The next self-report was Fu Shuo-chuan's. "In the past I couldn't get along," he said. "But after the Eighth Route Army came, I farmed 10 *mu* and kept a donkey. Then I sold the donkey and bought a mule, but that put me into debt.

"Our land yields 8 *dan* of unhusked millet a year. That's not enough for my family, since we have eight mouths to feed. So I'm always having to do short-term labor for other people or go to the kiln to make bricks. And when I'm at the kiln the kids are left at home alone.

"We have only a small hut, and no chairs, tables, or benches. But I have a plow, a seeder, and other tools, big and small. Besides my

so that the figures on all banknotes were divided by 10,000—i.e., 10,000 *yuan* became 1 *yuan*. At the same time each *yuan* was divided into 100 *fen*. These monetary units are still (1979) used in the People's Republic. For convenience' sake (i.e., to avoid the constant addition of four zeros to monetary figures) the present-day system had been backdated to the period covered by this book. Actually the speaker gave the figures 50,000, 70,000, and 130,000 *yuan*. The purchasing power of the *yuan* in the Liberated Areas is indicated by the prices quoted at various places in the book.

own land, I rent 7 *mu* from a widow and cultivate another 5 to 6 *mu* of wasteland on the mountain slopes. I'm pretty hefty, and I like to do trade-and-transport.

"So if you look at my life from the outside, it seems pretty good. But the fact is that I just put up a front; I'm a sort of half-and-half. If you say I'm a poor peasant, my position's a little too strong; if you say I'm a middle peasant, it's a little too shaky."

The crowd fermented and reunited. Some of the spokesmen referred to Fu's small amount of land or to its low yield; others emphasized his need to do trade-and-transport and work as a hired hand.

"As to his mule," said one, "it's only a paper mule. All it's done is pile up debts and hunger for him."

In the end Fu Shuo-chuan was classed as a poor peasant.

These first three cases were characteristic: though there were still some poor peasants in Ten Mile Inn, there were no longer any tenants or desperately poor hired laborers. In the main the villagers were partly fanshenned—or in Fu Shuo-chuan's words, "sort of half-and-half."

The fourth to report was Li Li-zi, who was seventy-four. "I have 12½ *mu* of land and a donkey," he said. "And I've got all the small tools—hoe and pick and spade—but none of the big ones except a plow. Then there are another 7 *mu* belonging to my grandson. We two have lived together for ten years now. There are two old mouths to feed—my wife and me. And there are three young ones—my grand-daughter, my grandson, and his wife." The grandson was only thirteen, his wife two years older.

"I've got no debts to speak of, but my wife's sick and we have to spend money on medicine. The average yield of the land is about a *dan* a *mu*. All of it was bought before the Eighth Route Army came.

"Our family divided up once, but then we moved back together. When we were apart, my son was counted as a middle peasant and I was a poor peasant. So I don't know exactly what I am now; but since the five of us are together, maybe I ought to count as a middle peasant. I don't mind what class I am—please decide for me. My trouble is that I've got no labor power."

"Let's put that point aside for the time," Geng Xi suggested. "We can decide what his class is according to the facts; then we can take up the question of his labor shortage."

Without that knotty problem, there was not much to discuss. Certainly 19½ *mu* was a lot for five people, its yield was high by local standards, and it had been acquired before the democratic reforms. So Li Li-zi was classed as an old middle peasant, with some approving comments that he had spoken up like the honest old man he was.

Some of the others who followed Li were also praised for their frankness with such comments as "He calls a spade a spade," "No need to strain your brain over his case," and "If they were all like that, we'd soon be through."

Almost all the cases were presented by men, since few women were heads of families. After a while, however, a widow rose to make her self-report. She was listed not under her own name but as "Li Lian-xi's mother."

Her son became the subject of considerable controversy. "He's rated as a full workhand," the widow said, "but the fact is that he's sick and really ought to be considered as half a hand."

"What!" someone exclaimed. "A nineteen-year-old not a full work-hand?"

Someone else said, "It's true that he's not very strong. All the same, you might consider him a full hand."

While no one disputed the fact that the young man was not a good worker, this did not affect the family's class. The people at the meeting concluded that Li Lian-xi and his mother were old middle peasants.

The decision followed from a basic principle of classification— that it was the ownership or nonownership of the means of production, and the exploitation or nonexploitation of labor, which determined class. Class was not measured by a family's standard of living. Both Li Lian-xi's mother and Li Li-zi hired labor from the mutual-aid group and paid for it at the established rate. This left little surplus for the middle-peasant employer; in fact, his employees often enjoyed a higher standard of living than he did. Nevertheless, both Li Lian-xi and Li Li-zi were undoubtedly middle peasants, for they owned abundant land and tools compared with the mass of villagers.

Many of the people at the meeting showed that they had grasped this principle of classification. There were still some, however, who confused class with the standard of living. When Li Liu-cheng was listed as an old middle peasant, his wife could not accept it. "How can you call us old middle peasants?" she asked bitterly. "I've never enjoyed a single good hour in my whole life."

The crowd, while acknowledging that this may have been true, said that the Lis were certainly old middle peasants, for they neither exploited nor were exploited by others. But since the wife disagreed with the majority decision, both opinions were recorded.

The last case of the morning session was that of Wang Xiang, who had been speaking for the other women earlier in the meeting. In her youth Wang Xiang had suffered bitterly as a home-raised daughter-in-law. When a girl was betrothed in childhood and sent to live with the family of her future husband, she was usually treated like a slave.

Later Wang Xiang had fanshenned and been elected a leader in the Ten Mile Inn women's association. Nevertheless she felt insecure in her position. She knew that many of the women looked at her askance because she mixed freely in public with the men, and even adopted some of their mannerisms. She realized that it was because of their own dread of speaking in public that they admired her daring and so had elected her a cadre of the association.

Would Wang Xiang be able to keep her position in the women's association if she lost her standing as a poor peasant? She did not know, and she was less confident than usual as she rose to make her self-report. But she braced herself on her small bound feet and said in a firm voice, "Until the Eighth Route Army came, I had nothing. Then I fanshenned, and now I have 5.9 *mu* with an estimated average yield of 6.2 *dan*. I have no animal, no house of my own, no debt. I think I'm a lower-middle peasant."

In this way Wang Xiang compromised, hesitating to call herself a poor peasant, yet unwilling to commit herself as a middle peasant. But the team member Geng Xi explained that this time there was no such class as lower-middle peasant, that she would have to decide whether she was a middle or a poor peasant. After a pause, Wang Xiang said boldly that she was a poor peasant.

The crowd began to murmur, and she tossed her head in embarrassment and defiance.

A spokesman for one of the small groups rose. "She has a widowed niece who can't cultivate all her land," he said. "So she has given 3 *mu* to Wang Xiang. She doesn't ask for anything in return; she only drops in for a meal now and then."

"Wang Xiang has quite enough. In fact, she can't eat up all her grain," said another. "And her son's in the army, so she gets all her land plowed. Her water is fetched for her, and the village supplies her with fuel."

A conciliatory spokesman from a third group said, "It's true that her yield is enough now. But if her son married, it'd be too little. So if we count two mouths as three, she hasn't got enough. And she has no animal. All in all, our group thinks she's a poor peasant."

But Geng Xi said, "In classifying we have to consider things as they are. We can't take two mouths as three; one mouth is one mouth, neither more nor less. So we must count the son in the army as one—. But we must consider him a workhand as well, because he'll come back. As to the fact that she has her land plowed for her, we don't count that in deciding her class. She has no animal, but that doesn't mean she isn't a middle peasant—though of course, if a middle peasant has a hole, it will have to be filled up."

As the discussion continued it became clear that after the arrival of the Eighth Route Army, Wang Xiang had risen to the middle-peasant class. In the end she agreed to be ranked as a new middle peasant.

It was understandable that Wang Xiang should be somewhat confused about the standards for classification, for the team had not coached better-off peasants. Instead they had concentrated on developing activities among the partly fanshenned poor peasants. The reason was this: they had foreseen that a small number of highly articulate middle peasants would think it in their own economic and political interests to be classified as poor peasants. For the view was spreading in the village that a new social hierarchy would result from the current campaign, with poor peasants at the top, new middle peasants in the middle, and old middle peasants at the bottom.

When the Fort villagers reassembled after the noon meal, it became obvious that a few people who had been classed as middle peasants had gotten together. The animal dealer Li Bao-hui reopened the case of the prosperous Fu Wei-shan, saying, "I don't know how it was that everyone agreed to class him as an old middle peasant. He told me just now that if the Eighth Route Army hadn't come, he'd never have been able to get along. He really fanshenned only after the army arrived. Isn't that so?" he asked Fu.

"I agree to whatever class all of you decide," said Fu Wei-shan. "But it's true that my life improved only after the Eighth Route Army came. They asked us to plant cotton, and I planted it. After that I was able to buy a donkey."

A little later, Fu Wei-shan spoke up on another peasant's behalf. "Li Min's land was bought only after the Eighth Route Army's arrival," he said. "It seems strange to classify him as an old middle peasant."

It was true that the lives of Fu Wei-shan and Li Min, as well as those of many other middle peasants, had improved following the arrival of the Eighth Route Army. Almost all the middle peasants had benefitted by the innovations that the Communists had introduced: cotton growing, spinning and weaving, mutual-aid groups, loans from the cooperative, and not least, restraints imposed on the landlords and rich peasants. Many had also profited from the incorrect handling at the time of the Black Lands Campaign, when the farmland taken from tax-evading landlords and rich peasants had been put on sale instead of being distributed free to the poor peasants. This "middle peasant" line had enabled Li Min and many other middle peasants to buy land.

The efforts of Fu Wei-shan and other middle peasants to get each other reclassified as poor peasants failed because, encouraged by the activists coached by the team, the poor peasants dared to stand up to the middle peasants and to uphold the decisions made in the morning. But, as the afternoon meeting went on, Fu and his friends made a fresh attempt. They now tried to get as many people as possible classified as middle peasants. Apparently they were anticipating a later stage of the campaign when the middle peasants would be invited to contribute land to fill the holes of poor peasants. They decided that the more middle peasants there were, the smaller the burden on each one.

Li Bao-qin, for example, had inherited a small quantity of poor land and a few tumbledown rooms from his father. On this flimsy basis one middle peasant tried to call Li an old middle peasant. After all, the speaker pointed out, Li had acquired his land neither by the sweat of his brow nor through the Communist-led reforms; he had simply inherited it. But most of the peasants reporting for their groups insisted that Li Bao-qin was a poor peasant, and the opposition collapsed.

As they went along, the villagers of the Fort gained considerable understanding of the principles of classification and the need to stand by them. At last Shao Hang of the work team slowly read out the final results of the first classification in the Fort:

| CLASS | NUMBER OF FAMILIES |
|---|---|
| *Unanimous verdicts* | |
| Poor peasants | 18 |
| New middle peasants | 13 |
| Old middle peasants | 24 |
| Workers | 2 |
| *Two opinions* | |
| New middle or poor peasants | 6 |
| New middle or old middle peasants | 2 |
| *Three opinions* | |
| Old middle, new middle, or poor peasants | 2 |
| *Accidentally omitted* | 4 |
| TOTAL | 71 |

"This is the first of three classifications," said Shao. "By the time the final classification is made, we must see that nobody has any prejudices or fears left in his heart. We must make sure that all opinions or objections have been freely expressed, for there must be no mistakes. If certain things are not clear or not correctly done this time, we must think them over and correct them in future classifications. We must speak out frankly about the cadres, whether they're Communists or not, and about the Party members, whether they're cadres or not. We must do away with the face-saving habit. We must not be afraid of kindling grudges or provoking reprisals, but we must make sure that what we say is accurate and concrete. We must stay calm and avoid being drawn into quarrels.

"When the whole village has finished the first classification, we'll put up a poster so that everyone can study it. Then they'll ferment and prepare to make corrections next time."

With this Shao closed the meeting, but it was the partly fanshenned poor peasant Fu Li-yong who had the last word. The classification had made a strong impression on him, for it had established the principle that people were not transformed into members of an enemy class simply by becoming prosperous. Provided they did not exploit others, there was no limit to the wealth a family could accumulate. "So far, I haven't tried as hard as I might to improve our lives," Fu said, peering from under his rakish towel. "But it won't be like that any more; I'm going to work like a mule."

Word of the Fort's classification quickly spread through the village, and every section was impatient to begin its own. Some met by day, others by night; some met in spacious courtyards or vacant lots; others crowded into rooms and filled the *kangs*, squatted on the doorsills, and leaned against looms and bins of millet and corn.

For three days the entire village was immersed in classification. On the morning of the fourth day, three placards giving the results were posted in various places. Opposite the name of each family head was the classification agreed upon in his section. Where there had been

Results of the classification are posted in the village.

different opinions, two or even three classes were recorded next to the name. This classification covered 330 of the 421 households in the village; objects of struggle and a few absentees were to be dealt with later. A breakdown of the figures shows the following distribution:

| | |
|---|---:|
| Poor peasants | 120 |
| Farm laborers | 2 |
| Workers | 2 |
| Handicraft workers | 2 |
| New middle peasants | 99 |
| Old middle peasants | 80 |
| Unclassified due to lack of agreement (either poor, new middle, or old middle peasants) | 25 |
| TOTAL | 330 |

# 7

# Electing Recruiters for the Poor-Peasant League

## March 7, 8

The core of the present task is the problem of democracy.
—The Central Bureau in a letter to Lou Lin, March 6, 1948

On the evening of March 7, the villagers who had been classified as poor peasants met to elect the people who would organize the poor-peasant league. The work team had chosen Geng Xi to act as chairman, because his simple question-and-answer technique had proved popular with the peasants. He began by emphasizing the need for unity.

"This is a meeting of all the poor peasants of both Fort and Street," Geng said. "Do the peasants classified as poor-and-hired all belong to one family?"

"They all belong to one family," was the reply from different parts of the crowd.

"Who had the power in the past?" said Geng.

"The landlords, the Old Moneybags," the crowd answered.

"Why was that, if all the poor-and-hired were members of one big family?"

"Because we weren't united."

"We hadn't fanshenned."

"And who should be the masters of the house today?" Geng asked.

"The masses."

"All right. So today we are to have a singlehearted meeting of the poor to discuss how they can become masters.

"Some of you say, 'We're always holding meetings. It would be better to get on with the job of filling the holes; then we can concentrate on

65

production.' But organizing the poor-peasant league is like laying the cornerstone of the house. After it's done, we'll work with the middle peasants to reorganize the peasant union. Then we'll elect new cadres. Only after that will it be time to fill the holes.

"How is the league to be organized? To begin with, it's just like selecting seed: we must choose the best of the best. Which means that today you must dare to speak out, or the wrong people will be chosen to organize the league. If we plant the wrong seeds, we'll get a bad crop.

"With classification it's different. If it's not done well the first time, it can be put right the second; but that's not the case when we're electing people. If we don't pick out the right ones today, we can't have another election tomorrow. Today everyone must dare to act as a master of the house."

Geng Xi listed the qualifications that had been put forward during discussion in the various village groups: Organizers of the poor-peasant league should be hardworking, simple and honest, happy to serve the people and not bootlickers of the landlords and rich peasants. The crowd agreed that these were the qualities to be found in the best of the best.

The recruiters, Geng said, would gather into the league all the poor peasants and hired laborers who were suitable for membership. As for people who were in some way undesirable, those with minor defects might be put on trial to see if they could reform. Those with more serious faults might be excluded for a longer time. Besides poor peasants and hired laborers, a certain number of new middle peasants might be invited to join the league. Eventually this class would make up about one-third of the membership.

"When enough members have been gathered in," Geng said, "the league will be formally established. Then everyone who has been proposed for membership by the recruiters will be considered by all the poor-and-hired to see if he's really suitable. A person can be proposed for membership many times until he's approved by all. Everyone must wash the dirt off his face before he's admitted to the league.

"From now on it's the poor-and-hired who must take the lead. That means poor-and-hired women too; the league wouldn't be representative without them. And if today's elections aren't successful, how can we make a good job of filling the holes?"

The candidates of the south end were the first to be called. Wang Wen-sheng, prodded by those who had chosen him, climbed to the head of the steps leading into the temple building.

"I've never spoken in front of an audience before," he said with his

Candidates for recruiters of the poorpeasant league were shaken by the experience of speaking to a large audience and hearing the audience criticize them.

shy, good-natured smile. "My group have chosen me as a candidate, but I don't think I meet the requirements. I used to be very poor, I've worked hard, and I've never been a woman-chaser. Yet I just don't have the courage to speak out, and you can't serve the masses unless you do. Some people say that I don't treat my father well—that I don't give him enough food and clothing. Well, your eyes are clearsighted; please tell me what defects I have; don't save my face."

The audience broke into fermentation groups and murmured, then came together again. "He's been poor since he was a child, and he was a hired laborer in Shanxi," said the spokesman of one group. "He's unselfish, and he's never run after women. He hasn't any faults."

"He fills all the qualifications," said another. "We're satisfied with him."

"It's not true that he doesn't treat his father well. The people who say so are just scandalmongers."

After everyone who wanted to had spoken, the next nominee climbed the steps. He was the fifty-year-old Wang Guang-xun, who had been discussed at the meeting of five peasants and four team members. These peasants had described him as foul-mouthed and as a person who preferred "food in his belly to clothes on his back." Nevertheless, he had enough standing in his own section of the village to be named as a candidate.

"I've never been a woman-chaser," he said. Having gotten this far, however, his tongue refused to work. Finally he muttered, "I can't say anything, so speak your minds about me," and hastily withdrew to the side of the temple porch.

After the peasants had fermented, they said:

"He was a poor laborer for many years. He was exploited by the landlords, and he's had a bellyful of suffering."

"He's a good man. He treats other people well, and he's never had power." (At this point in the campaign, the cadres had been so thoroughly criticized that the villagers considered it a virtue not to have held office.)

"He's never been a womanizer, even though his wife died years ago. And he's a hard worker."

"But he doesn't work so hard when weddings or funerals are going on. And he's planted hardly any winter wheat." This first unfavorable note encouraged other cautious criticism.

"He doesn't covet other people's belongings, but he never gives his own away without good reason."

"He's extravagant, though. He bought a sugar wafer last time he went to Yangyi." The discussion petered out, and the next candidate was called.

It was a militiaman who worked the ginning machine at the coop. "I don't meet any of the qualifications," he said bashfully. "Of course I work, because I have to. I've never held office or run village affairs. I used to chase women, but that was a long time ago."

The villagers' preoccupation with the subject of chasing women was a result of the shortage of women. Before the liberation, in times of famine, many poor families had been forced to kill their girl babies. The reasoning was: There was not enough food for all; but the boys, at least, would grow up to work for the family, while girls would marry, leave home and work for their husbands' families.

In general the discussion groups approved of the militiaman. "He was a loafer for a while," a man said, "but he reformed about five years ago."

"He's honest, loyal, and upright. And he never ran around trying to get into the landlords' good books."

"Yes, he never turned one face to the landlords and another to us."

"He's the sort of man who can serve the people."

The peasant whose turn came next apologized "because I'm a bit deaf. I don't know what other faults I have," he said, "so please point them out to me."

His deafness was the chief topic of discussion. No other serious objection was raised, but many people regarded his handicap as a disadvantage that excluded him from public duties.

The candidate who then climbed the steps had little to say for himself. One spokesman described him as a good worker and a straightforward, honest person. On the whole, however, his faults seemed to outweigh his virtues. People said that he had a bad temper, did not attend meetings regularly, and was unsociable.

The self-appraisal of the next peasant, an army veteran, was short and crisp. "My trouble is that I have a hot temper and often quarrel with my wife," he said, and stepped smartly to the side of the platform.

"He's loyal and generous," said one spokesman, "but he does have a temper. And he's not interested in other people. If a lot of visitors come to his house, he grabs his hoe and makes for the fields."

"After the struggle fruits were distributed, he became something of a spendthrift."

"He's a bit lazy, too. He hasn't even plowed all his land. And when the government asked us to grow wheat, he planted only one *mu* of it. If a man's not keen on planting his own land, it's not likely that he'll bestir himself to help other people. He needs to pull himself together."

These were all the candidates of the south-end section. Geng Xi stood up. "It's taken quite a while to discuss six candidates, considering that there wasn't much criticism of them. I think you're still hanging on to the habit of saving face.

"Everybody should speak out freely. Don't worry about whether the candidate will be accepted or not; don't be afraid of retaliation and grudges.

"Also, we shouldn't make any distinctions between candidates from the Fort and the Street. You can speak your mind about any candidate; just stick to the facts.

"Before we go on to the voting, please ferment. After that you have to elect three of these six candidates, so each person should raise his hand only three times. Don't look around and see how the others are voting; make up your own mind. And don't vote according to your personal relations with the candidate. Measure him by the four qualifications."

After a brief period of fermentation, the voting started. Members of the work team counted the upraised hands.

Wang Wen-sheng, who had spoken first, received 102 votes, while the second of the three successful candidates, Wang Guang-xun, was given only 59.

It was now late. Geng Xi rose to announce that the meeting would adjourn till the following afternoon. It was important to leave the morning free for work in the fields.

The following afternoon when people had reassembled, the candidates of the north-end section came forward for appraisal. It was as much as Zhao Zhen-fang could do to muster courage to climb the

The men vote for recruiters by raising their fists.

The women, sitting apart from the men by custom, also vote. The woman in the center holds a frame on which she is winding yarn.

steps. He stood at the top for a moment in silence, his tall, spare frame prematurely bent. Smiling in response to the good-natured encouragement of the crowd, he said, "I'm old." He was forty-six. "I'm afraid I'm no good at handling public affairs."

Wang Wen-sheng was elected a recruiter by an overwhelming vote.

The people's comment on him was equally simple: "He's a wholly honest man. He more than meets the four qualifications—he could meet double that number."

Li Bao-yu, a man as short and stocky as Zhao Zhen-fang was tall and thin, was approved in much the same way. "I work hard," he said, "otherwise I'd starve. And I've never had anything to do with the landlords."

The villagers called him "a completely good man, unselfish and generous," and "a person who meets all the requirements." Both Zhao and Li led the north-end candidates when the vote was taken.

The north end was the first section to nominate any women as recruiters. But the women candidates did not displace the men; they ran in addition to them. This arrangement had been made because it was felt that women would have no chance in direct competition with the men. Their position was far better than it had been before liberation, but it had not kept pace with other reforms.

Two women from the north end were elected, more because they were model housewives than because they fulfilled the qualifications.

The three they did meet—industriousness, good character, and ability to get along with people—would also have been praised in the old society. It was the fourth requirement—enthusiasm in serving the people—which was characteristic of the new. For the women of Ten Mile Inn, however, service still meant service to their own family, not to the bigger family that was the village.

Thus when it was the first woman candidate's turn to make her self-report, it was found that she had already left the meeting. Her baby had been peevish, so she had taken him home. In the discussion held in her absence people said:

"Wang Chui-de has never lost her temper once since she came to Ten Mile Inn."

"She's honest and faithful and gets along with her neighbors."

"She's never complained about her husband's poverty."

The other woman candidate, Song Ting-de, made a few halfhearted attempts at a self-report and lapsed into silence, hiding her embarrassment by tilting her head so that her black shoulder-length hair half covered her face. Like Wang Chui-de, she was praised for her domestic virtues—her skill and industry in spinning and weaving and her excellence as a wife and daughter-in-law. She, too, was elected with a good-sized vote.

Of the candidates put forward by the east-central section, Li Shu-tung had the most complex background. He had been born to a landlord family, but was driven out and forced to live as a hired laborer. To further complicate matters, he had later married the cast-off wife of a landlord. It was only after a great deal of discussion during the classification meeting that he had been ranked as a poor peasant and thus became eligible for nomination as an organizer. In the discussion that now took place it was clear that Li Shu-tung was popular with the villagers.

"His landlord family didn't like him—that's to his credit," "He follows the mass line," and "He has no faults," were the comments. So in spite of his and his wife's family origins, Li Shu-tung was elected.

Eventually candidates from the four sections of the Street had been voted on, and only those of the Fort remained. The first to speak was Fu Li-yong, the old man whose white towel almost hid his eyes. His self-appraisal was not as modest as those of the people who had gone before him.

"You can see that I'm active and hardworking. In recent years I haven't run after the women. I've overcome that fault. But still," he added ceremoniously, "I'm afraid I can't lead you."

"He works hard and has a good reputation," the first speaker said.

"It's true he works hard," said the second, "but when he was in charge of the co-op grain, he grafted by mixing dirt with it."

"Yes, and he mixed dirt with the yellow beans, too. He's selfish, not unselfish."

"Some say he's still a woman-chaser, too, in spite of his age."

"He can't meet more than two of the four qualifications."

A woman closed the discussion by saying: "This man's not good enough."

Fu Li-yong stood through it all without any hint of reaction. Below the towel his creased and sunburned face, covered with a sparse growth of stubble, showed no emotion.

The next candidate was the simple-and-honest Fu Bian-de, whom the team member Shao Hang had carefully primed to take an active part in the Fort's classification.

Fu spoke briefly of the hard life he had led, and there was little discussion afterward. "What he says is true," the peasants agreed. "He's a good man."

Then came Li Bao-qin. "I used to be called a first-class loafer," he said, "and I still don't manage my land well. After I got married I used to gamble, and my wife had to leave the door unlatched and wait up for me. When she tried to get me to stop, I beat her, and as a result she had two miscarriages. Afterwards I realized my faults and corrected them.

"I've never held office, and I've never grafted. Some people say that I'm not really a poor peasant and should be classed as a middle peasant; so maybe I should wait until my class is settled."

"Well, he's spoken up frankly. All of it's true," was the first comment.

"Yes, a man will make out all right if he admits his mistakes."

"Well, why didn't he tell us that he ruined the bean crop when he tilled the land of the soldier's family? He said he's a loafer, but his own bean crop came up all right."

"None of these candidates from the Fort are worth anything," said someone from the Street. "They had no business nominating them."

A ripple spread from one part of the crowd to another, and soon an angry hum rose.

"It's not a question of Fort or Street," someone shouted, "but of whether the candidate's good enough!"

But still the noise swelled, until at last Geng Xi took the meeting in hand. Even with his powerful voice and personality, it was some time before things quieted down.

When the hubbub subsided, the Fort's remaining candidate, a

woman, came up for discussion. Like most of the other women, Chen Chui-de was too timid to make a speech, but the others spoke up for her:

"She works hard and spins first-grade yarn."

"She takes good care of her mother-in-law."

There was no opposition to her, but the crowd showed considerable resistance when it came to voting for the Fort's candidates. Rumbles of discontent passed from one fermentation group to the next.

The reason was clear. Originally the Fort had put up five candidates —four men and Chen Chui-de. But one of the men was her husband, and at the last moment he had withdrawn. "It would be unsuitable to have both husband and wife run in the election," he said. Thus only three men were left, and since everyone had three votes, all three would automatically be elected.

Because there was such strong opposition to two of the candidates, Geng Xi proposed that the procedure be changed. He suggested that only the candidates who received at least half of the votes should be accepted. The audience unanimously agreed, and Fu Bian-de and the woman were elected. The other two were not.

The meeting had lasted nearly three hours, and people were edging toward the gate. The women especially were anxious to leave, because they had meals to prepare.

Geng Xi called them back. "Here are the candidates you have elected," he said. "What instructions are you going to give them?"

Most of the peasants stopped and looked at him thoughtfully. Some of those who were leaving began drifting back.

A peasant pointed at the newly elected recruiters. "You're the yeast to make the poor-and-hired rise," he said.

"Yes; mind you ferment well."

"Remember that in the classification some families reported on themselves again and again, but they never told the truth."

Advice flowed from every part of the temple courtyard. Then the recruiters were asked to reply. Most of them declined, saying that they had made enough speeches for one day, but after much friendly persuasion a few obliged:

"I'm not much good at things like this, but I'll do my best to fanshen together with the masses. And I hope you'll supervise me carefully. If you have any criticisms, just tell us; no need to wait for some special occasion."

"So far we haven't fanshenned well, but from now on we'll make a real effort. We'll all unite to serve the poor."

"Yes, we'll unite. The differences between Fort and Street aren't important. If the number of recruiters elected by the Fort is too small, we can have another election and choose some more."

On this note of unity Geng Xi brought the meeting to a close. "Can all the poor peasants unite?" he asked the crowd.

"Yes, we can."

"Can the poor peasants unite with the middle peasants?" he asked, looking forward to a future stage.

"Yes, we can." And they streamed through the gates.

# —8—

# Factionalism

Unity, however, was to prove no simple matter. In Ten Mile Inn factionalism had flourished for centuries as a tradition fostered by the landlords and rooted in the clans: the Fus, the Wangs, and the Lis. In theory, the clans had been social, even semireligious bodies concerned with the worshipping of the clan ancestors, the yearly sweeping of their graves, and the celebration of the lunar new year and other festivals. In reality, they had also fulfilled important political and economic functions, because they were an organized form for the rivalry between the landlords.

Various landlord cliques competed for all official and semiofficial posts, especially for jobs involving tax collection and other opportunities for graft. By keeping the ancient clan organizations alive, the landlords secured ready-made groups of followers.

The Communist-led reforms had eliminated the worst aspects of factionalism along with the landlord rule that had fostered it. But village life was still shot through with vestiges of factional spirit.

The work team encountered factionalism almost as soon as they arrived in Ten Mile Inn. During their house-to-house visits and the early meetings, the peasants often referred to the traditional rivalry between the Fort (where most of the people were Fus and Lis) and the Street (the Wang stronghold). There was also ill feeling inside the Fort (between the Fu and Li clans) and inside the lower village (between the north and south parts of the Street). And in time the team became aware of another rift. This was among the militants—meaning the people who were politically active in the village. One group of militants had rallied around the former village head, Wang Ke-bin, and those who supported the present cadres.

Factionalism intruded in many ways on the work of the team. During classification, people from the Street made remarks such as, "They're a tight little bunch up there in the Fort. They even classify old Fu So-and-so as a poor peasant, and he owns half a donkey." A small group from the south-end section got together and agreed to classify each other as poor peasants. Then people from other sections said that the south-end peasants were all "scratching each other's backs." When it came to criticizing the cadres, several people of the Fort wanted to know why all the big cadres came from "Wang Street," as they sarcastically called the southern half of the village main street.

The team members had different ideas about the best way to deal with factionalism. Some said, "We shouldn't bring it out in the open; that gives it official recognition." Others said, "Until we bring it into the open and thrash it out, we can't get anywhere."

The team leader Lou Lin was opposed to both approaches. At one of the work team's first meetings, he said: "Factionalism can't be overcome in a day; it's not an isolated problem. Whenever it comes up, we need to deal with it openly and tie it in with our current work."

Now the team met to decide how to deal with the factionalism that had appeared in the election of recruiters. The discussion was detailed and prolonged. Afterwards Lou Lin summarized the conclusions:

"First, don't make concessions on matters of principle; don't disregard incorrect opinions or shy away from mutual criticism. In other words, don't gloss things over for the sake of superficial unity.

"It's true that when the people from the Street criticized the Fort's candidates, their motives were partly factional. Yet a good deal of the criticism was valid. In spite of this, some of you shied away by suggesting that 'We should stick to criticizing ourselves and let others criticize themselves.' You should have led them in discussing which criticisms were sound and which were partisan.

"Second, we must take great care that we ourselves don't become involved in the mass's factionalism. For example, one or two of you who are working on the Street said, 'The team comrades up in the Fort don't know what they're doing,' and one of you from the Fort replied, 'The main responsibility for factionalism lies with the Street. It dominates the Fort, which is much smaller.' In saying these things you were tailing along behind the masses. This must be guarded against.

"When you see a suitable opportunity, openly criticize the few peasants who are engaged in factionalism. Some of you fear that if you do, you'll be taking over instead of letting the people fanshen on their own account. Of course we must guard against that. On the other hand, letting things slide doesn't unite us with the masses; it separates us from them."

When the newly elected recruiters met to make plans for choosing members, the team pointed out to them that factionalism must be overcome. At the same time, Shao called a special meeting of the

Fort's poor-peasant militants—that is, of the peasants who were beginning to be politically active—to discuss why only two of their candidates had been elected.

The two unsuccessful candidates—Fu Li-yong and Li Bao-qin—were there. So were the shaggy-browed Fu De, star trumpeter of the Fort's music club, and the handsome and hefty young oil-press worker, Fu Chan-ting. There was no formality as the meeting began. The little group sat on the *kang*, on the doorsill, or on benches borrowed from the kitchen of the border-region public relations department next door.

Shao Hang took no part in the talk at first, because he wanted to give the peasants an opportunity to vent any anger they might feel over the afternoon's meeting.

"It's no good," one old man said. "A big village always oppresses a small one. Our Fort is like the daughter-in-law in the family."

"The only thing for us to do," another peasant said, "is to divide the family—make two separate villages."

The talk drifted to the election. The general feeling was that the Fort candidates may not have been perfect, but those from the Street were no better. Fu Li-ku, the husband of the Fort's successful woman candidate, supported this idea. He took an active part in the meeting even though he had withdrawn his own nomination.

"Mutual-aid group 5 nominated Wang Shui-chen, didn't they?" Fu said. "What is he? Nothing but a loafer. And there's old what's-his-name who's having an affair with that widow. They all cover up for each other; that's how they're nominated as candidates. A new type of mutual aid."

"Besides, Fu He-qi is a second-class struggle object. Why did they classify him as a poor peasant?"

"They pointed out what was wrong with our candidates, but they never bothered about the faults of their own."

"The fact is," Fu Li-ku resumed, "everybody has some faults—even county magistrates. We've got to pick some smart young fellows who've got drive; otherwise we'll never get things done. It can't be helped if they're not perfect. Just insisting on their being simple and honest isn't enough."

"Yes," said the music club trumpeter Fu De, "a lot of people are saying that if we elect only simple-and-honest fellows like Fu Bian-de, it's going to be pretty tough. Look what happened with Li Hui; he's honest, but he never accomplishes anything." Li, the ineffective, henpecked vice-head of the village, lived in the Fort.

"None of the active young fellows are perfect. Look at Fu Chanting, here. He's active enough; he's done a lot for production in the mutual-aid group. But the people in the Street don't know about that. They only know he's a bit hot-tempered."

"It's true," said Fu Chan-ting. "I've offended a lot of people. I do have a bad temper."

It remained for old Fu Li-yong to take a more positive stand. Despite the harsh criticisms that the people from the Street had made against him, he said, "Anyway, two of our candidates from the Fort were elected—a man and a woman. That's something. And if our people here in the Fort think it's not enough, we can suggest that we elect some more." Gazing out from under the towel that made him seem so fierce, he said peaceably, "The thing is that we poor people of the Fort mustn't look down on those of the Street. It's the poor-and-hired who are going to run the house now. It's no good holding grudges."

The other unsuccessful candidate, Li Bao-qin, agreed with him. "How are we going to get on with the job? That's the question," he said.

Seeing that the peasants had got their grumbling done, Shao Hang took up the subject of factionalism. He spoke of the importance of unity for the village's current tasks of recruiting members for the poor-peasant league and criticizing the Party cadres. Unity demanded two things, he said. The peasants must look forward rather than backward, and they must be self-critical as well as critical of others. He reminded them that factionalism had been fostered by the Old Moneybags in order to divide and rule the peasants, who had all suffered as a result.

"This shows," said Shao, "that it doesn't matter what mutual-aid group you belong to, or whether you're from the Fort or the Street. The important thing is that all the poor belong to one family."

Similar meetings were being held in every section of the Street. Now that factionalism was in the spotlight, the villagers recognized it as a serious defect inherited from the old society. From that day, freedom from involvement with any small cliques became one of the qualifications for membership in the poor-peasant league and later in the peasant union.

But there was another and more dangerous form of factionalism which might erupt in the village—anti-Party factionalism. With the Party members under criticism by the masses, it was possible that those who had been offended by domineering attitudes of Party cadres, or those who were greedy for power or position might seize the occasion to form a special clique. Any sort of organized anti-Party factionalism would be a step backward from the advances achieved in the last eight years. Thus one of the most crucial problems was how to reorganize the Party branch without undermining its prestige and position. The unfanshenned poor-and-hired must be encouraged to criticize the Party members; but the process of criticism must not create an opening for an anti-Party faction to seize power. In the days following the election of the league recruiters, the reformation of the Party members became the crucial focus of the campaign.

# —9—

# The Fort Appraises
# Party Members

## March 9

The peasants had gained political experience during the period of classification, and the recruiting of the poor-peasant league that was already under way gave them a feeling of security. Now the work team wanted them to criticize the Party members publicly in order to expose the defects that the Party branch would have to correct.

But at the same time, the local Party members also had to participate in building the poor-peasant league. In spite of their failings, after all, the Communists had been the most courageous, consistent, and clear-headed people in the village through the dangerous years of struggle against the landlord class. Thus unification and criticism were not contradictory terms; both were necessary in order to organize the masses and reorganize the local Party.

Public criticism called for careful preparation. The poor and middle peasants began by having a rehearsal before an audience with which they felt comfortable—their own sections.

On the evening of March 9, 1948, all the Fort's poor and middle peasants, with the exception of the Party members, crowded into the room that was their established meeting place. The team member Shao Hang started things off by encouraging them to speak out. They could count on the work team's support, he told them, and they did not need to be afraid of retaliation from the Communist cadres after the team had left. By then the masses would have their own organizations—the poor-peasant league and the reorganized peasant union—to support them. Moreover, those Party members whom they trusted and had therefore approved for membership would also belong to these organizations and would give them full support. So there was nothing to fear.

To begin, Shao Hang pointed out that this was the time to present

81

criticisms of the old cadres—like the former village head, Fu Gao-lin, who lived in the Fort. "It's already been decided," he said, "that Fu Gao-lin is to have some education to straighten out his ideas about whatever bad things he did in the past. If the Party members or any of the cadres, past or present, have committed any serious crimes, they can be sent to the people's court for trial.

"So come on, now; say what you think. When everyone has given his opinions, we'll elect some delegates who can speak for the whole group at the meeting tomorrow."

The first complaint was made by the music club trumpeter, Fu De. He criticized Wang Shao-zhen, the political director, for selling the rifle that was given to him for the militia. During the evening the political director was also criticized for buying the courtyard of the ex-landlord Wang Ban-yan and for breaking off his brother's engagement.

Fu Li-ku, who had been so critical of the Street in last night's session on factionalism, complained about the village head, Wang Xi-tang: "He spent 30 *yuan* on his mother's funeral, and I don't know where the money came from." Fu spoke in the manner of the old society, with understatement that amounted to an accusation of graft.

Fu Li-yong spoke several times that evening, and so did other poor peasants. In fact, for the first time the poor peasants dominated the meeting. As the team had hoped, they were finding new courage now that the poor-peasant league was about to become a reality.

The middle peasants, on the other hand, often sounded politically backward compared with the poor peasants who had been groomed to serve as the backbone of the league. The new middle peasant Li Bao-hui, the dealer in farm animals, said of a former village finance director, "He was seen mixing earth with the black beans that the border-region government gave the co-op to distribute during the famine. He got away with it because he was in with the cadres on the Street. There's not a single cadre from the Fort to represent our interests up here."

Actually, both the vice-head of the village and the militia commander came from the Fort, and the poor peasants did not respond to this factionalist appeal.

Fu Li-yong, however, seized on the subject of earth and beans. "At the election meeting I was accused of mixing dirt in the beans," he said, "but I didn't do it."

Fu looked earnestly out at the peasants from under his towel. "This is the way it was: When I was put on trial, the village head insisted that I was guilty, and he said I would have to come clean. So in the end I was compelled to say that I had added a couple of bowlfuls of earth.

"Once they'd got that much out of me, Zhang Zhun went ahead and calculated that I had put four ounces of earth into every pound of beans! I was made to pay compensation, and from that day to this the whole village thinks that I mixed earth with the beans."

Everyone listened tolerantly to Fu Li-yong's explanation, but no one took it seriously. When he had finished speaking, someone began criticizing Fu Gao-lin, the former village head:

"When it was his turn to carry stretchers, he put plasters and ointment on his face to make it look as if he was too sick to go. But when I was really sick, he said I was trying to shirk my duty. The fact is that I've been sick from that day to this, as you all know."

Many charges were made against two other former village heads: Wang Ke-bin, now leader of a faction opposing the cadres in office, and Wang Ze-yin, who had left the village to work in the government of the county seat.

Now that the peasants were no longer afraid to criticize, the fact that they still had no serious complaints about the present cadres convinced the team members that their suspicions of collusion among the cadres had been unfounded. Whatever the faults of the current village officials, they were obviously much superior to the cadres of the past.

The criticism turned to a non-Party member, Li Bao-wu, the former chairman of the people's defense committee. "Li Bao-wu had my mother tied up and beaten," said Fu Xi-ang. "He claimed that she was an 'air-raid shelter' who hid goods for the landlord. Afterwards she was sick for ten days.

"And he said that I burned a light at night as a signal to the landlords who had stuff to hide. In fact, the light was burning because my child was sick. He died a few days later."

"Li Bao-wu made a good thing out of the famine," said Xing Heng-tai. "My family were starving, so I sold him 3 *mu* of my land; he's still got it. And he changed his poor land for good, and traded his plots far away from the village for some that were nearby."

"During the famine," a woman said, "my husband was away and I ran out of food and money. I went to Li Bao-wu to sell some land, and he took advantage of my troubles to try and force me to marry someone else. When I wouldn't, he said, 'You'd better watch out!' After that he picked on me whenever I didn't attend a meeting."

Li Bao-wu was now manager of the Fort's oil press, and the peasants complained that he grafted in that job too. "When I went to buy oil at the press," said Li Bao-qin, who was Li Bao-wu's clan brother, "he sold me only the dregs, saying that he had nothing else left. The fact is that he'll treat you well if he likes you, but not otherwise."

"He's always putting money in his pocket that ought to go into the oil-press accounts," someone said.

Charges that Li Bao-wu was corrupt surfaced in many parts of the village but were never proved. In general a number of the criticisms made at this stage were not well founded, although the work team refrained from pouring cold water on them.

Thus the members of the team let it pass when one of the hotheads announced, "All the cadres are alike. The village head, the public security officer, and the peasant-union chairman ganged up to shield the landlords so that they weren't properly struggled against."

However, the team members did intervene when they considered the criticism was completely unsubstantiated. The animal dealer Li Bao-hui called one of the Party members "a feudal tail, not qualified to be a Communist." Carried away, Li said, "In my opinion he's not even qualified to be a member of the peasant union."

"Is he really not good enough for the peasant union?" Shao Hang asked quietly.

"Of course he is!" the crowd replied.

The poor peasant Fu Shou-chuan, speaking of the public security officer Wang Lin-yong, said, "He was in charge of selling the struggle fruits, and there were three pairs of bracelets among them, but he wouldn't let any of the women buy. Nobody knows whether he took them for himself or turned them over to some special friend."

"It was the same with the bedding," said someone else. "A lot of people who wanted it couldn't get any, but he wound up with some."

Fu Yu-he, who criticized the local Party members incessantly. Fu was a militiaman on leave from the front.

"He got a share of the relief millet, too," said Xin Wei-ze, the oil-press foreman. "And where did he find the money to buy that mule?"

Fu Yu-he, a young man who was habitually antagonistic to the local Communists, complained about Li Song-ting, one of the two assistant secretaries of the branch and an ex-commander of the militia. "He's no leader of production," Fu said. "At weeding time he wouldn't go near the fields unless he had plenty of tobacco on him. In fact, he got his land weeded for him by the mutual-aid group. The group took his compost out to the fields for him, too. He owns enough land, yet he managed to get some of the relief grain the government sent. During the struggles he took an extra share of fruits, too."

Fu scowled. "It's all because the cadres and Party members looked after each other. This sort of thing has got to be straightened out if we're to answer the call of Chairman Mao."

The team attributed Fu Yu-he's endless grumbling against the village Party members to a mixture of personal ambition and jealous antagonism. "It's nonsense to talk about our criticizing the Party members and their not getting their own back," he had said repeatedly. "The only way to avoid that is to make sure that none of them are reelected."

Earlier, when classification started, Fu had said, "How can we expect to have a fair classification under the leadership of the Communist Party?"

"Then how do you think we're going to get one?" a peasant had asked him. "Under the leadership of the Guomindang?"

Though he was disconcerted by this question, Fu Yu-he had stuck to his argument. "It's human nature," he said. "As long as a man lives, he's bound to seek revenge if he gets a chance."

When men like Fu mixed freely with the simple-and-honest and were given latitude by the work team, there was always some risk that their provocative charges might end in violence. Of course, the more politically aware the masses became, the more unlikely it was that they would respond or allow violence to erupt.

But at this stage of the campaign the work team and the Ten Mile Inn Communists, as well as many of the peasants, were apprehensive about holding a public meeting of criticism. Would reason and fairness prevail? Or would the masses be swayed by exaggerated accusations made by men like Fu Yu-he? And if so, would they manhandle them, as they had the landlords and rich-peasant collaborators in earlier campaigns?

# —10—

# The Masses Criticize
# the Communists

March 10

The peasants assembling in the temple courtyard were elated, for even those who found most fault with the village Communists felt that it was an honor to be invited to a meeting of the Party. The Party members, on the other hand, were subdued and tense as they braced themselves for the grueling session ahead. They had to remind themselves that they belonged to the Communist Party of China which had led the people to victory over the Japanese invaders, and over the landlords and rich peasants. They had hung the temple steps and veranda with red drapery, which became the background for a huge portrait of Mao Ze-dong flanked by red flags. They had agreed that an open meeting of the Branch was an occasion for style and dignity, even when its purpose was to criticize the branch members.

As the peasants gathered in the courtyard, the village Communists were still in the temple talking earnestly with members of the team. Outside, the sixty-odd delegates who had been elected by the sections to present their criticisms sat in front of the steps which served as a speaker's platform. To the left of the delegates was an empty space that would be occupied by the Party members. To the delegates' right was the women's bloc. The rest of the villagers, with many of the team members scattered among them, sat in a large semicircle behind these three groups.

At last the Party members came out and squatted on the ground in the place assigned to them. The round, boyish face of the political director Wang Shao-zhen, which usually seemed ready to break into a smile, was solemn. So was that of his close friend, the peasant-union chairman Fu Chang-sou. Wang Xi-tang, who had been the village head for nearly four years and who generally carried himself with quiet

Open meeting of the Communist Party, with Leng Ping presiding. The villagers have been asked to criticize the local Party members.

The women's bloc at the open meeting.

assurance, seemed preoccupied and inattentive. After taking their places, the whole group sat with bowed heads.

Leng Bing of the work team climbed the steps. "In the village of Ten Mile Inn," Leng began, "there are twenty-eight members of the Communist Party. All of them have been publicly made known to you. There are no other members than these—no secret members. All of them are here this afternoon, except for one who is ill.

"All these Party members have their faults, and during the last ten days they have been thinking about their conduct and criticizing it among themselves. We did not ask you to attend the self-criticism meetings, but we have invited you to this open branch meeting. Warmly and with an open heart, the Communist Party asks you to help its members correct their mistakes.

"In the past we had a movement to Wash Faces and Rub Off Smudges, to help the Party members and cadres overcome their defects. But this present campaign is different. At that time the Party members were not required to reform; this time they will be.

"No Communist is allowed to seek revenge—ever. So you delegates need have no fear of retaliation.

"From now on the people are going to run the house themselves. In the past they were not well organized, but now we're going to set up the poor-peasant league and reconstruct the peasant union. Since the people will hold power, we can be doubly sure that there will be no retaliation. On the one hand, the highest ranks of the Party will never allow Party members to retaliate; on the other, the people themselves will not allow it—and they will hold power to enforce this rule.

"During more than ten days of education within the branch, we have discovered that there are three kinds of Party members.

"First, there are members who have been in the Party a long time and have served as cadres for several years. These are guilty of the more serious faults. Some of them have been dictatorial. Some seized more than their share of fruits during the campaigns and fanshenned too high. Some had improper relations with women. Some abused people, tied them up and beat them, and even denounced them as secret agents. Some of these old Party members have already made good self-criticisms; some have not and don't want to correct their mistakes.

"Second, there are members who have made less serious mistakes, such as taking a high-and-mighty attitude with the masses and acting selfishly. Again, some of these have made good self-criticisms and some have not.

"Then there are those whose faults have been minor. They are the ones who joined the Party quite recently. Their defects have been selfishness, inability to lead, or failure to serve others.

"Now it's up to you to say how you think these three types of Party members should be dealt with. They'll be criticized if they deserve it; they'll be dismissed from their posts if they should. If all of you say they have committed crimes, they'll be handed over to the people's court for trial. And if, after taking everything into account, the Party concludes that some of them are not qualified to be Party members, they'll be expelled.

"You have expressed a lot of opinions about former cadres, but today we will consider only the Party members; the ex-cadres' turn will come later. But you can be sure that we'll straighten everything out, based on the facts you give us. The team has already had talks with the former village heads, Fu Gao-lin and Wang Ke-bin, and has begun to deal with their problems.

"To make sure that today's meeting is well run, I would like to suggest a few rules to the delegates and the Party members.

"First, speak the truth.

"Second, no quarreling or fighting.

"Third, the Party members will listen to the criticisms of the masses humbly and consider them carefully. At this time they will not answer criticisms, even if they don't agree.

"Finally, the masses are asked not to make their criticisms directly. Please tell your delegates what you want to say, and they will speak for you.

"Now let's have your opinions of the Party members. I'll read out the names in turn.

"Wang Shao-zhen."

There was a moment of quiet; then criticism came thick and fast. As political director of the village and secretary of the Party branch, Shao-zhen was one of the two most active cadres in the village. The other, the village head, was an older man, more experienced and less impetuous. While carrying out the various campaigns and taking stands in the crises that had arisen in the past five years, Shao-zhen had offended many villagers and made bitter enemies of a few.

In all, the delegates raised thirty-two points of criticism against Wang Shao-zhen. The first complaint was about that rifle. It was brought up by several delegates, each time with a new twist. "The rifle was a gift to the people," one speaker said passionately. "Instead of presenting it to them, he sold it. So he took money from the people, yet he expected to be praised for bringing the rifle from the front." The subject aroused such anger because the militia was a matter of life and death, the villagers' means of defense first against the Japanese and now against the Guomindang.

Wang Shao-zhen was also accused of having taken more than his share of the struggle fruits—of having fanshenned too high. Not only had he bought a new courtyard (partly with the proceeds from selling the rifle) but, according to one delegate, "He got a tiara and an embroidered gown from the fruits and sold them in Yanghu. He got 6 *yuan* for them altogether and took 2 *yuan* for himself and gave 3 or 4 *yuan* to his pal the peasant-union chairman."

Besides taking too many of the fruits for himself, the delegates charged, Wang Shao-zhen regarded them as gifts that he could bestow or withhold as he pleased.

"When one of the women picked up something she wanted," a delegate said, "he cursed, asked 'What do you want with that?' and took it away from her."

"It was the same with me," said another delegate. "I wanted a wardrobe, and he swore at me and asked, 'Do you think you're entitled to that?'"

"His favorites had first choice of the fruits. During the Fill the Holes, Level the Tops Campaign, all he let me get was a torn cloth bag."

"He's bad-tempered, and people are afraid to speak to him."

"He slapped someone's face once for dozing at a Party meeting."

The women in the crowd brought up the matter of the broken engagement. Leng, who wanted them to take an active part in the meeting, allowed them to speak even though they were not delegates.

"His brother was engaged to a girl in South Yangyi," said a middle-aged woman brandishing a large steel needle in one hand and a half-finished shoe sole in the other. "But the political director got another girl for him and broke off the engagement."

"The second one was from Ten Mile Inn," another woman said. "She'd been married once too, but her husband went away during the famine and was never heard of again. She was going to marry someone else, but Shao-zhen forced her to marry his brother."

A delegate supplied more details: "Actually, she did marry a man from the village of East Harmony. She lived with him for three days, but the cadres forced her to come back. They annulled the marriage, on grounds that she hadn't waited the usual three years after her husband left. But then they let her marry the political director's brother."

"Shao-zhen thought that the first fiancée in South Yangyi was too small and scrawny; that's why he broke off the engagement."

Through it all Wang Shao-zhen sat motionless, his head slightly lowered, his eyes on the ground. At last the flow of accusations flagged and became repetitious.

At Leng Bing's suggestion, the political director's case was dropped and the second name on the list was read out. It was that of Wang Nan-fang, the labor hero.

The delegates began by insinuating that Wang Nan-fang had no right to his honorary title. "Every labor hero we've ever had has come from mutual-aid group 3," said one. Most of the cadres belonged to that group. "At weeding time it was mutual-aid group 7 that finished first and then helped the others. Yet Wang Nan-fang of group 3 became the labor hero."

Even Nan-fang's drive and industriousness were criticized. "He looks after himself," a delegate declared. "His group gave him the task of setting up a dye shop, but he wasn't satisfied with that. He turned around and opened a flour mill as well, just for himself and a couple of his pals."

Like his cousin the political director, Wang Nan-fang was involved in a marriage case. "His brother wanted him to marry a girl, but she wouldn't have him. So Nan-fang forced her to accept him."

"He got Li Xi-yuan to act as middleman." Li was the director of civil affairs and a Party member.

"Middleman! He just locked the couple up in a room and left them there. Then she had to marry him!"

"No, the fact is that it was marriage by purchase," said a delegate. "The girl was unwilling, so her family tried to prevent the match by insisting that he pay them something. But Li Xi-yuan said that he would come across with whatever they asked."

Thus the girl's family had been mercenary enough to take money and then allow the middleman to lock the couple up together. As in feudal times, the girl had been forced into the marriage; but at least she had put up some sort of fight.

The charges against Wang Nan-fang were only a fraction of those which had been brought against Wang Shao-zhen, for Nan-fang's role in village affairs was far less important.

The third man on the list, the village head Wang Xi-tang, was subordinate to Wang Shao-zhen in the Party branch but senior to him as an administrative cadre in the village. The first accusation against him was that he had acquired 6 *mu* of good valley bottom land in the face of competition from several buyers. Next he was charged with railroading a candidate into office against the wishes of the masses. Only one more point was raised against him, but it was supported by three delegates. This was the extravagance of his mother's funeral.

"He spent 30 *yuan* on it," said the first man. "Ordinary people couldn't possibly afford that much."

"I don't know how much money was spent," said someone else. "But I know it took five or six days to make the decorations."

The decorations had adorned the gateway to an empty lot which Wang took over for the funeral ceremonies. He had erected a canopy leading from the gate into the courtyard, where an altar was set up. On it were placed various offerings to the dead woman, including a pile of buns made of the finest white wheat flour. White pieces of cloth stitched with characters expressing condolence had been offered to the bereaved family by various villagers, who stretched them across the street in front of their own homes. When the funeral procession toured the village, it stopped under each banner, and the mourners kowtowed to the expensive coffin while the band played.

One delegate said, "When Wang Xi-tang buried his mother, decorations were put out on the road. But when the father of a soldier in another family died, no decorations were offered." The implication was that Wang should have taken the lead in arranging decorations for the other funeral.

After these complaints, there was a pause which stretched on. None of the delegates made a move to speak, and it became clear that there were no more charges against the man who had led the village for nearly four years of bitter struggle. Wang Xi-tang lowered his head to hide the smile that lit his face.

Leng read out the names of other cadres. Fu Pei-yu, manager of the village cooperative, was criticized for shielding his brother during the campaign to recruit soldiers as well as for the way he managed the co-op. The village public security officer, Wang Lin-yong, was accused of having an eye to the main chance when it came to business deals and the distribution of the struggle fruits. His affair with a soldier's widow was also brought up.

Wang Mi-shan, the organization secretary of the branch, was criticized for being domineering. The delegates also charged that he had used his position to get better housing.

A number of Party members were disposed of in rapid succession with comments such as "He's all right. He's just influenced by the others," "He's a bit stuck up," or "He's too selfish."

A few were even praised ("Nothing wrong there; everyone likes him"), though as the work team pointed out later, simply to be easygoing and likable was not to be a good Communist.

Several of the remaining names triggered long lists of complaints. Fu Chang-sou, who had become the peasant-union chairman a year ago, was not popular with the poor-and-hired, for in the old days his uncle had been a usurer.

"He won the election," a delegate said, "because the four big cadres forced the people to vote for him."

"And then he took more of the fruits than he should. Besides his regular share, he managed to get part ownership of a chaser mill. Now he tends to his milling business instead of working for his mutual-aid group."

"Besides, he sheltered the family of his uncle during the struggle. The uncle was away from the village, and Fu Chang-sou told his aunt to stuff some cotton wool under her clothes and pretend she was pregnant. So she wasn't struggled against, and when the time for the second struggle came, he told her to say that she had had a miscarriage and offer to buy her way out. But the people struggled against her anyway, and in the end she offered them 10 *yuan* and a jar of copper coins. Chang-sou is still keeping some silver for her."

"He's got one brother in the People's Liberation Army and one in the Guomindang Army." This was the accepted story in the village, though it had never been proved.

"When a widow went to him for a marriage permit, he said that he could fix her up, all right—if she'd marry him."

"Yes, he said he had plenty of money to give her anything she needed."

"All the big cadres backed him up. They promised that if she married him, she could go into Yangyi to buy anything she liked and she'd be able to eat whatever she wanted." Despite these inducements, Fu Chang-sou was still a bachelor.

"When Xin Ru-ling died," said a delegate, "Fu Chang-sou got hold of his belongings on the excuse that he was going to put up a tombstone. But he's never done it." It was the tradition that when a man with no close relations died, the nearest of kin, or failing that, a friend or neighbor would inherit his belongings provided he arranged the funeral and mourning as for a relative.

Another cadre, the twenty-six-year-old Wang Chi-yong, was accused of more wrongdoing than anyone else except the political director. Wang was commander of the militia, and the delegates claimed that he had abused his position.

"He always made himself scarce during recruiting drives. And just before the Japanese surrender when we went to the front to fight, he came home in no time with what he claimed was an injured leg."

"He got a house from the struggles, though he had one already."

An ex-soldier called from the back of the crowd, "And I still have no house to live in. He's always making cracks about us ex-soldiers, hinting that we left the army because we weren't loyal."

The bitterest charges against Wang Chi-yong arose from an occasion when four friends had taken a drop too much to celebrate the moon festival. Some companions from the militia joined them, and everyone drank a bit more. Then one of the original drinkers began to complain about having been classed as a feudal tail. He denounced the Communist Party, thereby arousing the ire of the militia commander.

"How were we to know that the militia commander was a member of the Party?" one of the four friends now asked.

But to continue the story, the drunken man had seized a gun and, according to some accounts, tried to bayonet the commander. The others restrained him. On the following day all four of the friends who had been celebrating were arrested, accused of stealing some bullets which had disappeared in the fracas, and denounced as a "clique of enemy agents." They were tied up in the temple courtyard and beaten.

"We were held for a day afterwards, and the village head said that we were a bunch of good-for-nothings and that we opposed the cadres. We insisted that we weren't guilty. In the end, they said we were enemy agents. We carry that label to this day."

The cadre Wang Wen-tang, whose turn came next, was treated very differently by the peasants, who seemed to regard him as a friend who had gone astray.

"Old Wen-tang," one delegate said, "you're a good man, but you've changed since you joined the Party. You bought a cow, moved into an ex-landlord's house, and found yourself a wife. Could you have done it all without being a Party member?"

Others suggested that Wang Wen-tang had become conceited since he was made one of the leaders of the newly formed cooperative committee. "When we go to the co-op to get our cotton ginned," a delegate said, "sometimes he talks to us, sometimes he doesn't. It depends on how he feels. What sort of attitude is that for a Party member?"

"When they gin cotton for you at the co-op," another said, "the weight always goes down. I lost half a pound on seven and three-quarters pounds."

"The co-op wouldn't let us put our grain on the open market; we had to sell it to them. And they paid a tenth of a *fen* less than the market price. The co-op belongs to the people, so why does it exploit them?" (The *fen*, itself one-hundredth of a *yuan*, was the smallest monetary unit.)

By the time all the Party members had been criticized, the meeting had lasted the whole afternoon and a good part of the night. Almost every aspect of the village government and Party branch leadership had been thoroughly covered.

Summarizing this phase of the campaign, Leng Bing made the following report to the work team:

At the open meeting a peasant voices his complaints about a local Communist.

"The thirteen-day period of closed-door Party education came to an end on March 10, when the people were drawn directly into the work.

"The majority of the masses were realistic in their criticisms of the Party members, but there was some question with regard to the most vociferous militants. The mildest thing that can be said about their accusations is that their motives were open to suspicion.

"Nevertheless, two important aims were achieved by the open branch meeting. First, the masses learned a lot. In hearing criticism of the Party members, they knew that they were also hearing criticism of themselves, because they realized that they were guilty of the same kind of wrongdoing. Second, the meeting helped the Party members to extend their self-criticism.

"In general, the delegates brought up no well-founded charges which the Party members had not already reported themselves during the closed-door meetings. In some cases, as with Wang Shao-zhen, the Party members had even accused themselves of weaknesses that the masses didn't mention. And when the delegates did point out something that a Party member had not already described, he was remorseful, saying 'Why didn't I think of that myself?'

"When the Party members heard criticisms that were just, they felt satisfied. But they did have to choke down the impulse to refute the false accusations. We had had a hot discussion beforehand in the

Party branch about this. Wang Wen-tang, for example, felt that the complaints about his arrogance on the cooperative committee were unfair. Still, he carried out the branch's decision not to murmur. After the meeting I reminded the Party members that their first task was to consider all the charges carefully and go more deeply into those that were just. They needn't bother about rejecting the unjust ones; that would come later.

"In a Party session we did discuss all the accusations to see which were justified and which were not. We discovered that in general, the delegates who spoke most excitedly and most vaguely had an axe to grind or an old score to settle. One who made many criticisms kept saying, 'I speak on behalf of all the people of Ten Mile Inn.' Of course he had no right to that claim; he was really speaking only for himself. So we must be sure to judge things from the standpoint of the masses. What affects them is important; mere personal spite is not."

# —11—

# Organizing the
# Poor-Peasant League

March 12, 13

The recruiters of the poor-peasant league had been elected on the afternoon of March 8, 1948, and that evening they met to discuss what they would do.

"If there are a few good people among the old middle peasants," some of the recruiters said, "we'd better let them in." The idea that the peasants who had been the most diffident in the past could form their own organization and make it into the backbone of village political life was too ambitious for them to accept.

But the majority of the recruiters said, "No, ours is going to be a league for the poor-and-hired, not for old middle peasants. They don't know what we've gone through, so their hearts are different from ours. They can join the peasant union."

With such arguments as this the more timid of the recruiters were persuaded to limit the membership according to plan.

Then other recruiters began to go to the opposite extreme. "Only thoroughly honest and unselfish people should be accepted," they said. "We don't want any good-for-nothings, or men who have played around with women, or air-raid shelters."

"That's too severe," Wang Wen-sheng protested. "All those who are of one heart with the poor should be accepted. Some people have bad mouths but good hearts."

"And if some are a bit selfish, we can still take them along with us and educate them," said Zhao Zhen-fang. "Then they'll have a chance to reform themselves."

"Some people were only very small air-raid shelters," said Li Bao-yu. "If they've already admitted it and realize it was wrong, we should accept them in the league."

Someone else said, "Those who gave presents to the landlords just a couple of times, or occasionally swept out a landlord's courtyard, shouldn't be considered landlords' running-dogs."

"And people who've been too poor to marry and have had an occasional affair with a woman shouldn't be written off as good-for-nothings," said one young man. "Not as long as they show that they can reform themselves."

So in the end the tightly closed door and the wide-open one were both rejected, and the recruiters agreed that everyone who had been classified as a poor peasant should at least be considered for membership in the league. Later, in accordance with directions from the Central Committee, a proportion of new middle peasants were to be admitted.

The recruiters settled on the following procedure for recruiting members. Each recruiter would make a list of likely people from his own section or mutual-aid group. Then all the recruiters would meet to discuss each other's proposals, weed out undesirables, and add names that had been overlooked. Next each would have a personal talk with everyone on his revised list to find out the potential member's attitude toward joining the league and toward his own defects. People who showed a sincere desire to correct their shortcomings would be put on the list which the recruiters would present at the inaugural meeting of the league.

The recruiters drew up four rules for their own conduct in this "linking up" of the poor-and-hired. First, they were not to be swayed by petty prejudice. Second, they must not shield friends and family or pay off old scores; whoever was unqualified was to be kept out, and whoever was qualified was to be let in. Third, they must not "stand on the masses' heads"—that is, adopt a high-and-mighty attitude—or lose their temper. Finally, they were to correct whatever defects they themselves had, and if they criticized others, they were to do it openly.

Several days later, after the open meetings to criticize the Party members, the work team met to discuss the progress in setting up the poor-peasant league. The team leader Lou Lin gave them some instructions that had arrived from the Central Bureau:

"First, one part of the poor peasants should be recruited, and another part examined. That is, those whom the recruiters consider qualified should be admitted straightaway, while those who are generally qualified but have minor defects should be told: 'If you correct your faults, you will be admitted.' The latter group will be under scrutiny, waiting for the league to accept them.

"Second, hold meetings with the recruiters and ask them to decide which of the poor-and-hired are suitable for membership.

"There are roughly three kinds of poor-and-hired: (1) those who should be admitted to the league—that is, those whom the league needs as members, (2) those who may be admitted to the league but who need some education first, (3) those who should not be admitted.

"The recruiters can also examine Communist Party members to consider which of them are qualified to join the league and which are not."

When the team members had noted these instructions, they filed into an adjoining room where the organizers were discussing who should or should not be admitted to the league. Finding the discussion there rambling and inconclusive, Lou Lin passed on the Central Bureau's point that there were three types of poor-and-hired. This formula was eagerly seized upon by the recruiters, who were talking mainly about the undesirables.

One man was turned down because "He's living with a landlord woman. He used her money to buy his house, and it's not right for a poor peasant to be dependent on a landlord."

Another was rejected because "he's a scandalmonger—always cooking up tales about people. And he holds grudges."

A poor-peasant couple who were living together without being married were excluded (even though the woman had a son in the army) "because their relationship is immoral."

Thus despite the policy that the recruiters had adopted, some groups' doors were far from wide open. The Fort's recruiters had found only one suitable member so far: the young oil-press worker Fu Chan-ting. They were obviously afraid of having their candidates for membership turned down the way their sections' nominees for recruiters had been. The north-end section, on the other hand, recommended thirty of their thirty-three poor-and-hired families as suitable for membership in the league. Each of the other sections had found six or seven acceptable poor peasants.

The recruiters who leaned toward the closed-door approach defended their decisions by saying: "So-and-so doesn't seem so bad now, but he may act up once he's safely in the league. Who knows?"

The majority opinion, however, was that in such cases "the masses can always throw him out again."

Finally it was agreed that the only poor peasants who should be kept out were those who were close to the landlords, those who formed cliques or factions, those who were swayed by petty prejudice, those who were "retaliation experts," and those who preferred maintaining questionable relationships with women to joining the league. Before the recruiters' meeting ended, every poor peasant in the village had been discussed and three lists had been drawn up, one for each of the three types of poor-and-hired.

The next step was for the recruiters to inform those on the first and second lists of the decision that had been made about them. Then those who qualified immediately to become league members would be asked to form themselves into poor-peasant groups within their sections. The groups were to help the recruiters in their remaining tasks: examining the poor peasants whose defects had to be corrected, bringing into the league the new middle peasants who were suitable for membership, and nominating candidates for the league committee.

There was a minor delay in taking these steps for on March 12 and 13 one of the traditional spring fairs of the region was held. This was in Yetao, some miles away—too far for the casual shopper, but those with important purchases to make could not afford to miss it. So Ten Mile Inn took a holiday during the daylight hours. After dark, however, the work of the campaign continued as the newly formed poor-peasant groups held their first meetings.

The Fort group assembled on the night of March 12. The dozen poor peasants who were expected drifted in by ones and twos, tired, happy, chattering about the fair. While waiting for the latecomers to arrive, Fu Zhi, who had worked for some years as a clerk in a wine store in Yetao, leaned close to the dimly flickering oil lamp and laboriously read aloud an article from the *People's Daily*. It was entitled "First Stage of the Work of the Ten Mile Inn Team. House-to-House Visiting, Propaganda, and Mobilization." Soon the last of the stragglers came in, and the peasants had to give up listening to an account of the campaign and get on with the thing itself.

The meeting was called to order by Fu Bian-de, who was painfully overcoming his timidity and mastering the art of chairmanship. He asked for reports on the progress that everyone had made in examining the poor peasants who had minor defects and in bringing in new middle peasants who were suitable.

The first report was made by Li Bao-qin, the unsuccessful candidate for recruiter. His defeat in the election had not diminished his enthusiasm for organizing the poor-and-hired. Li was a well-known figure in the village, for he followed his father and grandfather's ancient vocation of 'cupping,' which the villagers regarded as a cure for many ailments.

Referring to an old man who had been a farm laborer, Li said, "I had a good long talk with him, and he guarantees that he'll never be a 'leaky pipe' again." In working for various landlords and rich peasants, the man had occasionally passed on or "leaked" information which should have been confined to the masses.

"He says he knows he has a bad temper, but he'll control it in future. And as for his woman-chasing, he admits that he used to be guilty but he says he's already corrected it!"

The next to report was Fu Zhi, who had been reading the newspaper before the meeting began. "I've seen Fu De," he said, referring to the trumpeter of the band, "and he promises he'll guard against loose talk in the future."

A woman spoke up. "There's nothing wrong with Fu De's wife. She's a good woman. During the famine she had nothing to eat and so she took up with a few men, but she gave that up long ago."

Although there were several women present, few took any part in the discussion. One of them announced at the beginning: "A woman like me is neither a help nor a hindrance in affairs of this sort. I can't do good or harm."

Chen Chui-de, the Fort's only woman recruiter, agreed with her. "You men go ahead and work things out yourselves," she said. "We women don't know much about these things."

The chairman, Fu Bian-de, spoke of three peasants he had been in touch with. "One," he reported, "admitted that he used to chase the women, but says he's already given that up. Another agreed that his approach to people is bad and that he's been ill-tempered, but he'll behave better in future." And the third said that people had grounds for the complaints against him, but that he'd overcome his faults, and would attend whatever meetings he was entitled to in the future.

Most of the poor peasants who had been under scrutiny for minor defects had given satisfactory assurance that they would mend their ways. The recruiters agreed that their probationary period should be ended soon and that they should be proposed for membership.

As to the new middle peasants who were candidates for membership, the work team recommended that those who had fanshenned too high should be rejected for the time being, unless they offered to return the extra fruits of struggle. The recruiters agreed and decided to ask the other new middle peasants who seemed likely to be acceptable to come to the poor-peasant group the next day for criticism and self-criticism.

"The recruiters have done a good job of linking up the poor peasants," said the team member Shao Hang. "Now we must nominate candidates for the poor-peasant league committee.

"This committee won't be like the recruiting group, which has a short-term job. It will lead the work of the whole village and will exist as long as the league exists. It's very important to elect the right kind of people, because those who are not honest won't lead the masses well. Those who are elected must meet the four qualifications.

"You can nominate poor peasants from any part of the village, and put up as many as you wish; there's no limit to the number. You can nominate Party members too, as long as they are capable of doing a good job.

"After all the names have been put forward, we'll have some discussion of them. And when all the sections have made their nominations, we'll hold a big meeting to found the league. At that time we'll elect its chairman."

The first two names to be put forward were those of Communists. Then came some people who were prominent in the village: Li Bao-yu, Zhao Zhen-fang, and Wang Wen-sheng. The list grew until it contained twenty-one names, at the end of which were those of some people present at the meeting: the young oil-press worker Fu Chan-ting, the chairman, Fu Bian-de, and others.

The last of the last were the women, among them the two league recruiters, Song Ting-de, who had been too embarrassed to make a speech at the time of her election, and Chen Chui-de, who had said half an hour ago that women didn't know much about these affairs.

When the nominations came to an end, Chen Chui-de's husband Fu Li-ku, who had again declined to be nominated, said that he was not satisfied with the list. "All these working people are good," he explained, "but they're illiterate. The fact is that those who are too simple and honest haven't got as much ability as those who have defects."

"The question is," said Fu Chan-ting, "do they meet all the four qualifications or not?"

"They must also be able to speak well," Fu Li-ku insisted.

"Being literate and having ability as a speaker are not included in the qualifications," said the team member Shao Hang. "In the old days, the landlords were literate and spoke fluently, but they didn't work for the poor. The committee members of the poor-peasant league must be chosen realistically and carefully."

Fu Li-ku was overruled by the peasants, but he was not convinced. When it came to discussing Fu Bian-de's candidacy, he said, "Bian-de works all the year round. He gets along well with the masses and never loses his temper. Even if you were to give him a good punch he wouldn't turn a hair. He meets all four of the qualifications. He's poor-and-hired and *laoshi*, simple and honest. But," he concluded, "he's not a leader."

Li Bao-qin disagreed and added, "There's no question about it. We should nominate him for the committee." Both the men and the women supported him.

"I think Bian-de has plenty of ability," said the young oil-presser.

"Besides keeping his temper, he's unselfish and enthusiastic and works hard."

Bian-de soon gave evidence of his good nature, for he proposed once more that his critic, Fu Li-ku, should be a candidate. However, Li-ku stuck to his decision to decline.

When Fu Chan-ting was discussed, he pointed out that his temper was bad. "Even if I were elected," he said, "it would be no use; I couldn't lead you. Anyway, I have to work in the oil press."

"It's true that his manner with people isn't always too good," said the former wine-store clerk, Fu Zhi, "but that can easily be corrected."

"You're right," said Li Bao-qin. "He's a bit gruff, but he can get over that. And he's an upright man and a good worker." So Fu Chan-ting's protests were brushed aside and his nomination accepted.

Fu Zhi himself had also been nominated, and he seemed in two minds about accepting. "It's no good nominating me," he began, but apparently found it difficult to give up the honor. "My good points are that I'm no spendthrift and I dislike the ways of the bad cadres," he said. "And I work pretty hard all year from dawn to dusk."

He paused and then said without much conviction, "But still I can't meet all the four requirements."

Li Bao-qin agreed with this last statement. "He works fairly hard," he lied tactfully, "but the fact is that he's been a clerk ever since he was a boy, and the lower village are bound to say he won't do. We must be realistic."

In fact, Fu Zhi was a notorious loafer. Having been a clerk in a small town for almost forty years, he felt that he was too good for manual work. Ever since he had returned to his village home, he had left the bulk of the farming to his fourteen-year-old son. Consequently his fields were among the worst cultivated in Ten Mile Inn.

No one, however, was willing to press Li's criticism further. The only people who spoke were those who wanted to gloss things over.

Fu Bian-de said, "It seems to me he's always very busy. And he keeps his temper under control."

"He takes an interest in other people," Fu Li-ku put in.

Li Bao-qin, however, held out with his vague objections. In response Fu Zhi began saying that his health was not really good, and in the end he declined the nomination.

Of Li Bao-qin himself, Fu Chan-ting said, "He's been a good worker over a number of years. He pulls his weight in public affairs. And he hasn't done anything wrong." The last was a strong statement considering Li Bao-qin's admission at the recruiters' election that he was "a first-class loafer," that he had been a gambler, and that he had beaten his wife and caused her to have two miscarriages. But the poor peasants of the Fort evidently felt that he had really reformed, and he was accepted without protest.

There was little discussion of the two women candidates, though the young oil-presser said that Song Ting-de was "not much concerned about other people and did not always attend meetings when she was supposed to." But it seemed as if the women had been nominated only to comply with the work team's wishes, so that they were approved as a mere formality.

The team member Shao Hang closed the meeting with some critical comments:

"This session has had some shortcomings. For one thing, we haven't yet overcome the habit of face-saving. Naturally we all have our weaknesses, but tonight we didn't speak up about them. Friendship and a spirit of harmony have caused us to cover up defects.

"You seem to have felt embarrassed in mentioning other people's faults, and you didn't pay much attention to the four conditions. This is a serious shortcoming and will have a harmful effect upon your work in the future.

"As you know, the candidates are for the whole village, so you should be very careful in making your nominations. You must be frank and unselfish in order to serve the village.

"If there's a man who is well known for his idleness but we cover up this defect by talking of other things, is this good for him, or harmful? Defects should be exposed, not hidden. If a person does not fulfill the qualifications, he should not be accepted.

"So the trouble with tonight's meeting was that frankness and realism were missing. In future we should be as open and realistic as we were in nominating the recruiters."

The meeting broke up in a subdued spirit, and the peasants promised to put to good use the thirty-six hours that remained before the formal inauguration of the poor-peasant league. They still had to examine the new middle peasants who seemed likely to be acceptable as league members.

The procedure for the new middle peasants was much the same as it had been for the poor peasants who had minor faults to overcome. Possible candidates were proposed in each section and had to be tentatively approved by all the recruiters. Then the candidates were visited by their sponsors, who reported back, not to the recruiters, but to their poor-peasant sections. Those whom each group agreed upon then appeared before the section for criticism and self-criticism.

By the evening of March 13, the stage of criticism and self-criticism was completed by the new middle peasants who were candidates. The recruiters then calculated the grand total of all those who had been linked up by the poor-peasant league: 209, of whom 142 were poor peasants and 67 were new middle peasants.

The benefits of absorbing the new middle peasants were immediate. The poor peasants lost their feeling of isolation, the middle peasants their feeling of exclusion. Compost that had lain piled up in courtyards in the early days of the campaign was now being spread on the fields. Even the middle peasants who had not been recruited into the poor-peasant league shared the cheerfulness that spread among all the "basic masses" as the day approached for the league's inauguration.

# —12—

# Founding the
# Poor-Peasant League

## March 14

For the inauguration meeting, the temple courtyard was gaily decorated with slogans written on strips of colored paper, as well as the usual red drape and the great portrait of Mao Ze-dong. "Closely unite with the middle peasants," said one streamer in gracefully brushed black characters on a background of brilliant red. It was pasted on a monumental slab of stone, which recorded the contributions made by the landlords centuries ago when the temple was built.

The meeting was haltingly called to order by the recruiter Li Bao-yu, whose usually agile mind seemed blank now that he faced a large audience. At last, with a little prompting from other recruiters and members of the team he stammered through the agenda.

First a presidium of five was approved by the crowd. This was a relief to Li Bao-yu, who could now share the burden of chairmanship. Next the village band energetically played a "congratulation tune" which, like a good deal of the music in Ten Mile Inn, bore a remarkable resemblance to jazz.

Wu Xiang, the front-line correspondent who had conducted the team's first meeting with the villagers, mounted the steps. As the crowd clapped for him, a few flakes from a long-threatened snowstorm drifted from the leaden sky. This was a good omen because snow was needed for the winter wheat, and the peasants smiled at one another as Wu Xiang began speaking:

"The work team is here only to help you carry out the Agrarian Law.

"Now the poor-and-hired are going to run their own affairs. Those of you who have been accepted as members of the league are the best of your class. As for the poor peasants who are not yet members, they can be admitted after correcting their faults.

106

Li Bao-yu, a house builder, elected chairman of the poorpeasant league.

"From the members you have chosen candidates for the league committee, and this morning you will elect the best of the best.

"In future you will run your own meetings and manage your own affairs. In running things, you must pay great attention to unity with the middle peasants. In the past the landlords stirred up disunity, but now the poor-and-hired will unite with the middle peasants to form the peasant union."

The snow had begun to fall steadily, and the peasants did their best to squeeze into the main building. A part of the crowd overflowed onto the veranda, which had just been serving as a platform for the presidium.

Settled into new quarters, the meeting went on to the criticism and self-criticism of Party members who were candidates for membership as new middle peasants. The Communists who were poor peasants had already been considered for membership by the recruiters, and four out of nine had been admitted. With the new-middle-peasant Party members, the procedure was much stricter. Not only had they made their self-criticisms to the poor-peasant groups, but they were now required to repeat the process at the league inauguration meeting.

Wang Xi-tang, the village head, began. "It was wrong of me to bury my mother in such an extravagant fashion," he said. "You know that my father, though he earned good money as a brickmaker, took to spending it on opium and heroin. He died when I was still young, and my mother looked after my brothers and me, spinning, weaving, washing, mending, and making clothes for other people. So I wanted to show her some gratitude and respect, even though I knew that it was wrong to spend money extravagantly.

"And after the people had put out so many white cloth banners for my mother, it was wrong of me to forget to do the same for the ex-soldier's father.

"Another weakness is that I'm not democratic. I'm from the poor-and-hired class; in the past all I knew was how to pick up stones." This referred to the stony land that the poorest peasants had to farm. "But when I began to manage the people's affairs, I didn't remember my origins and stick to my convictions. They weren't solid enough."

Wang Xi-tang turned to the case of the drunken moon-festival party that had ended in arrests and beatings. "I didn't believe that the four men should be arrested," he said, "and I went to the militia commander and told him so. But one of them was a relative of mine, and the commander accused me of protecting my family, so I gave in. I didn't stick to my principles."

Wang also criticized himself for his role in the rifle-selling episode. "I didn't believe that the political director should sell the rifle," he said. "We argued about it and finally took the dispute to the district leader, who couldn't make up his mind. He said, 'It seems wrong in a way, but Wang Shao-zhen needs the money. The best thing would be for the people to make him a gift by buying the rifle.' " Thus the district head implied that Wang Shao-zhen deserved the money because of his service to the people. Though Wang Xi-tang knew that this reasoning was unsound, he acquiesced in order to keep his peace with the village cadres.

Wang Xi-tang continued, "I didn't agree with the political director when he wanted to break his brother's engagement, either. We had a furious argument about it, and I ended by throwing the village seal on the ground. Then Shao-zhen picked it up

The village government in session. Wang Xi-tang on the right; Wang Fu-xin, the village clerk, on the left.

and used it to seal the letter he wrote to the girl's family. Again I didn't stick to my principles; it was a case of 'officials protecting officials.' That's my weakness, and that's what has made me defective in my service to the people.

"Last summer I bought 2.6 *mu* of land in the lower valley, which caused me to fanshen too high. I became a mound, for my family had 1 *mu* per head more than the village average; I was aiming to become a new rich peasant. Now I would like to return the 2.6 *mu* to the masses. If you can forgive me and admit me to the poor-peasant league, I'll be very happy. If you cannot, then I must stay out of it. It's up to you to decide."

For the most part, people seemed satisfied with the village head's self-criticism. He had spoken with sincerity and humility, but where there were extenuating circumstances, as in the case of his mother's funeral, he had said so. A chorus of approval followed his speech.

However, one of the men who had been arrested following the moon-festival party said, "You should have known they were going to beat us up. What would you have done if one of us had died?"

"When I heard that the militia commander had been knocked down," Wang said, "I thought it was very serious. But in the main, I was at fault for being in with a small group of cadres."

"We never did knock him down," the speaker replied. "We had taken off our shoes and were sitting on the *kang*. One pair of shoes was near the rifle, and my friend was just going to put them on. When he reached for them, the commander thought he was going to grab the rifle and start a fight."

"And all because of that," said another victim, "I was beaten as cruelly as if a landlord had done it. Even if I had been in the wrong, I shouldn't have been treated like that. I should have been given some education."

On this angry note the discussion of the moon-festival party ended. The chairman asked if there were any more comments about Wang's self-criticism.

"When the political director and the public security officer got angry and glared at us, the village head never corrected them for it," said one man.

"Yes, he looked down on the people and sheltered the cadres," said another.

"That's true. Even when he knew something wasn't right, he gave in. He has soft ears." This meant that he was easily swayed.

"And he didn't make the struggle-fruit accounts public so that everyone could know how things had been distributed."

One of the poor peasants complained at length about his treatment during the campaign to Dig Out the Air-Raid Shelters. "My sister married into a family in Blue Smoke Temple, but after her marriage she left a lot of her things in our house. They had been given to her by my mother in the first place, so we didn't think they were the same as other air-raid goods. When the air-raid shelters were being dug out, the militia came to our house and asked for my sister's belongings. After her clothing had been taken by our peasant union, some people came over from Blue Smoke Temple and made us give them something as well. The cotton padding for my bed quilt was taken, and my sister got a beating for being an air-raid shelter. The whole thing was unfair and undemocratic and that the village head should have seen that justice was done."

"It's quite true," said Wang Xi-tang, "that you ought not to have been made to give those things to Blue Smoke Temple. But the trouble was that you weren't straightforward; every time the militia went to your place, they discovered more air-raid goods. I'm sorry that I didn't do my duty, but for your part, you weren't always simple and honest." Having learned that he had been wrong not to stick to his principles, Wang was now taking a firm stand on them.

There was a long pause. At last Wang himself rounded off the discussion by saying, "As village head I didn't do my job well. As a Party member, however, I was under the leadership of the political director and had to influence others through him. Still, in the long run we were all guilty of the same thing; we covered up for each other. It was a case of officials protecting officials."

Now the peasants had to decide whether, in spite of his faults, the village head could be admitted to the league. When it came down to the vote, an overwhelming majority was in favor of him. So Wang Xi-tang became the league's first member who was both a new middle peasant and a Communist.

Three more cases were considered and settled in short order. In his self-criticism one Party member said that a small package belonging to a struggle object had been hidden in his house during the Air-Raid Shelters Campaign, but that he had turned it over to the village government as soon as he discovered it.

"Yes, he's a good man. We have no criticisms," the peasants said, and he was admitted without discussion.

The next Party member was a young militiaman. "My attitude's not good, and sometimes I can't control my temper," he said. "Once I borrowed a harrow and broke it out in the fields, and I said nothing when I returned it. That was wrong. And when I was in charge of the militia, I didn't call meetings very often. That was a shortcoming."

The crowd laughed, for the Communists' frequent meetings were a joke in the Liberated Areas. Some peasant poet had composed the couplet:

With the Guomindang, it's more taxes to pay.
With the Eighth Route Army, it's meetings all day.

"He's just a young chap who's never held any responsible post," the peasants said of the militiaman, and he was unanimously admitted. The fourth Communist was also accepted, and these newly admitted league members were asked if they had anything more to say.

Wang Xi-tang spoke up. "I went astray, like a messenger who loses his message. But I promise that in the future I'll stand together with the people. So please make further criticisms of me. If my presence makes this difficult, then I can go."

"No, no. We've got no more criticisms. You stay here," people shouted from the crowd. The mass of the poor peasants knew in their hearts that Wang Xi-tang was a source of strength to them. The minority who bore personal grudges or had axes to grind were no match for the newly organized league.

Next the secretary of the work team read out the entire list of the league's members. The crowd was supposed to discuss each one before giving their final approval, but after they listened to the list the general feeling was, "They've all been discussed and examined at their group meetings; no need to go over them again." As one man said, "Not a single name grated on my ears." So the audience unanimously agreed to accept the entire list.

Wang Wen-sheng came to the front of the room with a slip of paper in his hand. "The recruiters have drawn up some regulations for the poor-peasant league that they ask you all to consider." He handed the paper to the team secretary to read out.

There were five points. "First, what does the league do? Second, who can join it? Third, the procedure for joining: applicants should be introduced by a member, should criticize themselves at their poor-peasant group meeting, and then, if the group passes them, should be submitted to the committee of the league for final approval. Fourth, what sorts of rules should there be? (For instance, obeying the leaders, attending meetings, not being a 'leaky pipe.') Fifth, what is to be done when there are breaches of discipline?"

This mixture of problems and proposals had been worked out by the recruiters themselves, and as such it was a turning point in the campaign. For with it the poor peasants were taking over the management of their own league, and the work team would gradually withdraw to an advisory position.

Li Bao-yu now introduced the last major item on the agenda: the election of the league's committee. Because he still felt ill at ease before so large a crowd, Li asked the team secretary to explain the details of voting.

"The recruiters propose that the committee should have thirteen full members and two reserves," said the secretary. "Forty people have been nominated, but the suggestion is that you should vote only on those who have been nominated by two or more poor-peasant groups. That would leave twenty-one candidates." This procedure was accepted, and each of the candidates was asked to speak.

"I did have affairs with women once or twice in my youth," the first said, "but not since."

'The crowd applauded him, calling, "He's all right. We've got no criticisms of him."

"I'm not famous for my laziness," said the next, with a cocksure smile.

"No, but you'd better cure your woman-chasing habits," said someone in the crowd.

The third candidate, Wang Guang-xun, admitted at the outset, "My defect is that I'm lazy. And since my wife died, I've had to spend a lot of time looking after my child.

"People have criticized me for not planting enough winter wheat," he went on. "Well, it's this way: My land is on the Yangyi Plateau, and I said to myself, 'It's no good for wheat; better just depend on the autumn crops.' But I should have followed your advice and planted more wheat, because I could sell it and get the cash I need for clothes.

"It's not true that I bought a sugar wafer in Yangyi that time." Apparently this accusation that had come up at the recruiters' election still rankled.

But the peasant who had originally made the criticism still grumbled. "He's a spendthrift, anyway. Always sitting around on the Street."

"I'm afraid that I don't have the ability for this job," Wang concluded. "But whatever you want me to do, I'm willing to try."

"Brother Guang-xun's all right," was the general verdict, and he was accepted as a candidate.

Next came Wang Wen-sheng. "My price was too high," he said. "I weighed things up too carefully before putting myself out to do people favors.

"And my treatment of my father has not been right." The peasants had rejected this charge at a previous meeting, but evidently Wang had been mulling it over as the self-criticism movement swept the village. He said, "I've often lost my temper with my father. Once he took a bit of someone else's fodder and was locked up for two days.

I was angry because I thought he had ruined our reputation, but really I ought to let him eat as much as he likes." In fact, the whole family was not far above the subsistence level.

"Anyway, I'm afraid that I can't speak well and that I have no ability." But Wang Wen-sheng was accepted by the crowd.

Fu Bian-de of the Fort rated himself even lower. "My memory is no good, I can't talk well, and I have no head for business.

"In the past when I didn't have a water crock, I borrowed one from a landlord. That was wrong. And my wife hid some goods for a landlord, though I reported it as soon as I found out."

It was clear to everyone that Fu Bian-de was no running-dog of the landlords, and he was quickly approved.

One speaker acknowledged that his greatest shortcoming was a weakness for women. But the crowd overlooked this defect and praised him for his even temper and good-natured way with everyone, men and women, young and old alike.

Wang Xi-tang, however, was not inclined to let him off lightly. He insisted that the easygoing philanderer ought to tell them which women he had had affairs with, but the crowd was against this, and the names remained a secret.

When all the candidates had been considered, the genial Geng Xi mounted the platform to present the work team's ideas about the coming election. He also took up the recurrent question of sexual morals, for the narrow-minded views of many peasants on this subject warped their judgment on more important matters. Although censoriousness about sexual lapses was stronger among the women than the men, Geng Xi dealt with the matter from a male angle.

"We must distinguish between serious defects and petty ones— between different types of woman chasing," he said. "If a poor man who couldn't afford to get married has improper relations with a woman, that's a small defect. Just think how many concubines the landlords used to keep, while poor men had to stay single all their lives. So whether woman chasing is a serious fault or a minor one depends upon the particular case. Are there some people who think that woman chasing is always a serious defect?"

"Yes, I do," said Wang Xi-tang, "because it undermines the relations between husband and wife."

Although he came from a poor-and-hired family and, as he had said earlier, used to understand nothing but picking up stones, Wang's outlook had changed with his improved economic position. As a new middle peasant he had been able to marry, and now he thought like a man anxious to guard his own wife from the womanless poor-and-hired.

But Wang Xi-tang did not speak for the majority of league members. "Woman chasing is not such a serious matter if it's done by the poor," they insisted.

A few days before, the work team's supervisor at the Central Bureau had explained the Party's view of woman chasing. The bureau disapproved of sexual irregularities among its own members, he said, because there was always the danger that the cadres would abuse their power by taking other men's wives. But where the poor-and-hired were concerned, the Party took a sympathetic view of woman chasing as long as it did not create discord.

The next point that Geng Xi made at the meeting concerned the relationship between the Party and the poor-peasant league. "What should this relationship be?" he asked. "The Party is the long-term laborer for the poor peasants—for all the peasant masses. So the people have to assign tasks to the Party.

"At the same time, the Party should be the leader of the league. But it cannot lead simply by giving orders—though it may make criticisms. It must set an example, educate the masses, and convince them.

"Still, some of the Party members have weaknesses. Those with small ones can be reformed. But if there are some who have committed crimes, they can be handed over to the people's court.

"So now I want to ask you which is better: to have Party members in the poor-peasant league, or not?"

"They should be in the league," many answered.

"Is it a good thing to have Party members on the league committee, or not?"

"There should be some on the committee," a few answered.

Geng Xi went on to other aspects of the election. "In electing the committee members, we should have a broad outlook in order to make sure that the committee is really representative. It should contain someone from each of the mutual-aid groups, and it should include some women.

"Altogether there will be thirteen members on the committee, plus two reserve members. The reserve members will attend committee meetings, where they can discuss things but not vote. And they can fill the vacancies if someone is absent or dies.

"Now let's vote by show of hands."

Zhao Zhen-fang and Wang Wen-sheng came out well toward the top of the fifteen successful candidates, with Fu Bian-de of the Fort close behind them. Four women were elected, one of them as a reserve member. Of the three Communist candidates, one came within three votes of being elected as a reserve member; the other two made a poor showing.

The successful candidates, as had now become the custom, made modest speeches asking the people to criticize them whenever they showed signs of failing in their duty. And the crowd in turn called out that they should serve the people "with an upright heart" and warned them not to have "soft ears" or allow anyone to pay off old scores.

"Committee members who fail in their duty may be dismissed by the people who have elected them," said Geng Xi in closing. "And the members of the league should listen to the leadership, just as the leadership should respect the people."

And so the poor-peasant league was formed.

Later that evening when committee members met to allocate responsibilities, Li Bao-yu was chosen to be chairman of the league.

# —13—

# The Party
# and the Masses

It often happens that the masses need a certain change but are not yet conscious of the need, not yet willing to make the change. In such cases we should wait patiently until, through our work, most of them have seen the need and want the change. Otherwise we shall isolate ourselves from them. . . . There are two principles here: one is that the actual needs of the masses may be different from what we fancy they are, and the other is that they must make up their own minds instead of having us decide for them.*

In the opinion of the team members, the fact that no Communist had been elected to the poor-peasant league committee was a serious reflection on their work. Subsequent analysis by the Central Bureau also assigned some of the responsibility to the Party leadership higher up. The Communists had exaggerated the "impurity of the Party" throughout the Taihang subregion. They believed that the poor-and-hired had not fanshenned in this area because the Party cadres were influenced by landlord and rich-peasant ideology.

In reality, however, much of the land reform had been satisfactorily carried out. As soon as the Party leaders in the Central Bureau realized their mistake, they began issuing guidelines for forming an accurate estimate of the good and bad points of local cadres. A member of the Central Committee stated:†

Among our local cadres are many who carry on the fight despite hardships. . . .
But there are also a few who have done things contrary to the best interests of the people. Some of them did these things because they

---

* For the full quotation see: Mao Ze-dong, "The United Front in Cultural Work," October 30, 1944, *Selected Works*, vol. III. Translated directly from the Chinese.
† Ren Bi-shi, "Several Questions Arising from Agrarian Reform," delivered January 12, 1948. Because of disruptions in communications caused by the war, copies were not available in Ten Mile Inn until March 27.

used bad methods in fulfilling tasks assigned them from above. For example, in collecting grain and fodder and providing stretchers, when time was pressing and when they had not learned the democratic way of working, they simply resorted to enforcing orders, beating and shouting at the masses and thus alienating them.

The responsibility for this sort of thing cannot be placed solely on the local cadres. The upper levels of leading organs are also responsible for assigning too many tasks, setting too short a time limit, and for giving too little education during ordinary times in the democratic way of working.

But for such things as distributing too much of the fruits of agrarian reform to themselves, misappropriation, graft, corruption, and committing unlicensed acts which run counter to the directives issued time and again by the leading bodies, the responsibility must be borne by the cadre himself. If the upper levels have any responsibility, it is that they did not immediately discover these things, put a stop to them, mete out punishment for them, or remove the cadre from office.

Often it is not easy for the masses to make these distinctions.

In addition, a directive issued by the Communist leadership discussed the relations between the Party and the masses:*

[Where] feudalistic forces have generally been eliminated, the dissatisfaction of the peasants is frequently focused on a handful of Party members and cadres who misuse their political position and usurp the fruits of agrarian reform. In such areas, land adjustment must be combined with reorganization of the ranks of the Party. . . .

While paying serious attention to the phenomenon of impurity within the Party, we should not forget that our Party has undergone long-term tests, registered victorious advances, and possesses great prestige among the masses.

The application of these policy statements to local cases, however, called for expert judgment and left considerable possibility for error. For example, the diary of the work team at Ten Mile Inn contains the following entry for March 1:

Lou Lin and Leng Bing had some difference of opinion regarding the work of reorganizing the ranks of the Party. According to Lou Lin, we should explain that the chief purpose of this work was to make it clear that the Party members harbored landlord and rich-peasant ideology and call on them to admit it. Leng Bing said that this would be going too far.

Leng Bing proved to be correct. The branch had eliminated its impure and feudal elements in 1944, when it was reorganized. What-

* "Directive on Agrarian Reform and Reorganizing the Ranks of the Party in the Old and Semi-old Areas."

ever their faults, its members could not be characterized as harboring "landlord and rich-peasant ideology." Individually and collectively, the Communists of Ten Mile Inn had shown themselves to be the most selfless, courageous, and resourceful men in the village. Their shortcomings were their secondary, not primary, characteristics.

The situation was complicated by the fact that in the past the branch had been partly underground, and the peasants did not know who all of them were. So while the village masses appreciated the role of the Communist Party in general, they did not always give full credit to the Communists in their own village. And the work team had been so eager to correct the Party members' mistakes that it had failed to set the villagers right. Indeed, the team had taken such pains not to pour cold water on the masses that it had poured cold water on the Party members.

In addition, the timing of criticism and classification had gone awry. Lou Lin's Central Bureau supervisor had written him:

> You must let the masses think over their criticisms of the cadres and Party branch members while classification is going on. You should let them make criticisms and mull things over whenever they feel like it. In doing so, their enthusiasm will be raised, and the work of reorganizing the ranks of the Party will be pushed forward.

The work team's original plan had been that classification would go on by day and criticism by night. Once classification had begun, however, the masses did not want to do anything else but classify. So the criticism of the cadres and Party members was temporarily postponed. The point was not driven home to the peasants that the education of the Party members was vital to the development of democracy, and that democracy was vital to the adjustment of landholdings. In the early stages of the campaign the connection between these three things was not fully understood even by some of the team members, let alone by the mass of the peasants.

The relationship which the peasants did see very clearly was that between classification and land adjustment. In their minds, classification became simply a matter of who was to own the land. They assumed that if a person was classified as a landlord or rich peasant, he would have land taken away; if as a middle peasant, he might voluntarily offer up a little, receive a little, or simply keep what he had; if as a poor peasant, he would receive land. They wanted to finish the classification quickly because they were in a hurry to settle the question of land, and it took time for the work team to convince them that democracy must come first.

These factors—the exaggeration of the Party branch's impurity, the failure to point out its accomplishments, and the unavoidable departure from the original timetable—all had an effect upon the inaugural meeting of the poor-peasant league, particularly on the failure of Communists to win positions on the league committee. Of the three Communist candidates, one was a man about whom the peasants had said, "No complaints," at the open branch meeting four days before. At the league inauguration meeting, however, someone criticized him for being standoffish and lazy.

Another Party candidate had been discussed by the crowd at some length. "He's all right," said one man, "but his wife's not so good."

"He has soft ears," said another.

"He was always letting information leak out to the landlords."

"He's *too* simple and honest."

"I don't know about that," someone objected. "I think he's selfish. He didn't report all his family's housing at the classification."

"That was only because I didn't understand the instructions properly," the candidate replied. "And I don't think it's true to say that I leaked information to the landlords." There the matter rested, but neither of these two candidates made much of a showing when it came to the vote.

The third Party member, Fu Pei-chang, was a popular man in the village. Most of the peasants said that he did a good job in the difficult position of director of rear service, where he had to supervise stretcher bearing, grain transportation, shoe and uniform manufacture for the army, and so on.

When his name had come up as a candidate, Fu Pei-chang had made a long self-criticism. "I have the weakness of putting my own interests before those of the masses," he said. "For example, last winter when the hostel wanted a cook, I thought it was a good chance to make some money during the off season, so I took the job myself. And when you used to come there to settle up for your rear-service coupons, I often said I was too busy to bother about it. So I was selfish and wasted your time.

"And when some of you asked me to take part in the new year's play, I said I didn't have time. I wasted a lot of time in our mutual-aid group, too. All these things were mistakes on my part, so now I'd be glad if you'll criticize me. Don't think that you can't speak your mind because I'm a cadre."

This advice was unnecessary; the complaints had begun at once. "Last year when all the fruits were spread out on the threshing floor, there was nothing much of any value. So you turned up your nose and wouldn't take anything."

"During the frugality week last July to celebrate the birthday of the

Party, Pei-chang proposed an unrealistic quota for himself: he said his family could get along on ten ounces of millet each per day."

There was some objection to this criticism from the crowd, for in reality it was possible to get by on ten ounces a day, and Fu Pei-chang and his family had done it.

Fu Pei-chang defended himself against the charge that he had scorned the fruits of struggle. "The reason I didn't take my share," he said, "was that the members of the Party branch had agreed not to. It certainly wasn't because I turned up my nose and thought I might manage to get something better."

The sound of chatter welled up and filled the courtyard.

"He's spoken the truth."

"He made a good self-criticism."

"His ears are a bit soft, but there's nothing else wrong with him."

Practically all the objections had been raised by militants with axes to grind or old grievances in their breasts. The majority of the peasants, however, were not blindly critical of the Party members. They were affected by the strong tide of criticism but did not float along with it.

In fact, the poor-peasant league's inauguration meeting had proved to be a turning point in the relations between the Party and the masses, for it was the first time that the Party members had made any reply to the charges leveled against them. Previously they had only listened quietly, no matter how heated or inaccurate the criticism became. But when Wang Xi-tang was being considered for membership in the league, he set a precedent by stating his own side of the case with objectivity and strength. And the poor-and-hired had backed him up, approving his membership by acclaim.

However, membership in the league was one thing; leadership was another. So in the election of committee members Fu Pei-chang, for all his popularity and loyal service, lost by three votes.

The defeat was not serious, but it warned the team that the relationship between the Party and the masses needed cementing. In future there must be a higher standard of criticism, more discussion, and deeper analysis of past events and of the role that the Communists had played in them. And there must be a realistic appraisal of the accusations flung out by the militants who belonged to opposition cliques. Above all, the branch would have to make a better showing when it came to electing the committee of the new peasant union.

The poor-peasant league was formally established on March 14. The Central Bureau wrote to the work team: "When the poor-peasant league has been inaugurated, the middle peasants will feel uneasy. So the peasant union should be organized just as soon as the league has had a brief period for mulling things over and building its membership."

For their first sixteen days in the village, the team's job had been to awaken and then to organize the masses. As soon as the poor-peasant league was established, however, the team was expected to limit its functions increasingly to those of guide and adviser. From then on, as much of the work as possible was to be done by the people themselves through their organizations: first the poor-peasant league, then the peasant union, and later the people's congress.

If the Party branch in its turn were to function correctly, it would have to play a leading role in these organizations and in village life. So before the team could effectively withdraw from village affairs, the relations between the Party and the masses would have to be straightened out.

This meant that as many of the branch members as possible should quickly complete their reeducation so that they could resume their normal place in day-to-day activities. The ten poor-peasant and new-middle-peasant Party members who had been accepted into the league were already back in circulation. Now Leng Bing arranged for another eight Communists whose shortcomings were considered fairly minor to prepare their self-criticisms. They presented their statements on March 15 at a branch meeting attended by elected delegates of the people.

The attitude of the villagers toward the Party members had already changed since the open branch meeting five days before. Then, urged on by the work team and influenced by the more dissatisfied activists, the masses had tended to be overcritical. But at the league inauguration meeting, when the Party members had begun to present their side of the case, a more balanced approach began to emerge.

Also, the older men were beginning to make their influence felt in opposition to the young militants who had been making the sharpest attacks. Men who remembered vividly what conditions had been under the landlords and the Guomindang knew that the Party branch had improved the peasants' lives. They felt that the present militia commander and the public security officer were tough—they had to be, in order to do their jobs—but they pointed out that compared with the Guomindang army officers, the cadres dealt gently with the people. This view was held by a number of the delegates sent to the Party branch meeting.

Many with strong dissatisfaction also came to the meeting. They included a handful of ex-soldiers who felt that their services had not been adequately rewarded by the cadres and that their families had not been treated well enough. There were some delegates who had been punished, justly or unjustly, by the authorities. Finally, there were militants who wanted to replace the Party members in office and were trying to start up a movement for a clean sweep.

But as the evening wore on, the sincerity of the Party members' self-criticism had its effect. Though they had prepared their statements in advance, most of them were illiterate and found it difficult under the stress of the occasion to remember what they had planned to say.

In making his self-criticism Fu Pei-yu, the manager of the cooperative, came to a pause and muttered to himself, "Is there anything else?"

"Woman chasing," prompted one of his comrades.

"And that land-buying business," another added.

"Oh yes," Fu said, and resumed.

Besides criticizing themselves, the Party members gave their opinions of the villagers' charges against them. Their manner was calm and modest, but they refused to accept accusations based on hearsay or personal spite.

The result was that all eight of the statements were accepted by the delegates, four of them without question and four with the grudging consent of those whose criticisms had been answered. The work team felt that more than half of the branch members were now well on the way to regaining their place in village life. But the team also realized that the masses judged the Party members too much by their conduct in trifling personal matters and overlooked the part played by the Communists in the struggle against feudalism, Japanese imperialism, and the Guomindang.

Before the new peasant union was formed, the team would somehow have to bring the villagers to a fair evaluation of the Party branch and a better relationship with the Communists. The old middle peasants posed the greatest difficulty, because many of them resented the rise to power of the Party cadres who had become new middle peasants. Furthermore, there were a number of rival militants among both old and new middle peasants. However, the poor peasants had made such rapid political progress that they could be counted on to display a realistic attitude toward the Party branch. The middle peasants were now backward in comparison.

As the middle peasants were now backward compared with the poor, the team asked the members of the poor-peasant league in every section to arrange meetings with small groups of middle peasants— old or new, male or female—who were simple and honest and had no old scores to settle.

In the Fort, the new activists of the poor-peasant group called together some twenty middle peasants. The chairman of the meeting, the young oil-press worker Fu Chan-ting, turned to the team member Shao Hang and asked his advice on how to get things started. Shao suggested that people might clarify their attitudes by sorting out the various Party members into good ones and bad ones. They might even single out the worst and the best.

The proposal was accepted, and the twenty-eight Party members were discussed in turn. The group decided that seventeen were either good or had no serious defects, and that eleven were bad. Of the bad ones, the peasants agreed that five were under the influence of the other six, and that these six were the worst.

"Now we've sorted the Party members into good and not quite so good, bad and not quite so bad," said the chairman. "The question is, can they join the peasant union?"

The meeting broke into smaller groups for fermentation. The verdict was that all should be considered qualified to join except for the six worst, and that for the time being, these six should be kept out.

"Well, and should the others be allowed to run for office as cadres?" There was more fermentation.

Then Shao Hang spoke. "I would like to explain the proper way for the Party to work.

"The members of our Ten Mile Inn branch are members of the Party led by Chairman Mao. It is their duty to offer leadership to the people. The proper way for them to do that is to put ideas and suggestions up to the poor-peasant league and the peasant union. They should ask the members of these organizations to discuss their proposals to see whether they are good or not. If the proposals are turned down, then the Party members must not try to force them on the poor-peasant league or the peasant union.

"Sometimes the league or the union will decide that the proposals are partly acceptable and partly not. Then the branch can modify them, as long as they stick to Party policy.

"So you see, the only right that the Party members have is to make proposals and ask you to consider them. Neither the Party members nor the branch may give orders. In the past, it was not right for the Party member cadres to make you do things their way."

When Shao had finished, the groups fermented again. Then the chairman asked them, "What use do you think we should make of the Party members in future?"

"The village head Wang Xi-tang is a Party member who knows how to lead," said the father of a soldier. "Last year at weeding time, the village was short of labor power to tend the fields of the soldiers' families. So Wang called a meeting of all us soldiers' families to mobilize whatever labor we did have. And we found that we could get a lot done by mutual aid among ourselves, so we didn't have to put too much of the burden on the village."

"When the work team first came here," an old woman put in, "I was afraid that they wouldn't make any distinction between our good village head and some of those rotten cadres. What I think is this: we should use people according to their abilities, whether they're cadres or Party members or not."

"Yes, only the bad ones should be expelled from the Party."

"But if they make good confessions and reform, there's no need to expel them."

"Yes, give them a little more time to criticize themselves. If they do it all right, there's no need to expel them. We can admit them to the peasant union, because we need able people."

This was the sense of the meeting. Shao's idea of sorting the Party members into good and bad had blocked the antagonistic militants' drive to make a clean sweep. Not only was the dividing line between the Party and the masses being erased, but people were beginning to acknowledge the need for leadership from the Party branch. With minor variations, this was the result of the meetings held in all the sections.

In the next series of section meetings, the delegates who had heard the Party members' self-criticism at the branch meeting were to report to the masses, and the masses were to nominate candidates for the new peasant-union committee. Everyone except the struggle objects was entitled to attend. The broad attendance, of course, meant that the general level of political understanding would be lower. So in preparation, Shao Hang suggested beforehand to the Fort delegates that in their reports they apply the grading process to the Party members' statements, singling out the best from the good and the worst from the bad.

The delegates agreed, and after the reports were made at the meetings, the masses were asked to apply the same standards of good and bad, best and worst, to the Party members. In this way Shao hoped to raise the level of the sessions. But the attempt was only partly successful, for many peasants still harped on trifling details and personal feelings. In all the sections there were people who had not yet grasped the principle of judging the Communists by the role they had played in the political struggle. Just how much progress had been made would be seen when the committee members were elected at the meeting to inaugurate the new peasant union.

# —14—

# Building the Peasant Union

## March 18

While the work team concentrated on the relationship between the Party and the masses, the masses were expanding the poor-peasant league and using it to organize the new peasant union. Some of the poor-and-hired underestimated the importance of the union—as when one old hired laborer opposed the nomination of Wang Xi-tang for membership on its committee. "We'd better reserve the village head for some more important post," he said.

In reality, the head of the peasant union would be one of the most important officials in the village. As the masses became politically more conscious and active, less initiative would rest with the cadres and militants than in the past. The rank and file of peasant-union members would have much more to say about village affairs.

Although the new peasant union was for all the laboring masses, poor and middle peasants alike, it would serve the interests of the poor peasants more effectively than the old union had done. The poor-and-hired were to be its backbone.

Not only the poor-peasant league's committee but its entire membership were now mobilized to recruit for the union. All old middle peasants, and all new middle peasants who were not already in the league, were discussed by the league members in the various sections. Some were immediately approved as being *laoshi*—simple and honest —and as fulfilling the four qualifications for membership. Others were rejected until they could provide evidence that they were correcting their faults. Others who were borderline cases were invited to go before their section's poor-peasant group for criticism and self-criticism. Some of these were accepted; others had to go through a period of reform. All the work of building the new union was carried out by the members of the poor-peasant league, who were automatically to be members of the union.

Very few middle peasants were considered unsuitable for the union. In the Fort there were only five, including the oil-press manager, Li Bao-wu (who was still under suspicion of graft), Li Bao-hui, the "slippery-headed" animal dealer, and Wang Xiang, the outspoken head of the peasant women's association.

As the great majority of their class was signed up for the new peasant union, the middle peasants, both old and new, began to lose their sense of isolation. They had felt left out when the poor-peasant league was formed and the emphasis was on the poor peasants as the backbone of the campaign. Now, however, the theme was the unity of poor and middle peasants. The campaign was standing firmly on both its feet, and the minds of the masses were at rest.

The one group of middle peasants who remained ill at ease were the eleven Party members who had not been admitted to the poor-peasant league or recruited for the peasant union. A feeling of doom weighed them down. Those who were cadres regretted that they had ever accepted office, for it was this, they felt, which had brought them to their present pass.

Years before, the political director Wang Shao-zhen had braved the fury of the ancestral ghosts by leading the villagers to farm graveyard land. Now he looked as wan as the spirits themselves. He had lost the heart to repair the terrace walls of his land across the river in South Mountain Field. He no longer took his bowl out to eat with the crowd that gathered at mealtimes in front of the co-op. He spent his days examining his thoughts.

As for Li Xi-yuan, the director of civil affairs, he was so absorbed in introspection that he could not tolerate the slightest interruption. One day as he was driving his donkey to the fields, he untied the bell from its neck because the tinkling interrupted his train of thought. And the branch's propaganda secretary, Wang Wen-tang, even struck himself in remorse for his misdeeds.

In contrast, Wang Mi-shan, organization secretary of the branch and director of the people's arms committee, said dryly to his wife, "I seem to have become an Old Moneybags all of a sudden."

In spite of their diverse reactions, these eleven Party members had a common feeling of unease and anxiety. But the spirits of most poor and middle peasants rose steadily following the inauguration of the poor-peasant league. Their good humor reached a peak on the morning of March 18, when a huge crowd met to establish the new peasant union.

The crowd's size alone showed that the poor and middle peasants were once more together, as they had been at the first meeting in the temple courtyard. And though the middle peasants were out in force, it was the chairman of the poor-peasant league, the short, stocky house-builder Li Bao-yu, who opened the meeting. The poor-and-hired were in the lead.

"It's about ten years now since the Eighth Route Army first came to our village," Li said. "There have been great changes here since then, though there are still some of us who haven't fanshenned properly.

"But now we've gone ahead and organized the poor-peasant league. And today we and the middle peasants are going to set up the new peasant union.

"We know that there are twenty-eight Party members in our village, and we have made our criticisms of them and of the bad cadres. We've admitted good Party members to the poor-peasant league, and now we're taking good ones into the peasant union. It doesn't matter whether a person is a Party member or not, or whether he's a poor peasant, a new middle peasant, or an old middle peasant. If he's a good man, he should be admitted to the union.

"As to those who can't be admitted yet, we'll decide later whether to accept them. In any case, peasants who have received an unfair share of the fruits should return them, and those who've done wrong should be suitably dealt with."

Li Bao-yu came to a stop and turned around uncertainly to look at Geng Xi, who prompted him on a final point. "Yes," said Li Bao-yu, "later we'll elect the peasant-union committee. First, though, we'll ask our work team comrades to say something."

Geng Xi, who had been appointed the team's spokesman for the occasion, came to the head of the steps, where he stood towering above little Li Bao-yu and smiling until the applause died down.

"When the poor-peasant league was organized, there weren't as many people here as there are today. So the league members looked around and thought: 'Hm, there aren't very many of us. How'll we manage?' Then they felt that the only thing to do would be to unite with the middle peasants.

"Meanwhile, the new and old middle peasants were thinking: 'Why don't they ask us to their meetings?'

"So both the poor and the middle peasants have the same demand—to come together and work together. The poor-peasant league has been like a matchmaker; it has joined the two in this new peasant union. The main task of the new union will be the same as the main task of the league—to lead all of you who didn't fully fanshen in the past to do so now.

"Maybe you'll be thinking: 'Well, we had a peasant union before, didn't we? Is this one any different?' Let's compare them. How were people admitted to membership in the old peasant union? Both the good and the bad were allowed to join, weren't they? But now we've set new conditions.

"In our new union we don't want any leaky pipes. We don't want good-for-nothings, or woman-chasers, or people who get all worked up over nothing.

"The new union is also going to do a better job of dividing the fruits." Geng Xi was referring to the fruits of an earlier campaign which had not yet been distributed. "Everything that the new peasant union does will be just and fair.

"Now I'd like to say something more about the relationship between the poor and middle peasants.

"Among the poor peasants are those who have big holes to be filled up. Those holes could never be filled until the poor peasants became masters of the house. Now they are running it. And they have known suffering, so they will be able to act with justice.

"But it's not only the poor peasants who've suffered. Some middle peasants suffered too, because they didn't dare to speak out. The poor peasants worked hard on the land, and so did the middle peasants. Because they have labored together and suffered together, they are both of one family. They can never be separated.

"In the poor-peasant league, nothing can pull the league members apart, because they've all been poor. But the poor peasants can't run the house alone; there are too few of them. So they must unite with the middle peasants, and all the poor and middle peasants together can become masters of the house.

"How's it going to be when they run the house together? Well, it will be like running a business, with the poor-and-hired as the manager in chief and the middle peasants as the assistant manager.

"In the old days, weren't there a lot of loafers and rascals in the village? Weren't there cases of women being abused? Weren't there people who smoked opium or took heroin?"

"That's true," someone called.

"That's how it was, all right."

"We used to have all sorts of riffraff."

"But after the Communist Party came to Ten Mile Inn," continued Geng Xi, "what happened? The masses learned from the Communists and reformed themselves. And now the Communists are learning from the masses and reforming themselves. It was the same with our work team. We had to learn from you in order to give you help and advice. Ability comes from the masses.

(*above*) Candidates for the peasant union committee. Li Bao-yu in the center; young Wang Ru-tang at the left; Wang Wen-sheng standing in the doorway.

(*right*) The crowd at the inauguration meeting of the peasant union in the snow.

"Now, with the poor and middle peasants united and the Party members reformed, the peasants will be sitting on the throne. Together all will fanshen, make a better living, and become prosperous."

Geng Xi stepped to the back of the temple porch and Wang Ru-tang, who was joint chairman of the meeting, came forward to conduct the election of the peasant-union committee. For a moment, Ru-tang, the youngest member of the poor-peasant league committee, stood tongue-tied in front of the crowd, then said, "Well, now we have

A group of women at the inauguration meeting.

to elect the committee members. First we'd better see who the candidates are."

Seventy-two people had been nominated, twenty-five of them by more than one section, and it was agreed to limit the voting to the latter group. Ru-tang asked the team secretary to read out the list of names. As each candidate heard his name, he mounted the steps to the porch so that the crowd could see him and give their opinions about him if they wished.

The peasants made some complimentary remarks about the candidates whose names came first on the list, including Wang Ru-tang. In his embarrassment at hearing himself publicly praised, he scratched one ankle with the other and clasped his hands behind the back of his neck. He was clearly thankful when a diversion came in the form of a suggestion from the crowd: "Let's divide into small groups and ferment a little before we go any further with this."

After a few minutes' fermentation the consensus was that all the candidates had been discussed in their own section meetings, and that everyone was ready to go straight on to the voting. So each candidate rose from his seat on the platform as his name was called, and the crowd raised their fists to be counted.

When the votes were tallied, old middle, new middle, and poor peasants were all represented on the committee. Poor peasants were in the majority, as was fitting. Six members of the poor-peasant league committee had been elected to the committee of the new peasant union, among them Li Bao-yu, chairman of the league, Zhao Zhen-fang, and Wang Wen-sheng. Three of the successful candidates were women, and a fourth woman became a reserve member.

Moreover, five Party members had been elected. In fact, one of them—the village head Wang Xi-tang—came out at the top of the list, thirty-seven votes above the next-highest candidate and at the meeting of the committee which took place shortly, he was chosen to be chairman of the new Peasant Union.

# —15—

# Taming the Tiger

## March 18

The very day of its election, the new peasant union committee launched a series of meetings designed to attack one remaining obstacle to fuller democracy: the lingering factionalism of the former cadres and their cliques of militants. In all, there were forty or fifty of these militants. Some of them supported the Communists and were helpful in village affairs. Others were inspired mainly by dislike of the people in power or by personal ambition to replace them. The most formidable of all the cliques was led by Wang Ke-bin, who had been head of the village government in 1942.

In 1940 the first Communist work team had come to Ten Mile Inn. It was an armed team, for the Japanese were not far away, and its purposes were to organize the peasants for resistance and to set up a Communist Party branch. The most powerful weapon that the team entrusted to the village leaders for mobilizing the people was the "mass line." It was a weapon not easily mastered, however, and both Wang Ke-bin and Fu Gao-lin, who succeeded Wang, governed the village by traditional authoritarian methods.

Though the two men were both from poor-peasant families, they had powerful personalities and took easily to authoritarian ways. If the Communist Party branch had been a strong one capable of disciplining and educating them, they might have developed into model village heads. But during the years of their rule the branch was sabotaged from within by landlords and Guomindang supporters.

Wang Ke-bin and Fu Gao-lin did help organize the people of Ten Mile Inn to protect the village against the Japanese. However, they did not encourage the popular initiative in resisting the enemy as called for by an ideal Communist-led village. At the same time, the two village heads genuinely supported the Communists' system of progressive taxation, but in carrying it out they practiced a certain "flexibility." While they never exempted a landlord or rich peasant from paying taxes, they often lowered his tax bracket for a bribe or raised it out of spite.

In 1944 the village branch was dissolved because it had been infiltrated by landlord, rich peasant and Guomindang elements, and the Party membership of all those who had belonged to it, including Wang Ke-bin and Fu Gao-lin, was annulled. When a new branch was established, neither of them was asked to join. New leaders like Wang Xi-tang and Wang Shao-zhen were recruited instead.

The old leaders were left largely to their own devices, and they set off on two different roads. Wang Ke-bin tried by fair means or foul to regain his influence in village life. Fu Gao-lin settled down to take advantage of the new opportunities to become prosperous after the Communist reforms.

The new village leaders had some of the same personal qualities that Wang Ke-bin and Fu Gao-lin showed, but the new Party branch was fundamentally different from the old one. It had no class enemies boring from within, and it was more closely tied to the higher levels of the Party. The result was that the talents of the new village leaders were combined with something of the accumulated experience of the Chinese Communist Party.

Under these conditions, the new branch was able to lead the village in carrying out the Reduction of Rent and Interest Campaign and the successive land reforms. In doing so the new village leaders made some progress in applying the mass line, but they too failed to master this complex tool. They did not realize how far short they had fallen until the work team led by Lou Lin came to the village and began their education.

By the time the peasant union had been established, the Party members no longer considered themselves the best-qualified leaders in the village. Their loss of confidence was reinforced by the work team's insistence that from now on, the masses themselves must be masters of the house.

The masters-to-be, however, were inexperienced. With the work team's encouragement they had tentatively asserted themselves in criticizing the cadres; yet it was these very cadres who had taken the initiative against the excesses of Wang Ke-bin and Fu Gao-lin. Thus the situation on March 18, 1948, was delicately balanced. Wang Ke-bin still had influence, and many villagers were afraid of him. He was skilled in the arts of political campaigning, he spoke fluently and well, and he hoped to make a comeback. If he were to become influential once more in the village government, would not democracy deteriorate under his authoritarianism?

The best move seemed to be to hold a grievance meeting, where the people could confront Wang Ke-bin and make their charges against him. They already had experience with public criticism, and their new organizations furnished safeguards against the old cadres. A grievance meeting would pave the way for righting old wrongs and would clear the air of some imaginary ones, so that the villagers could put their whole minds on the tasks of the future. Furthermore, a final careful look at the past would give them a chance to compare the cadres of those days with the present village government and appreciate the progress that had been made.

That evening all the members of the peasant union and the work team gathered in the temple courtyard under a brilliant moon. The atmosphere was charged. The team members, realizing how much was at stake, were as keyed up as the villagers.

The new masters of the house were represented by the poor peasants Li Bao-yu and Wang Wen-sheng. Diffident in their role, they stood at the head of the steps together. The housebuilder Li Bao-yu regained his composure first and began to speak.

"This morning we established the new peasant union. And it's the new union which tonight is calling this fanshen and grievance meeting. We've already given our opinions about the Party members. Now we're going to talk about the former cadres. They are a rock which has been weighing down on us for many years."

Li turned to Wang Wen-sheng, who said haltingly, "This morning we established the peasant union. What is the union's main task? To lead all of us to fanshen; to unite the poor and middle peasants." He paused, caught the reassuring eye of the team member Wu Xiang, and continued:

"The good Party members have been picked out, and we'll go on having our say about the others. Their cases will be solved in the future. We're not going to deal with them tonight.

"What are we going to do tonight? We're going to reveal our grievances, to make accusations. Who will we accuse? The former cadres, Wang Ke-bin and Fu Gao-lin.

"The complaints you make tonight," Wang Wen-sheng said with increasing confidence, "will be acted upon. The peasant union will carry out your wishes on the cases. Accounts will be settled according to the grafting these men have been guilty of, and what they have seized must be taken back."

The other chairman, Li Bao-yu, took over again. "Both the peasant union and the poor-peasant league will guarantee to do whatever you want," he said, and went on to outline the procedure for the meeting.

"First we'll ask Wang Ke-bin and Fu Gao-lin to speak. We'll see

whether what they say is true, and if it's not, we can give our own
views. We must get everything off our chests, but it must be done in
an orderly way. We can't allow any quarreling or fighting."

The two chairmen whispered to one another. Then together they
walked to the end of the porch, where there was a pool of darkness
cut off from the light of both the moon and the lamp. There, practically
lost from sight, they leaned over the edge of the porch and called to
Wang Ke-bin, who was sitting on the ground in black shadow.

Wang Ke-bin shuffled to the foot of the steps, dragging his cloth
shoes along the ground, his hands buried in the sleeves of his quilted
winter clothes, his head bowed. Even after he had stepped into the light
he remained a somber figure, for his great shock of thick, disheveled
hair merged with many days' growth of beard and almost covered his
deeply lined face. The people had said that this man was a fierce tiger.
Wang Ke-bin started to speak in a low, uncertain voice which contrasted with his loud self-confidence and fluency in former days.

"From the Thirty-first Year of the Republic [1942], when I became
village head, up to the present, I have done a lot of wrong."

"Speak louder," shouted the people at the back of the crowd. "We
can't hear you."

Wang Ke-bin raised his voice a little. "At that time we had not yet
had any struggles. But the landlords were trying to get out of paying
their taxes, and they used to invite us to eat dumplings with them. We
ate in the homes of many of them.

"During the famine years when I ordered the militia commander to
see that the crops were protected, a few people were tied up and beaten.

"I've done a lot of grafting. My attitude toward the people has been
bad, and I've been ill-tempered. A few years ago I had immoral relations with women. And I forced people to carry stretchers against their
will."

Wang Ke-bin paused. There was no sound from the crowd. After a
moment he went on:

"During the famine when the old man Wang Chen-fang didn't
have enough to eat, he pilfered a little grain. Although he was almost
seventy years old, I made him go around the village beating a gong
so that everyone would know what he had done. And when Tie Xun-
zhen didn't pay back some millet he owed, I had him locked up for
half a day."

Again Wang Ke-bin paused, then broke the silence to mutter, "If I
can think of anything more, I'll speak again." And he shuffled into
the darkness.

Wang Ke-bin's place at the foot of the stairs was taken by the
second former cadre, Fu Gao-lin. His tall, imposing figure emerging

from the darkness had none of Wang Ke-bin's disheveled look. Fu wore well-padded winter clothes and a clean white towel wound neatly around his head. He gave an impression of self-respect—though he seemed somewhat at a loss.

At last he said in a quiet voice, "I did many bad things when I was village head and chairman of the peasant union." Thrusting his hands up his sleeves, he began to enumerate them.

"When the cadres ate dumplings in the landlords' homes, I went too. I permitted a number of divorce cases." The peasants knew that this was an understatement, for Fu Gao-lin had encouraged and even compelled couples to divorce so that the woman could marry one of his friends. He said blandly, "I myself helped arrange some of the remarriages, and I was often invited to feasts.

"Then I bought some land that was going cheap during the famine. Chang Chang-he also wanted it, but I managed to get it because it lay alongside the rest of my land." In other words, he had taken advantage of his position as a cadre to cut out his competitor.

"When I was peasant-union chairman, I was in charge of seven or eight distributions of relief grain. The scales were soft," meaning that light weight was given, "and part of the grain went astray. Together with some of the other cadres, I had a few meals out of it. There was some buckwheat left over, too. I ate part of it and ground some into flour, with which I made noodles that I sold.

"In the famine year I ran an inn for three months and found many ways to use it for making profit at others' expense.

"I also bought a whole courtyard, although the owner wanted to sell only the building on one side of it. And later when I no longer had any use for all the rooms, I sold them to someone else instead of giving the original owner the option.

"The year before last I divorced my first wife, and last year I married again. Many people in the village disapproved of this, and I myself realized that it wasn't right.

"When the wall of my terrace needed repairing, I took some stones from the public embankment, which then collapsed and blocked the roadway. I should have repaired it right away, but I didn't and it became a public nuisance.

"During the famine years I got a share of more than ten sheaves of millet which had been confiscated by the cadres and militiamen who patrolled the fields to prevent pilfering." A certain amount of this grain was indeed confiscated from pilferers, but some of it was taken from anyone carrying grain whom the patrollers regarded as suspicious characters. Personal spite and dislike played a part in many of these cases.

Fu Gao-lin rounded off the catalog of his misdeeds with the statement: "At the beginning of one new year's celebration, someone sent me a gift of several pounds of mutton. I accepted it. That was wrong."

He stopped and looked first at one chairman and then at the other. After a moment they motioned him back to his place in the dark.

"Now it's time to get things off your chest," Li Bao-yu told the crowd.

Wang Wen-sheng said, "We guarantee that the complaints you make will produce results. After the grievances have been listed, we'll decide how to deal with them."

"Remember to speak one at a time," said Li Bao-yu, "and keep good order. First let's have criticisms of Wang Ke-bin." The tiger was summoned back from the shadows to face his accusers.

He had scarcely taken up his position before a voice choking with anger came from the darkness. Wang's name was spat out with an explosion of hate: "Wang Ke-bin, when you were village head you tried to make my mother kill my dad." The speaker was a young man barely out of his teens.

He continued in a shaking voice, "She said that she would never do such a thing. And when she was on her way to Younger Wang Village for her mother's funeral, Wang Ke-bin waylaid her and threatened her with a big stick. And he made her promise that she would kill my dad. Next day, she and my sister both hanged themselves. The people who cut their bodies down are still here in this village. The whole of my family, all three of them, were driven to their death by Wang Ke-bin." The speaker ended with a stifled sob.

Wang Ke-bin hung his head so that his mane of uncut hair fell over his eyes. No one in the temple courtyard stirred. The rumbling of a cart's wooden wheels on the highway floated up to the meeting place.

A second man rose and spoke in reasoned tones that contrasted with those of the grieving son. "When Wang Ke-bin was village head, the people gathered to have a reckoning of accounts with him. But he said it was impossible to straighten them out, so the matter was dropped. How much did he make out of it—that's what I'd like to ask him now. How much did he graft?"

Next a woman spoke. "He's a buyer and seller of women. He sold his own adopted sister for 50 *yuan*. That is, in arranging the marriage Wang Ke-bin exploited the shortage of women by demanding 50 *yuan* from the groom's family."

"When my daughter-in-law wanted to marry again," a middle-aged man said, "she went to Wang Ke-bin to ask for a permit. And he said he'd give her one if she'd sleep with him first."

An old woman struggled to her feet and stood supporting herself on the shoulders of the people on either side. For two years she had scarcely left her courtyard, but tonight she had been so insistent on attending that her son had carried her on his back.

"My brother went out to gather the green beans from my field," she said in a quavering voice. "And Wang Ke-bin said that while he was doing it, he stole some ears of corn. So he had my brother tied up and beaten, and he fined him 50 *yuan*.

"And when I went out myself to gather wild herbs in the famine years, Wang Ke-bin said that I'd been stealing his turnips. He called me a thief and took away my sack and basket. He used them himself and never returned them, and he fined me 10 *yuan* as well." She sank back to her little wooden stool, shaking all over.

The next speaker said, "Once during the famine years, my husband's little niece went out to the fields to gather green beans. And on the way back, Wang Ke-bin, you saw her and said she had been stealing. And you had her hands tied and had her beaten on her bare back, although she was weak and sick from hunger. And her father was at home, too weak from hunger to move. After the beating, my niece also became too weak to move. So for four or five days she lay in the house and had nothing to eat, until she died."

The speaker concluded, "And instead of the new basket that she had been carrying, you gave us back an old broken one."

"I was practically starving during the famine," said another peasant, "but he made me pay over 20 *jin*\* of millet in taxes without leaving anything for me. One day he told me: 'The district office has sent a man here who wants you to pay up on the grain you owe the village government.' I didn't know that I owed the village government anything, but I was frightened out of my life. So I took some of my belongings to Yangyi and sold them, and I was able to hand over 10 *jin*. After the autumn harvest I had to pay another 10 *jin*."

"When Wang Ke-bin was village head," the next speaker said, "he handled the distribution of relief grain, and I don't know who got any of it."

"I remember once when 700 *jin* of relief grain was assigned to our village," said someone else, "and it was sold in one lot. I'd like to know just what he did with the money."

"There was a holdup case near Stone Cave Village during the lean years," said another person. "A man driving a donkey was beaten up, and the donkey was stolen. Wang Ke-bin said that it was Li Kai-ming who had tipped the bandits off, and he and two other innocent people from this village were locked up. And if the district hadn't sent some-

---

\* 1 *jin* equals 1.1 pounds or half a kilogram.

one here to make an investigation, all three of them might have been killed."

"When Wang Ke-bin's terrace wall crumbled and some of the earth fell onto the plot below, he moved the boundary stones of his land down onto the neighboring plot. That way he stole a whole strip of land. What's more, he sowed the strip with castor bushes and sorghum." The peasants believed that these crops depleted the soil.

The accusations that had been made, though penetrating, had not come freely from the crowd. It was only with constant encouragement that the villagers had spoken up. The once timid and wavering Wang Wen-sheng strode from one side of the porch to the other, imploring people to have no fear, to show courage and rely on the strength of their newly formed league and union. But for all this, the stream of complaints ran slower and slower until it dried up.

Wang Wen-sheng asked bluntly, "What's the matter; are you afraid to speak up?" Some people in the crowd were frank enough to say yes.

Wu Xiang of the work team climbed to the top of the steps and said, "Many things came out about Wang Ke-bin in the small-group discussions before this meeting, but these things haven't been mentioned tonight. The team has just learned that Wang Ke-bin has been telling people that he reached an agreement with us. He says that everything's going to work out all right for him as long as he makes a confession.

"That's not true. We want to make it clear that the peasant union is in complete charge of this case. It's up to the people to decide how to deal with Wang Ke-bin.

"And there's no need at all for you to have any fear. This matter does not concern Ten Mile Inn alone. All over the border region the people are conducting a democratic campaign Here, too you can pour out your grievances freely. If Wang Ke-bin were to try and retaliate, he would only be adding to his crimes.

"My suggestion is that you should ferment for a while over this. Then continue to tell your grievances."

The reminder that the people of Ten Mile Inn were allied with more than thirty million others in the border region was reassuring, but it was still not enough for some of the more cautious villagers. They suggested that Wang Ke-bin be sent away so that the people could speak more easily. Grateful for any suggestion which promised to loosen the peasants' tongues, the chairmen agreed.

Without waiting to be told, Wang Ke-bin was off like a flash. He skirted the edge of the crowd, went down into the lower courtyard, and headed for the temple gate.

Before he could reach it, however, a voice rang through the courtyard: "Wang Ke-bin. Stay where you are." It was the team leader Lou Lin, who seldom spoke in public because of his strong Hunanese accent. But there was no mistaking what he had said this time, and Wang Ke-bin halted in his tracks.

Lou Lin turned toward the crowd. Speaking slowly and clearly, choosing every word, he said, "Now that the masses are united and organized, you have nothing to fear from twenty Wang Ke-bins. Let's bring him back and face him. And let the people utter the grievances that have been locked in their hearts."

"That's right, bring him back. We're not afraid of him any more," people shouted from all over the courtyard.

So the tiger returned once again to face his accusers. And this time the charges flowed thick and fast.

A man spoke of the time when the peasants had had to run the Japanese blockade in order to obtain salt and other necessities. "Once forty-eight of us (three from this village) got safely past the enemy blockhouses. We took the stuff we had brought back into Yangyi to sell, but we didn't manage to sell everything. Then Wang Ke-bin framed us so that he could lay his hands on some of it: he said that my partner, who came from another village, had had relations with one of our women. As a matter of fact, my partner had never been alone with her; on the evening that Wang said it had happened, the woman's mother and her brother were present. In the end Wang admitted that the man wasn't guilty. But after that I had to spend money on a feast for my partner, to put his heart at rest.

"When that trick failed, Wang Ke-bin accused me of being a conspirator. He said I had received stolen goods, and he took a lot of my salt as a punishment."

"I used to go through the enemy lines to bring back salt too," said another man. "Once after I'd come back, Wang Ke-bin took 12 *jin* of salt from me without paying, and I didn't dare ask him for the money. But now I dare. Before this meeting Wang Ke-bin was afraid that I'd tell on him, so he went around the Street saying what a good fellow I am because I once gave him a present of 12 *jin* of salt!"

The next speaker, who had been waiting impatiently, said, "After my father died, my mother had a hard time getting along and had to sell some land. Wang Ke-bin wanted it and paid her only 100 *yuan* for it. If anyone else had bought it, she'd have gotten 110."

"It was the same with Li Kui-wu's cow," said someone else. "He couldn't get along during the famine and had to sell the animal. It was worth 130 *yuan*, but Wang Ke-bin gave him only 80. He promised old Li that he'd give him some extra relief grain, but he never did."

"Yes, Wang Ke-bin bought the cow, and he also bought houses and land during the famine; but my brother starved to death," a young man said bitterly.

"The autumn before last when Wang Ke-bin was looking after his mutual-aid group's herd, he just drove them anywhere—as if they were a herd of Guomindang cattle."

"When I looked after the herd," piped a young boy, "Wang Ke-bin said that I had lost his cow and that I was a secret agent's calf."

"He said I was a secret agent too," a young man put in. "He said to me, 'Young Yun, you think you're pretty tough, don't you? But d'you know what you are? You're just a stooge of the secret service men.' After that I was so scared I didn't dare open my mouth."

"When Wang Ke-bin was head of the village, any family that had good-looking women could get relief grain," said one man. "But my brother was a bachelor, so he starved to death."

"Of course a couple of bachelors like you two would just be a nuisance as far as he was concerned," said a worldly adolescent.

"The boy's right. Wang Ke-bin carried on with the wife of Chen Chun, and Chen caught them in the act. So the woman threw herself into a well and drowned herself."

"He's free enough with other people's wives," said a woman, "but he guards his own like a watchdog. He never allowed her to attend a meeting, and he cursed anyone who went to fetch her. None of the women of his house ever made shoes for the army. They don't even spin."

A Party member, the new middle peasant Li Bao-en, began a story of Wang Ke-bin's iron rule in the famine years. At times as he told it, he had to stop and weep.

"We were starving during the lean years. One day my boy came to me—he was twelve years old then—and said, 'Let me ride the old donkey out to our field, and I'll see whether any of the corn is ripe enough to eat.' It was over a mile from the village, and the boy was so weak he could hardly walk that far. So he left on the donkey. I went out peddling after that, and it was noon when I got back. But the lad hadn't returned, and I was worried. At last he came slowly along the path—the old donkey was on its last legs—carrying a bag. There were twenty cobs of corn in it. How happy we were! And my wife began to grind the corn into a paste, kernel and cobs and leaves and all. We were starving and didn't want to waste a scrap.

"While she was grinding it, Zhang Qi-zheng came in—his field's just next to mine—and he said that my boy had taken some of his corn. So I went with him and another man to the fields to see. I was very humble with them, because I thought perhaps the lad did take some of the corn. None of us had eaten, so I bought them each two corn cakes. I got one for myself as well, I was so hungry from having walked around peddling from dawn till noon. And when we got there, we saw hoof marks in his field, and there were signs that some corn had been plucked from his field as well as from mine.

"In the end we found out that when the boy got to the field, he tied the donkey up near Zhang Qi-zheng's plot. And somehow the animal broke loose and ate some of the crops in Zhang's field. Seven or eight cobs were missing, either eaten by the donkey or stolen. So I had to admit that it was my boy who had done it." Here he wept.

"I went straight to the village office and reported what had happened, and Wang Ke-bin said, 'It's a terrible crime to steal.' I said I was sorry and waited to be fined. They told me to go home.

"On the way back as I went along the Street, I saw four or five ropes slung over the branch of the overhanging tree." He wept again.

"By the time I got back, I was so tired and hungry that I sat down to rest on the bed.

"Then all of a sudden, three or four militiamen came in and told me I was to go back to the lower village. When I got there, they took me to the tree. Then they said, 'Take off your coat,' and they lashed my hands together and hoisted me up.

"When they had gone, my neighbor came and held my legs to take the weight off my arms, and afterwards he got some others to untie the ropes and take me down. I'll never forget him for doing that.

"And I was fined 100 *yuan* and 50 *jin* of unhusked millet, and I had to beg for time to pay. They took away the green paste that my wife had made from the cobs of corn and took it to the inn, and Wang Ke-bin ate it and invited the militiamen to join him. And we didn't have anything to eat in the house for two days.

"I'm only one of the people that he treated that way. He hung up practically everyone in the village at one time or another, from the north end to the south, from the Street to the Fort."

"Let's hang him up now," shouted a young man.

Whispering spread through the crowd. The people had been moved and shaken by Li Bao-en's story, coming as a climax to the others. Would they now treat Wang Ke-bin as savagely as he had treated them?

Lou Lin spoke quietly for a moment with the two chairmen. Then Li Bao-yu said, "It's nearly midnight. We've heard many grievances from the masses. Now let's consider carefully what we should do about the case of Wang Ke-bin."

"Let him cough up what he's swallowed," someone shouted. "And if he can't, let's confiscate his property."

"Ferment, ferment," came shouts from several parts of the court-yard. So the crowd broke into little groups to discuss what should be done.

After a while the chairman called for suggestions.

"The money he grafted and the house he bought from the fruits should be handed back to the peasant union."

"And the land as well."

"And the cow, too."

"Tomorrow morning he should start to straighten out his accounts. And until he's finished he should be made to sweep the street every day."

"It's all right to make him sweep the streets, but he's a vicious char-acter and shouldn't be allowed to roam around them, or there's no telling what he'll do."

"Send him to the people's court!"

"First I want him to take off the secret agent's cap that he put on my head."

"Let's keep him under lock and key while we find out more from the masses."

As the suggestions slowed down, Wang Wen-sheng said from the platform, "The masses have made a lot of suggestions, so we'd better sum them up."

The two chairmen conferred for a few minutes with the team secre-tary, who had been taking notes. Then the secretary read:

"First, he must clear up the accounts and disgorge what he has swallowed.

"Second, he is to sweep the streets in the morning. The rest of the time, when he is not working his land, he is to stay at home and not loiter about the streets.

"Third, regarding the men whom he accused of being secret agents, he is to give proof or admit that he was wrong.

"Fourth, he must guarantee not to seek revenge.

"Fifth, in the future he is to be handed to the people's court."

Wang Wen-sheng took over. "It was wrong for the bad cadres to hang people up and beat them," he said. "That was the landlords' way of doing things. We must not follow their example. If you have other demands, you can put them to the committee members of the poor-peasant league or the peasant union."

Then he turned to Wang Ke-bin and asked, "Do you have anything to say?"

"What has been said about me tonight has been strong medicine," Wang Ke-bin answered. He thought for a moment and said, "That quarrel I had with Mi-chuan's wife was in the house, not on the street."

"What!" screamed the woman. "Didn't you curse me right in front of the co-op? Didn't you go to the village head to complain about me?"

Wang Ke-bin let this matter drop. He then turned to the young boy. "I don't remember saying that you were a stooge of the secret service."

But the boy shouted, "You cursed me right in the middle of the street and said I was a secret agent's calf!"

Wang Ke-bin fell silent.

"He's just trying to wriggle out of things," said an old man. The suspicion was shared by many that Wang Ke-bin was still up to his tricks—that despite his talk about strong medicine, he was far from cured. Clearly the people's anger was rising again.

Once more the work team took a hand. Geng Xi assured the crowd that the meeting had not been held solely so that they could let off steam. "We guarantee that tonight's session will have results," he said. "It is you, the people, who are to decide things from now on. But it will take a little time for the people's court to be set up, because we have to get a representative from the government to sit on it, as well as a representative that you elect. But you'll see that the court will carry out your will."

The meeting over, people rose from the little stools and bricks that they had been squatting on for hours. Stiffly they stretched and stamped. The sick old woman was once more hoisted onto the brawny back of her son. The crowd flowed through the temple gate and along the paths across the fields which led to both Fort and Street. "Remember," the two chairmen shouted after them, "tomorrow afternoon we deal with Fu Gao-lin."

# —16—

# The Case of
# Fu Gao-lin

## March 19

At the grievance meeting to discuss Fu Gao-lin on the afternoon of
March 19, no other topic received so much attention as his divorce
and remarriage. Before the Eighth Route Army came, Fu Gao-lin had
been a poor peasant who could barely eke out a living in spite of his
hard work. And of course he had no wife, though he was tall and handsome. But he fanshenned when the army arrived and lost no time in
finding one. She bore him several children, but none survived, and he
finally bought a son from a starving poor peasant during the famine.

Fu Gao-lin prospered politically as well as economically, becoming
in turn chairman of the peasant union and village head. Meanwhile he
grew increasingly dissatisfied with the wife he had wed in his less
prosperous days. In time he found a woman more suited to his taste
and his new condition, even though she was already married. Her husband had neither a robust physique nor a forceful personality, and the
wife had henpecked him even before Fu appeared on the scene.

As Fu Gao-lin's scheme for divorce and remarriage took shape, he
worked untiringly to undermine his rival's marriage. With Fu's encouragement the wife subjected her wretched husband to a daily barrage
of curses, refused to cook for him, and openly flaunted the fact that
she slept with the village head. Finding life intolerable, the henpecked
husband left home and soon afterwards conveniently died. Fu Gao-lin
immediately divorced his first wife and married the second. But as the
sordid affair became common knowledge, village resentment increased
until it "tied a knot in the hearts of the people."

The story came out piece by piece at the grievance meeting. The
last to speak was the mother of the man who died. "Fu Gao-lin drove
my son away so that he died far from home," she said. "Then he took
all my boy's belongings into his own house. Before my son left the

village, he was afraid to go home to eat. He had been locked up by Fu Gao-lin several times, and many times he had tried to commit suicide. Now the dead man is dead, and the living woman has been taken by Fu Gao-lin. As for me, I have wept until there are no tears left in my eyes; only my heart weeps."

Fu Gao-lin had also created a string of wrecked marriages in the village for purposes not of sentiment, but business. As prosperity spread, more and more poor peasants who had been bachelors from poverty became prosperous new middle peasants seeking wives. Women were scarce, and Fu Gao-lin let it be known that for a consideration he would do what he could to find wives for these men.

In the interests of his matchmaking business, Fu kept an eye out for unhappily married couples and promoted discord wherever he could. Then he approached the woman and suggested that in his official capacity he could arrange a divorce, provided she married the bachelor he recommended.

"When I was lying sick in bed," a young man said, "Fu Gao-lin persuaded my wife to divorce me. She was taken away to Horse Village, where a divorce paper was issued, and then sent to marry someone in Three Princes Village. For this Fu Gao-lin got 50 *jin* of husked millet and 300 *yuan*."

Not all the accusations concerned Fu's abilities as a marriage broker.

"When I was away from home peddling secondhand clothes," said one man, "he seized the key to my house and set up a bakery in one of the rooms. He burned all my chaff and wheat stalks and even sold some of my bricks. When I came back and protested, he tried to make me back down. In the end he said he'd get out in a month." During the famine Fu Gao-lin gave people bread from his bakery on credit. When they couldn't pay the debt, he demanded their labor or even their land, just as the landlords had done.

"Two months after opening the bakery, he had made enough money to buy land and a son," one man declared. "My own son bought some biscuits from him on credit and couldn't pay up, so Fu Gao-lin tried to seize our courtyard. In the end he made the boy do weeding for him. He made me do his weeding too, by giving me 5 *jin* of black beans as relief and then asking me to weed. What could I say? Those who have their mouths sealed with favors cannot speak."

"People who had land could always go and eat his biscuits and cakes," said another man. "One day Wang Jin-xin, who was the militia commander then, was in my place eating cornbread. He said he'd had bread and cakes from Fu Gao-lin's shop several times, and that now Fu was demanding land as payment. He had even singled out a particular plot where the millet was ripening. But people who had no land couldn't get credit from his shop, even if they were starving."

The guiding principle of Fu Gao-lin's conduct was personal gain. In the struggle against the landlords this had thrown him on the side of the people. But later as increasing numbers of villagers began to fanshen, his quest for riches put him in conflict with those he was supposed to serve.

In 1944 when Fu lost his Party membership, he withdrew from village affairs and concentrated on farming. His misdeeds belonged to the past, and in many cases he had already made compensation to people he had harmed. He had not become a model character, of course. But if the grievance meetings had not been necessary because of the threat posed by Wang Ke-bin, Fu Gao-lin might have been dealt with privately by the work team and the new cadres.

Yet the grievance meeting on Fu Gao-lin was almost as long and bitter as the previous night's session on Wang Ke-bin. Later, in analyzing the reason for this, the work team concluded that this meeting had given the old, politically backward militants an opportunity to capture the limelight. Some of them maligned him from personal spite; others did it in the hope of improving their positions in the coming village elections.

When criticisms had finally petered out, decisions on handling the case had to be made. The consensus was that the question of referring Fu's case to the people's court should be delayed for further consideration. Meanwhile he was instructed to vacate any property which he had occupied against the owner's will. The general principle was that he should "cough up what he had swallowed" in graft and extortion.

But in addition, the militants proposed that Fu Gao-lin be separated immediately from his second wife. Some of them even wanted him to remarry his first wife, although she already had two children by her second husband in Three Princes Village. The militants claimed that they were speaking for the masses, but when Leng Bing asked for a show of hands on the proposal, only five went up.

A peasant then suggested that Fu Gao-lin be required to do some work for the soldiers' families, and there was general agreement.

"Maybe Wang Ke-bin should do that too," someone said, "instead of sweeping the streets. It's been raining every day, so sweeping is a waste of time."

"Wang Ke-bin would love that idea," said Li Bao-yu. "He'd rather work on the soldiers' families' fields for ten days than sweep the streets for three."

For that very reason, the people turned the proposal down. Their hatred for the tiger demanded a feudal punishment, even though the labor wasted in sweeping the muddy streets could have been put to good use. As Lou Lin pointed out to the work team, the peasants' intense prejudice in this matter showed that the difficult process of building democracy is closely tied to ideological reform.

# —17—

# Some Ideological Problems of Revolutionary Intellectuals

After reading your letter of yesterday, I felt that there were several problems in connection with the work in Ten Mile Inn. Please note the following points:

1. So far as the present situation is concerned, the work should not get bogged down in the problem of the former cadres but should turn to a new central point. Any other opinions that the masses have about those cadres can be handed over to the new cadres to deal with. It must be understood that if the masses are not properly reorganized, the problem of the former cadres cannot be solved.

2. For the most part, the measures proposed by the masses for dealing with the former cadres are inappropriate. For example, the proposals to make Wang Ke-bin sweep the streets and to separate Fu Gao-lin from his wife resemble the "old ruling method." Have you tried any persuasion or education on this subject?

3. The focal point at the present time is the adjustment of land-holdings, not the people's court. No matter how great the crime of a former cadre, it must be dealt with after the people have been properly reorganized; otherwise the land adjustment will be affected. You will have to explain this to the people and convince them that it is right. If some of the comrades on the team also need convincing, then you should hold a discussion to straighten out their ideas. In a word, the proposal to send the cadres to the people's court should not be stressed from now on.

I'm still ill. When I'm better, I'll ask you to come over here to report.

Zhang

—Letter to Lou Lin from Zhang Pan-shi, his supervisor at the Central Bureau

At his headquarters in West Harmony, Zhang watched over the day-to-day work of three teams, giving them directions by telephone and messenger. In addition to monitoring their constant reports, he or his deputy, An Gang, regularly visited the villages where work was under way, and twice in six weeks Zhang called day-long conferences of the team leaders. He himself reported to the Central Bureau of the Communist Party at Yetao.

In Zhang's opinion, many of the difficulties that arose in the field reflected ideological problems on the part of the team. The majority of its members were intellectuals, which in China meant any person having enough education to read and write with facility. At this time such people numbered only about 5 million in an estimated population of 400 million. The Communist Party considered these people exceedingly precious, but at the same time very much in need of remolding. Although in most cases their educational attainments were modest, in general their sense of superiority to the illiterate peasants created a gulf between them and the peasantry. Thus the ideological remolding of intellectuals was an integral part of the campaign.

In a summary written in the middle of March, Zhang said that the chief defect of the Ten Mile Inn team was "the working style of the intelligentsia." On some occasions, he pointed out, team members launched "like learned professors" into theoretical discussions which to the villagers had no direct bearing on their problems. At other times they explained things over and over "like kindergarten teachers," fearing that the masses would not be able to understand.

Zhang said that both approaches were out of place: "The working style of the masses is accurate, simple, and clear. No need to tell them everything in exhaustive detail and in a roundabout way. That's not the people's way of thinking."

When it was time to organize the poor-peasant league, for example, the work team did not say straight out that the league should be formed. They thought it would be better if the demand for the league could come "spontaneously" from the people. As Lou Lin said later, "We talked and talked, trying subtly to convey the germ of the idea so that the villagers themselves might initiate it. But the more we talked and the more time we wasted, the more confused they became. They wondered what on earth we were up to. Wang Xi-tang never approached problems like that. Whenever he had a point to make, he did it in a plain, straightforward manner."

Another failing that was characteristic of members of the intelligentsia was their tendency to do things in a formal way, divorced from the mass movement. For example, at the time of the first classification not all the team members followed the method of self-report and public appraisal that was demonstrated by Geng Xi in the Fort. The team members in charge of the work in the east-central section studied the village statistical records and worked out the class of each family in advance. Then they submitted the classification they had decided upon to a meeting of the section for approval. This saved a lot of time, but it made the classification a static, technical affair. The process of sorting people into classes was supposed to be part of a political upsurge

(*right*) Zhang Pan-shi, representative of the Border Region Central Bureau, was in charge of all the work teams in the ninth district of Wu An County.

(*below*) The staff of the External Affairs and Public Relations Department of the Border Region Government eating lunch together. Li Huan-shan on the far left; Li Di-hua with glasses; Isabel Crook on the far right.

in which the peasants learned to break with feudal face-saving and to assume political responsibilities.

Although this mistake was made only in the east-central section, Zhang was not satisfied that any of the sections had fully integrated classification with the mass movement. During that period he wrote to Lou Lin:

> The special characteristic of your work is its precision. This is good and necessary, but it is among the masses that you must be precise. And on the whole, there seems to be too little movement in Ten Mile Inn. Your report reads like an account book.
>
> Precision is useless if there's no movement. The masses will only be left with a feeling of vagueness. The classification must be closely coordinated with concrete village issues—at this moment, the setting up of the poor-peasant league.
>
> It is only through the masses' activity that we can give them education and raise their political level.

Related to the team's leaning toward formalism was its tendency to become bogged down in trivialities. Quibbling arguments sometimes arose between the members over the use of a certain term—for example, whether they should refer to "class origin" or "class background"—instead of over matters of basic principle.

Talking with some of the team members, Zhang once said, "Some of you comrades like to split hairs. It's good for you to have discussions about your work, but you must learn to distinguish between minor matters and matters of principle. It's not good for the work if you get into endless arguments. Some members argue even when the work is in an emergency period."

Certain team members tended to place the blame on others whenever anything went wrong. At one meeting Lou Lin observed, "It's a funny thing that when everything is going well, no one seems to have anything to say; but as soon as a difficult situation arises and defects appear in our work, some comrades start blaming each other."

"You shouldn't complain about each other," Zhang told them. "Don't look only at people's shortcomings—nor, of course, only at their strong points. The thing to concentrate on is how to overcome our shortcomings."

Zhang also said, "In policy decisions the opinion of the majority must be carried out by everyone. The opinions of the minority can only serve to urge us to think more deeply. If some people do not abide by the majority decision, and the unity of the team is not maintained, the work will suffer."

There was no deliberate flouting of discipline on the team, for all the members were loyal and conscientious. But some had deluded themselves by disguising breaches of discipline as "creative initiative." This ability to disguise defects under a cloak of virtue was recognized as a tendency that intellectuals were especially prone to.

All the members of the team had faced danger, and some of them torture. Most had left comfortable homes in order to do revolutionary work. For years they had lived in peasant homes and, except on high days and holidays, eaten little but millet and pickles or cabbage. Their living standard was that of middle peasants. A few of the team members had been through the famine years in the Liberated Areas and had kept alive mainly on grassroots, bark, and leaves. For the revolution they were willing to give up their health and their lives; but this willingness alone could not solve the ideological problems they had brought with them from the old society. To become steeled Communists called for constant struggle.

# —18—

# The People's Congress and the New Village Government

March 20, 21, 22

On the morning of March 20, Lou Lin met with the committee of the poor-peasant league to talk about setting up the village people's congress. Then the committee members called section meetings at which people from the team explained the nature of the congress. It was to be a broadly representative body whose deliberations would be less unwieldy than a meeting of the entire village, yet it would keep in closer touch with every family than the village government committee could. It would leave routine government to the cadres or the committees of the league and the union, but it could be summoned quickly when a special issue arose.

The congress would have the right to criticize the cadres and even dismiss them from office and hold new elections. It would handle the payment of taxes and other obligations to the border-region government. The representatives of the congress would also mediate quarrels among their constituents and help solve their personal problems. They would play an important part in the coming election, the adjustment of landholdings, the allocation of housing, and the distribution of the remaining struggle fruits.

As a first step toward the congress, the villagers began to organize "people's groups." It was decided that each group would have twelve to fifteen families. In some cases a dozen families living in adjoining courtyards decided to form a group because they were a natural unit; in others a group of neighbors made up the nucleus but drew in one or two families living farther away. Whatever the arrangements, all the groups were formed on a voluntary basis.

On the day the groups were being organized, little knots of people gathered in courtyards, children ran importantly back and forth with

154

messages, and animated discussions were held wherever neighbors customarily gathered to eat their meals together. By evening the village had organized itself into thirty-one groups. When each was formed, it held a meeting to discuss how it could play its part in running the house. And each named a representative who went to the Communist Party branch meeting held that night for the continuing self-criticism of the Party members.

The next morning before breakfast, the people's groups nominated candidates for election to the people's congress. One or two groups contained an outstanding person, so that their choice was easy. But in most cases three candidates were put forward, and their names were submitted to the committee of the poor-peasant league.

These tasks were briskly accomplished for this was the day for the fair in Zhao Village, only three miles away, and everyone was eager to get away. Wearing their best clothes, old and young alike set off for the fair—with more money to spend than ever before. Every type of farming tool and household equipment used in the region was on sale. The new middle peasants in particular were anxious to buy. They inspected wooden saddles for their newly acquired animals, plows and seeders to work their new land, wooden bellows, iron cooking pots and many other goods. There were toys for the children as well, and snacks. The fair offered entertainment, too, with storytellers and plays in the old and new fashions. There was fun for all.

By evening, laden with new rakes, forks, bellows and cooking pots, and full of talk of the events of the day, people hurried home. By then the league committee had gone over the lists of candidates, eliminated eight undesirables, and made everything ready for the election of group representatives. The groups voted immediately, holding their discussions before, during, or after the evening meal. The final choices were a fair cross section of the village: nine poor peasants, sixteen new middle peasants, and six old middle peasants.

That evening the village people's congress and the people themselves met in the big hall of the temple. The thirty-one successful candidates were scattered through the huge crowd. Slogans painted on pink and red paper said "All Peasants Arise in Unity" and "All Power to the People's Congress."

"A meeting of all the peasants in Ten Mile Inn has the supreme voice in village affairs, hasn't it?" asked the team member Geng Xi. The crowd agreed.

"But we can't be calling meetings of the entire village all the time, or we'd never be able to get on with the farming. So we have to elect delegates to do things for us while we keep working. Except when we

Everyone took time off from the people's congress election to go to the fair at Zhao Village.

have a meeting of the whole village, the village congress will have the highest power. It is even authorized to dismiss the village cadres if the people demand it.

"In all the villages of Liberated China, the people's congresses will form the base of a government pyramid. On this base will be set district, county, and border-region people's congresses. When the whole country has been liberated, the pyramid will be topped off with an all-China National People's Congress,* which will elect the Central People's Government.

"In organizing the Ten Mile Inn people's congress, we have laid one of the foundation stones of the Chinese People's Government."

Geng Xi closed with a slogan. "All Power to the People's Congress!" he shouted, adapting the Russian Bolsheviks' old slogan, "All power to the Soviets."

As chairman of the new peasant union, Wang Xi-tang took the floor. This was the first time that the former village head had officiated at a public meeting since the work team arrived in the village, and he did so in high good humor. "Today the people of Ten Mile Inn have fanshenned," he said. "Now the assembled delegates can start their work for the people by making suggestions about how to set up the new village government. All of you please give us your ideas."

The thirty-one delegates, who had been elected only two hours before, spoke in turn for the families they represented. Not all of them were well briefed; one man said, "We haven't done much fermenting

* This congress was formed in 1954 with 1,226 delegates from all parts of China.

Buying wooden pitchforks at the fair. The peasants had more money since the reforms, and they all wanted more tools.

Inspecting spinning wheels at the fair.

yet, because most of us went to the fair today." But most of them already had decided opinions on a variety of subjects.

Their tendency was to urge that the village government's structure should be simplified by eliminating certain offices. This idea was popular not only because the governing apparatus was slightly unwieldy, but also because some people's impulse was to abolish the posts of any officials who had given them trouble in the past. Others calculated that the fewer cadres there were, the more people would be available for rear service. The cadres were commonly excused from rear duties at busy times of the year, so that the other villagers had more work to do.

Rear service was in fact a special problem for Ten Mile Inn, since

(*above*) A woman bargains for a wooden saddle.

(*right*) A blind musician fiddles at the fair. Blind musicians were organized by the Border Region Government to sing songs of great deeds in war, land reform, and production, in addition to the well-loved traditional ballads.

the village had been chosen as a relay station both for wounded soldiers being transported to the rear and for government grain and other supplies going to the front. "Either we should be exempted from long-distance transport service," said one representative, "or other villages should help. They do far less than we do, just because they're off the main road."

"Yes, Stone Cave Village and West Harmony and the others up Willow Spring Valley should help us out," said another.

"If we do so much rear service, we won't be able to produce enough even if we get more land," said a poor peasant.

With the tact and skill of an experienced chairman, Wang Xi-tang brought the discussion back to the new village government. Eight posts were finally agreed upon, and the people decided that all the officials would be on an equal footing. The masses' concern with democracy had grown so strong since the arrival of the work team that they did not want to give the village head any more authority than the other members of the government.

Before breakfast on the morning of March 22, the people's groups met to propose candidates. Eighteen people were nominated by four or more groups, and the committee of the poor-peasant league met for an hour after breakfast to scrutinize their names. At the suggestion of Lou Lin, who was acting as chairman, the list was shortened further.

"My guess is that people holding such big jobs as chairman of the poor-peasant league and the peasant union will be too busy to take on other responsibilities," he said. The committee members, already tired after eight days in office, agreed heartily and dropped Li Bao-yu and Wang Xi-tang from the list.

Wang Wen-sheng, who had been elected vice-chairman of the league, also tried to secure an exemption. He was the only able-bodied member of his family, for his father was old and crippled, his wife an invalid. "My wife says we'll never be able to make ends meet if I spend all my time on village affairs. How can I disobey her?" he joked, though he was in earnest as well. But the committee would not allow him to withdraw.

To ease the burden of office, Lou Lin suggested, perhaps there should be nine officials instead of eight. The ninth could function as a reserve to help whichever cadre had the most time-consuming job. The idea was unanimously accepted.

Someone asked whether the village head's secretary should be picked by the cadre himself or elected by the people. The latter alternative was chosen as a safeguard against graft.

The final question was how to conduct the voting. The committee decided that the sixteen candidates should sit on the platform, and the voters should all sit in their people's groups. Tellers circulating among the groups would read the list of candidates to each person, who would then whisper his choices to the teller. In this way the people would be able to vote as secretly as their illiteracy permitted.

Notes taken at the election that afternoon describe it as a happy occasion:

> The meeting starts in the usual way, with the women all together up near the porch, winding yarn and making shoes for the army, and the men occupying the rest of the courtyard. The announcement is made that all who belong to the same people's group should sit

together, regardless of sex. There is a certain amount of hesitation and some giggling, but most of the women move over to sit with the men of their group. A few of the more conservative women remain together at the front and form little grouplets of their own. When everyone has settled down, there are huddles of people dotted here and there like shocks of grain on a field at harvest time.

The work team members and border-region cadres go around among the groups reading the list of sixteen candidates to each person in turn. The peasants listen with intense concentration—as if they were trying to catch the sound of something far away—and pick out the nine names of their choice.

One old woman starts off with Li Bao-yu, manages to pick out one or two more, then comes back to Li Bao-yu again. After another couple of names she returns to her favorite, though he was not even a candidate.

At last the results are read out. The "clean sweep" principle has been rejected, for five of the winners are former cadres. Factionalism also has subsided: three of the new cadres are from the Fort. Both poor and middle peasants are well represented; there are even three old middle peasants among the nine elected. The team considers the Party's showing satisfactory, for three Communists have been voted in.

Zhao Zhen-fang tops the poll. When all nine names have been read out, he is asked to say a few words. He refuses for a long time, but the crowd jollies him along, and in the end he mumbles something. Wang Wen-sheng also has to speak, while his white-bearded father looks on, his face crinkled in smiles. The whole crowd is in higher spirits than we've ever seen them before. They push toward the platform to shout jokes at the newly elected cadres, who grin uncomfortably.

Although it's over, a large part of the crowd stands around gossiping in the courtyard. The successful candidates move inside the school building with members of the work team, and Geng Xi launches a discussion of their new status. They are a gloomy-looking bunch, weighed down by the thought of their heavy burdens.

Geng does his best to cheer them up, saying that all new cadres feel like this at first. Squatting around him on bricks, they seem anything but encouraged. Wang Wen-sheng says that his family is short of labor; some say they already hold other offices; others stress their illiteracy and lack of speaking ability.

Geng Xi says that they are like a bride getting into the sedan chair —at first she is heavyhearted, but later she feels happy. Zhao Zhen-fang remarks that the bride weeps the whole time. Geng changes his metaphor: "Well, it's like riding a horse for the first time. You'll soon get things under control and feel confident, like experienced riders."

When the newly elected government met the following evening, the cadres still had not reached the stage of confidence. Nevertheless, they

Some of the candidates for the peasant union. Li Bao-yu in the center; Li Di-hua in the doorway; He Yan-ling on the right.

The villagers huddle into small groups for the voting.

Wang Wen-sheng (third from left) was elected village vice-head.

He Yan-ling records the number of votes for each candidate.

had to decide who should fill the various government posts. The universal opinion was that the poor-peasant Zhao Zhen-fang, who had topped the voting, should be the village head.

Zhao protested vigorously. "No, no. Absolutely impossible. I can't handle the job. Anyone can see that I'm only a crossbeam. You can't make me into the ridgepole."

"Don't worry. All nine will work together."

"It's not you who have to decide what's to be done; it's the people."

"You won't have anything much to do. The rear-service committee can see about getting official letters sent, and you'll have a secretary to write them. The finance committee can count up the money for you. All you have to do is plan."

"Plan!" said Zhao in agitation. "I can't plan. Why, at this very moment I have no idea which of my plots I'll cultivate tomorrow."

"The people have eyes. They can see that you're simple and honest, and capable too."

"I don't agree at all!" Zhao cried. "I haven't a thing in my belly." The peasants regarded the belly as the seat of wisdom.

"It's true you haven't many holes in your heart," admitted a candid friend, "but you haven't any bad qualities either." It was an old belief that an ordinary person had one hole in his heart. Clever people had more, and wise ones had as many as seven, or even nine.

"Just because you keep your eyes glued to the ground, you'll never trip up. The thing is not to oppose the people, and be brave in serving them."

"You can be village head and Wang Wen-sheng vice-head. You'll make a good pair. You're simple and honest, and he's got plenty of plans."

"Better let him think it over for a while," said Lou Lin, for Zhao Zhen-fang seemed increasingly upset. But there was no escape for him; the committee decided that Zhao Zhen-fang should be village head and Wang Wen-sheng vice-head. Li Bao-en, the man who had been beaten at Wang Ke-bin's orders because his son had let the donkey eat the corn, was to be in charge of finances, together with Li Bao-xi, who was known for his skill with the abacus. Li Bao-en was a Communist, and another Party member, the ex-soldier Zhang Zhao-lin, was made chairman of the people's arms committee. Wang Chou-huo, the third Party member on the nine-man government committee, was to be in charge of education.

The next day the government committee's recommendations were presented to the village assembly for approval. It was cold and clear, with a coating of snow on the hillsides and patches of green winter wheat on the fields. As the allocation of posts and other recommendations were read out, the crowd was quieter and more expectant than it had been during the election. The entire audience fell silent during the formal transfer of office. Wang Xi-tang, still wearing white trousers and white-trimmed hat and shoes as signs of mourning for his mother, came to the center of the platform carrying a wooden box tied in a kerchief. In it was the village seal—the symbol of the office he was giving up.

Wang Xi-tang prepared to hand the box over to his successor, but Zhao Zhen-fang was half hidden at the farthest edge of the porch. The new vice-head of the village pushed him forward, and he awkwardly stretched out his bony hands for the box. Suddenly there was an outburst of clapping, shouting, laughing, chattering, and cheering. The new village government was in office.

# —19—

# The Second Classification

March 23–28

Huge snowflakes fell from leaden skies on the morning of March 23, but the streets and alleys of the lower village and the Fort were filled with little groups of men and women picking their way through slush puddles. They were bound for meetings in their sections, to discuss mistakes made during the first classification and to decide the class of the struggle-object families.

The east-central section met in the home of Li Bao-shi. The women crowded onto the *kang* in the alcove at the back. Forty-odd men filled the rest of the dimly lit room, those who arrived early sitting on two benches provided by their host, the rest squatting on the floor on the bricks or small stools they had brought with them. The raw March air was soon dense with smoke from the *kang* stove and from the long-stemmed, tiny-bowled pipes which were sociably passed from mouth to mouth.

The first four cases to be taken up had provoked controversy from the moment the first classification was posted. The case of Fu He-de had created conflict because he had been so anxious to be classed as a poor peasant that he did not make an honest self-report. He implied that 3 *mu* of his land belonged to his mother, though she had long since given it to him. Also, he failed to mention that one of his relatives who ran an inn allowed him to take manure from its stables.

These facts had been known to the people in Fu's section at the time of the first classification, but they were then still in the grip of face-saving and did not challenge him. Three weeks of activity under work team leadership had changed their outlook, and this time they were determined that no one would get away with anything. They brought Fu's deceit into the open and set about determining his class. In the end, all his maneuvering proved to have been unnecessary. Even with the 3 *mu* of land from his mother and the manure from his relative's stables, Fu He-de remained a poor peasant.

In contrast, Fu Pei-chang had insisted at the first classification that he was not a poor peasant but a new middle peasant. Although most people had the impression that he was a poor peasant, they were not prepared at that time to support their opinion, and the case had been left open. This time several people scolded him for indulging in self-sacrifice at the expense of facts.

"Just because you're a Party member, you're trying to be a model," said one man. "But all we're bothered about is getting your class right." And finally Fu Pei-chang agreed to be classed as a poor peasant.

Fu Chou-kui had agreed at the first classification that he was an old middle peasant, but later he had claimed that he was really a new middle peasant. Though his case was taken up again, no new facts were brought to light. In the opinion of everyone except Fu himself, his first classification had been correct. People pointed out, for example, that he had recently sold some land which he had received in the struggles because he could not cultivate it all. In the face of all the evidence Fu Chou-kui once more agreed that he ought to be classed as an old middle peasant. He did it grudgingly, however, and it was clear that he was still dissatisfied. Since the goal was not simply the correct classification of each family by majority decision, but the genuine conviction of the individuals concerned, this case was referred to the peasant union for further consideration.

The fourth case was that of Fu Lun, who had modestly described himself at the first classification as a new middle peasant. The general verdict then, however, was that he was a poor peasant, and he had been more than willing to fall in with it. Now the chairman said, "I've heard that a lot of people are dissatisfied with the decision that Fu Lun is a poor peasant. They claim that his elder son does good business in Yangyi and brings home a lot of money."

Once having been labeled a poor peasant, Fu Lun wanted to stay in that class. "It's just Wang Ke-bin's rumor mongering," he said indignantly. "I know he's got a grudge against me. It's true that my son used to be in business, but now he's serving the people in a government office. All he gets is his food and clothes and 6 *jin* of millet a month for pocket money."

Whether Wang Ke-bin was responsible or not, many people still felt that Fu Lun was not a poor peasant. The discussion was becoming heated when the Party member Fu Pei-chang suggested a solution. "He's a bit fatter than a poor peasant, but a bit thinner than a new middle peasant," he said. "So I suggest that we classify him as a new middle peasant, but if he has a 'hole,' it can be filled up during the adjustment."

This suggestion was accepted, and the meeting turned to the struggle-object families. The first to be called on was Fu Pei-min, the younger brother of a man who had been a notorious usurer in the old days. Fu Pei-min had found himself as inconspicuous a place as possible in the darkest corner of the room. He began making his self-report in a hesitant, scarcely audible voice, and he was asked to come to the front so that he could be heard. There he squatted by the chairman's desk and played nervously with a bit of straw as he tried to recall the details of his economic situation before the arrival of the Eighth Route Army.

Although Fu Pei-min's report was incoherent and contradictory, his listeners were patient. One of them said, "He's not like us. He hasn't been to meetings for two or three years, so he's not accustomed to speaking out."

They tried to help him by making the calculations for him. "He says he had 26.7 mu in the Twenty-eighth Year of the Republic [1939]. He admits that he often hired labor by the month, and by the day during rush seasons. Since even the best worker can't cultivate more than 15 or 16 mu, at least 10 mu must have been tilled by hired labor. So well over one-fourth of his total income came from exploiting labor. In the past he was clearly a rich peasant."

Wu Xiang of the work team was anxious that Fu Pei-min should feel that he had been correctly classified. At his suggestion the case was adjourned until the afternoon session, so that Fu could have time to recall any other points related to his classification.

The meeting turned to the mason Wang Er-he, who had been struggled against out of resentment toward his father. When Wang Er-he was a child, he had been kidnapped and held for a ransom of 400 yuan. The father had raised part of the money himself, but had used his official position as secretary to the village head to extort the rest from other villagers. This was the reason why Wang Er-he had been classed as a struggle object. Now that the peasants understood the principle that class was determined by economic relations, it was not difficult for them to see that Wang Er-he was a new middle peasant.

Similar meetings were taking place in other sections on March 23 and 24. By the afternoon of the second day, the present class of all struggle-object families had been at least tentatively determined. The great majority were now old middle peasants except for two families, one of whom belonged to the rich-peasant category while the other was still a landlord family. Although they no longer exploited anyone, these families had not yet changed their class by laboring for the required time (which was five years for a landlord and three years for a rich peasant).

The next stage of the campaign was reported in the *People's Daily:*

On the evening following these meetings, the poor-peasant league and peasant-union committees met jointly to examine the classification of each of the struggle-object families. . . . Although most cases had been correctly settled by public appraisal, some false reports and consequent inaccurate classifications were discovered.

On the nights of March 25 and 26, general meetings of the poor-peasant league were held to discuss and approve the classification of the whole village, and more than twenty cases were corrected. . . .

On March 28 the results of the second classification were posted. During the next two days the work team watched the effect on the masses of the corrections in the struggle-object classifications. The team members also visited the struggle-object families and sometimes met with a group of them in order to make clear the new spirit of the Party's policy. . . .

At first some of the poor peasants felt dismayed at these re-classifications. They said, "Haven't we a single landlord in our village?" And "If we're not allowed to struggle against middle peasants, where are we going to find houses to distribute to the poor peasants?" Some exclaimed, "It's a strange thing that even a landlord can become a poor peasant!" Others were depressed at the thought that the struggles of the past had been wrongly conducted. But there were still peasants who maintained, "The son should repay his father's debts. He didn't get his land through his own labor, so it isn't wrong to trace families back for three generations."

The correct view prevailed in the end, however. One man rose to his feet and said, "In the past the struggles were carried on just any old way. I didn't dare become prosperous. I ate up everything I earned. I spent what I got from the struggle fruits as well as what I raised on my own land. But from now on there aren't going to be any more struggles, so we'll all dare to make our families prosperous without fear of being struggled against."

Another man said, "You all know that I don't have enough food on hand to feed us, and I have no cattle to plow my land. In the past I had no trouble borrowing food and cattle from You-wang (an old middle peasant who had been taken as a feudal tail). But after he was classed as a struggle object, I didn't dare borrow from him any more. How difficult life has been!"

As for the middle peasants, their minds were generally at rest, because they knew that there wouldn't be any more struggles against them. One said, "It's reasonable to let the landlords and rich peasants change their class. They deserve fair treatment. They really don't work so badly." Another said, "If the struggles went on in the old way, we middle peasants would produce less and less." All the middle peasants agreed: "If the struggles were continued, all of us would be struggled against sooner or later. Who could avoid it? To work would mean working for the benefit of others. In that case it would be better to eat and drink all we have." . . .

As for the struggle-object families, most were very happy. They got rid of their bitterness in talking with the work team members. They asked to be given back their civil rights and the freedom to carry on production. Some of them asked to have their land, houses, and animals returned.

These understandable demands of the victims of an earlier ultra-left trend posed a problem for the new leaders who were already faced with the difficulty of finding land and other property for the newly fan-shenned poor peasants.

# —20—

# The Objects of Struggle

More than a week before the second classification began, the team had started talking to the people who had been the objects of recent struggle. A few team members made house-to-house visits to the struggle-object families and began holding regular small meetings of several families at a time. And as these people told their stories, it began to dawn on them that the root of their trouble lay in feudal society itself.

In the old Ten Mile Inn, the single way to prosperity had been on the backs of other peasants. The iron law was that a man had to exploit or be exploited. There was no permanent middle way: the middle-peasant class was in constant flux. Most middle peasants eventually declined and became poor peasants. A few managed to lift themselves into a higher class by usury, sharp practice, and service as "running-dogs" for the landlords and rich peasants.

The reforms introduced by the Communists created conditions for a different kind of social order. But though the poor-and-hired and the village leaders saw that the new society was designed to benefit the masses, they did not realize that the prosperous old middle peasants were essentially part of the masses and might have been made into allies. They saw only that they behaved the same way as the exploiters. In fact, because they had functioned as henchmen for the powerful, these old middle peasants were better known and sometimes worse hated than the landlords and rich peasants.

"I was really struggled against because of my father," Li Bao-yong said at a small meeting of the struggle-object families in the Fort. "When he was a boy at the clan school, Dad was one of the best students and became skillful with the abacus. So when he grew up he managed to get a job as an accountant with a big landlord in Stone Cave Village. In the end he was sent out to collect rents. When people couldn't pay, he was the one who had to drive them out and seize their land. Of course he didn't like the job, but he didn't have enough land of his own to get along. So he did it for three or four years, and in the end he managed to save enough to buy a bit of land himself."

Rather than employ literate middle-peasant rent collectors, some of the big landlords in Stone Cave Village preferred to rent their land to prosperous middle peasants in fair-sized lots, at rentals low enough to permit subletting. Li Bao-yong himself had acted as this type of middleman. "Someone I knew in another village," he said, "bought some land here in Ten Mile Inn and asked me to rent it out for him. The rent was a bit high, of course, and I was struggled against during the Rent and Interest Reduction Campaign. But I was only the middle-man, not the real owner. The tenant didn't seem to grasp that, and he struggled against me anyway. Basically he was a good sort; someone must have put him up to it." Though Li Bao-yong now supported the reforms, he apparently still saw nothing wrong with making profit out of his services to the absentee landlord.

Another peasant at the meeting, Li Bao-cai, said that his family had been struggled against because his father had served as a middleman in moneylending. "My dad used to borrow money from a landlord at the rate of 1 percent per month. Then he would lend it out in smaller amounts—usually less than 100 *yuan*—at 3 percent per month. Well, maybe sometimes it was a bit higher: a copper a day on each *yuan*." At 400 coppers to the *yuan*, this worked out at 7½ percent per month.

A number of the struggle objects were from declining or bankrupt landlord or rich peasant households. Li Feng, a one-time rich peasant of the Fort, sold his good land to forestall his creditors. Then he bought and rented out stony hillside plots (which no creditor would wish to foreclose on) and rented in fertile land from landlord relatives. Fu Xin, another one-time rich peasant of the Fort, succeeded in staving off bankruptcy by collecting a landlord's debts.

Declining or bankrupt landlords or rich peasants were constantly joining the ranks of the middle or even poor peasant class. A number of these strove to save themselves by turning to the legal profession. Drumming up business by playing on frictions and conflicts inevitable in feudal society was a recognized technique of the craft. And once started, a case was drawn out as long as possible by the lawyers. Clients were given to understand that success was assured if substantial bribes were offered to the judge through the lawyer, whose fingers were pro-fessionally sticky. Practices such as these made the feudal lawyers, or petition-writers, hated by the ordinary people, and earned them the nickname of "pen-and-knife officials."

Li Huan-ran, the son of a bankrupt landlord, had nothing left from his family's ruin except a classical education. This he tried to turn to account by writing legal petitions. He soon found, however, that a love of literature and art was not the stock-in-trade of a successful petition writer. Unable to make a go of it, he became a clerical and financial assistant to the landlord Wang Ban-yan. He was appointed accountant of the Temple Association (which was headed by his employer), and supervised the secret transfer of Temple Association funds to the Guomindang. In 1937 Commander Huang of the Guomindang Eleventh Column set up his headquarters in Ten Mile Inn. Wang Ban-yan became his local liaison officer and Li Huan-ran was made accountant to the Column. This could have proved a gold mine, but Li failed to enrich himself.

Well-off peasants or members of declining families also took on petty government office. They became *bao* heads (officials in charge of one hundred families), *bao* clerks, village heads or village clerks. In these positions of local power, they had carried out tax collection, conscription, maintenance of "law and order" for the Guomindang, and even had dealings with the Japanese. Consequently such people had long since been dealt with, and often were repudiated by their own sons and daughters. But in a number of cases the younger generation became struggle objects in subsequent campaigns.

Some of these now expressed bitterness at having to expiate their fathers' sins; others said they could understand why they had been made to do so. In the main they were more than ready to set their faces toward the future.

One of these was the thirty-four-year-old son of a landlord. He had joined the Eighth Route Army in 1940, but when the struggles began in Ten Mile Inn he had been summoned to answer for his share in family misdeeds. His commanding officer sent him home, advising him to bow his head humbly before the people. He was rated a struggle object, and accordingly was barred from returning to the army. He stayed at home to work the land and serve the soldiers' families. So well did he do this service, including tasks such as emptying the families' latrines and spreading the excrement on the fields, that the cadre in charge said, "There's not a man in the village who does better work for our soldiers' dependents."

Although some thought he had joined the Eighth Route Army only to strengthen his family's position, this landlord's son had evidently experienced a change of heart. He said of his father, "He was an enemy of the people, so he was an enemy of mine. I came back to bow my head humbly before the masses," he declared at a meeting of struggle-object families, "and I believe in the government's policy. So I don't think it was right to grade me a first-class struggle object. Whatever my father did, I myself have tried to serve the people, not to undermine the reforms.

"I've never said this before, but I always felt that the government's policy was one of bigheartedness, and that our village ought to be big-hearted too. I've been thinking that the best thing would be for me to ask for a trial and accept whatever punishment I'm given, so that I can start again."

Another who suffered on account of his forebears was the son of Li Huan-ran, the unsuccessful lawyer who had become an accountant. This son had been a traveling cloth dealer when the Communists first came to Ten Mile Inn. He took no active stand for or against the reforms until 1942, when the Japanese caught him on his travels and confiscated his stock. Then he came home with such a burning hatred of the invaders that the new village leaders encouraged him to join the militia. Within a year he had become one of its officers, and in 1945 he entered an anti-Japanese political and military academy. After the Japanese surrender he returned to Ten Mile Inn, took part in the struggles against the landlords and rich peasants, and received a share of the fruits.

At the same time his father, Li Huan-ran, who had also come to support the Communists, was appointed a librarian in the Mass Education Institute of the county government in the town of Wu An. Here this mild-looking, scholarly old man came to be respected for his careful work.

During the Feudal Tails Campaign, Li Huan-ran, being absent from home and in good standing in his institute, was not touched, though his name was brought up once or twice as a possible target. The son, however, became a struggle object solely because of his father's and particularly his landlord grandfather's record.

This young man did not have as hard a time as other struggle objects and had in fact been reaccepted by the masses before the arrival of the work team. This was due to his popularity as a writer and star performer in the dramas, ballads, and other entertainments that were customarily performed in Ten Mile Inn during lunar new year festivities. In the celebrations that took place in early February, 1948, he had been asked by one of the village cadres to compose a patter (a rapidly spoken, strongly rhythmic, rhymed verse) on the theme "The poor-and-hired must become the masters of the house." At first he had protested that he might make some political mistakes, but in the end he had not only written but also performed the patter to the applause of the whole village.

Now at the meeting of struggle objects called by the team, this man said, "Before the land law I thought everything was hopeless; it seemed as if I'd be a 'feudal element' all my life. Then after the law came out and I learned that those who work can change their class, I began to hope again."

Like the rest of the villagers, the struggle objects had learned from the classification that it had been wrong to struggle against the old middle peasants. Yet both groups could understand how it was that the struggle objects had been singled out. And now both were willing to wipe the slate clean without having an item-by-item accounting. There was no general demand by the struggle objects that all the property which had been wrongly seized should be returned. Any attempt to do this would have thrown the village's economy into chaos. Like the rest of the villagers, most of the struggle objects were confident that filling the holes would give them enough land and other resources to earn a living. It was their political rehabilitation that they prized.

# —21—

# Measuring the Thin and the Fat Land

## March 26, 27, 28

At a meeting of the joint committees of the peasant union, the poor-peasant league, and the village government, the main subject of discussion was how to find something to fill the holes.

"We'll have to measure the land first," said the peasant-union chairman Wang Xi-tang.

"Yes," said the vice-chairman, "we'll have to go over it plot by plot."

"We'd better get a standard measure from the district office," Wang Xi-tang continued. "Ours here may not be accurate. And we'll have to organize all those who can write and reckon."

"The owners can put a sign in each field giving its size and the average estimated yield," said Li Bao-yu, the chairman of the poor-peasant league. "Then we can check that against our calculations."

"It'll mean stopping all farm work and mobilizing the whole village," said the village vice-head Wang Wen-sheng, who was already hard pressed by the demands of public service upon his time.

"It won't take long," said Wang Xi-tang.

But a number of the new cadres and committee members felt that the job of measuring the hundreds of fields which made up the village's 4,000-odd *mu* was too much to take on just now, when the cotton had to be planted. The work team leader Lou Lin supported them, and in the end it was decided to get each of the village people's congress representatives to find out from his constituents if measuring the land was really a mass demand.

The next day at a mass meeting of the village the delegates came to the platform to report. "Do the people want to measure the land or not?" Wang Xi-tang asked them.

"Yes," said one of them definitely. "No question about it."

"They want to measure it, all right," said another.

Lou Lin drew Wang aside and whispered to him. The team leader suspected that a number of the old militants who had been elected as representatives might be expressing their own ideas rather than those of their groups.

Wang Xi-tang turned once more to the representatives and said, "This matter should be carefully discussed in each group, so that you can go deeply into the wishes of the people. Don't be subjective; get the facts."

So the thirty-one representatives went back to the crowd for more fermentation with their groups. The discussions lasted a good half hour, but at last the representatives returned to the platform. The decision was practically unanimous: all the land should be measured.

"Right!" said Wang Xi-tang, bursting with energy and enthusiasm. He knew that the measuring done when he had been village head was scrupulously honest, and he was eager for everyone to find this out.

"Then we'll have to go to the people again," he said, "and see how to organize ourselves, how to be quick but just, how to carry on measuring and farm work at the same time. Or should we put aside the farm work until we've got the measuring work done? We'll do whatever the people want; democracy's the thing today."

"Measure in the daytime, reckon at night," was the people's verdict.

Proposals came fast and were unanimously agreed to. "Whoever can write should write. Whoever can reckon should reckon. Those who can neither write nor reckon can measure and haul the string. Those who have no other job can stand by and supervise. Everyone must take part, and every people's group can be a working unit."

The general opinion was that even done this way, the job would take five days. A count was made of all the people in the village with the necessary skills.

"In the whole village," Wang Xi-tang announced, "there are twenty-nine people who can both write and reckon, fifteen who can reckon, ninety-nine who can measure and haul the string, and ninety-seven who can be checkers."

In courtyards and at sunny street corners the next morning soon after dawn, there were little groups of peasants crowding around the few literate persons. At the dictation of householders, these scribes recorded the area and yield of each plot on a piece of cardboard. Almost everyone who could write was in demand, and many former struggle objects found themselves at the center of a friendly crowd for the first time in years. An ex-schoolteacher in the Fort was using the chaser mill outside his father's former home as a writing desk. Down on the Street, a once-wealthy young landlord was busily taking the peasants' dictation. Later these two were among the many ex-struggle objects who acted as clerks to the land-measuring teams.

The most crowded place of all was the courtyard of the village government office. Inside, the village clerk Wang Fu-xin was writing furiously. The conversation of those waiting their turn was animated but not entirely cheerful. Measuring the land appealed to them, but they regretted the loss of planting time.

When breakfast was over most of the signs had been written, and the peasants rushed off in all directions to plant them in the fields. They headed for the lush plots beside the stream bed and bordering the main road; the terraces at the back of the Fort, along Willow Stream Valley, and on the far side of the dry riverbed; and the stony hilltop plots on the Yangyi Plateau. The landscape was dotted with hurrying figures.

Back in the village, the joint committees again assembled for a meeting. Wang Wen-sheng reported, "I heard some of the people saying that if the area of our village land turns out to be smaller than the district records show, then we can have our tax assessment reduced." He smiled with satisfaction, then said severely, "If any people with ideas of this sort try and fiddle with their measurements, we can look into the matter."

"I agree," said Wang Xi-tang. "We should be against that calculating sort of attitude. We're measuring so that the district will have correct records; it's not a matter of trying to get our taxes reduced."

Lou Lin too broke his silence to oppose any attempt to treat land measurement as a tax-reducing device. "The question of tax assessment," he said, "can always be taken up at the district or county people's congress; we'll be holding elections for them at the end of this campaign. Meanwhile, this afternoon I suggest that we ask Wang Xi-tang to explain the purpose of measurement clearly to the people."

The committees examined the measuring implements, which had been assembled in the village government office. The most important were the wooden "bows," which looked like large, squat tuning forks, with a distance of five feet or so between the tips of the prongs. The village had nine bows, and Wang Xi-tang picked them up and measured each in turn against one which had been obtained from the district office. The Ten Mile Inn bows turned out to be slightly larger than the standard. With everyone's approval, a carpenter was summoned to saw a fifth of an inch off each prong.

Within an hour the news of the shortening of the bows had spread through Ten Mile Inn. The almost universal hope that land measurement would somehow make it possible to lower the village's taxes was shattered. In its place came fear that the shortened bows might result in a tax increase.

When it was time for the village meeting, a crowd assembled more rapidly than the team had ever seen. It was also the largest crowd of the campaign, and the atmosphere was tense. Not only was measurement of the land closely related to taxes, but in the old days it had been one of the methods by which the landlords and rich peasants cheated the masses. Thus measurement was a subject that aroused strong emotion independent of the particular issues.

Wang Xi-tang announced that the purpose of the meeting was to organize everyone into groups for the measuring. A hubbub immediately broke out.

"There's no need to measure all the land," one man shouted.

"The estimated yield of my land is too high! I want it measured," shouted another.

"If your land's thin, you can put in a claim," the first speaker retorted. Thin land had a smaller area or a lower yield than the record showed; fat land had the opposite.

"Those with thin land will report it, all right, but those with fat land won't say a word."

"Then others can report the fat land for them. There's bound to be someone who knows about it."

"No, let's measure all of it. Our village's estimated yield is too high. We can have it reduced if we do a good job of measuring."

This was Wang Xi-tang's cue. From the top of the porch steps he launched into a condemnation of the idea that measurement was for the purpose of obtaining a reduction in taxes.

"Measurement is for the sake of justice, not taxes," he said in closing. "We must be just and realistic; we must measure from one row of border beans to the other." The peasants planted a border of beans to make use of the few inches around the edge of each field that the plow could not reach.

"If we find that the area or yield is wrongly recorded," Wang said, "we can take it up with the district. And now let's put the whole matter of measuring the land to a vote."

"Better let the people ferment a little first," suggested Lou Lin quietly.

"Ferment, ferment!" A low buzz of excited talk filled the courtyard. At last the murmuring died down, and Wang Xi-tang once more mounted the steps.

"Those who want all the land to be measured, go to the east. Those who want only the thin and fat land measured, go to the west," he shouted.

There was a scuffling and a moving of stools and bricks as the whole crowd rose and voted with their feet. There was no need to count. A good four-fifths of the villagers thronged to the side of the courtyard nearest the river—to the west. Only the thin and fat land was to be measured; the previous day's decision was overwhelmingly reversed.

The next thing to settle was how the thin and fat land was to be reported. The crowd decided to hold meetings of the people's groups on the spot. The members of each group were to report whether any of their land was thin or fat. If anyone who had fat land failed to say so, others in the group were to report it. However, there would be no reprimanding of people whose land was fat.

Meanwhile, Wang Xi-tang seemed thoroughly perplexed. Evidently the reversal of the decision to measure all the land had taken him by surprise and caused him considerable dissatisfaction. As one of the representatives came up to the platform with a question from his group, Wang told him to go and round up the thirty others. He wanted to discuss the decision to see whether some misunderstanding lay at the bottom of it. Lou Lin intervened, however, and said that Wang Xi-tang himself had put the whole matter very clearly in his speech, that there could be no possibility of a misunderstanding, and that the masses obviously did not wish to take the time to measure every piece of land. After all, everything indicated that most of the land in the village was neither fat nor thin.

Wang Xi-tang said stubbornly, "But it's got to be measured under the new village government, hasn't it?"

"Yes," said Lou Lin, "but it can be done at a more convenient time. The masses have spent a long time on meetings recently, and more meetings will be necessary to fill the holes. We should leave the people time to finish planting their cotton."

Wang Xi-tang remained silent. It seemed that he wanted the complete measurement carried out for the sake of his personal reputation, to prove to the most doubting poor peasant that the village had been run with integrity and honor under his leadership. Newly elected cadres like Zhao Zhen-fang and Wang Wen-sheng lacked experience, but Wang Xi-tang had spent years in office. Yet he had not correctly gauged the feelings of the people. He appeared nonplused.

After a moment his curiosity got the better of his mortification, and he leaped down from the porch to talk to the people. He passed from one group to another, always receiving a friendly welcome, always ready with an apt remark. And he listened all the time; now he was getting the facts.

When the fermentation was over and the group representatives handed in their reports, Wang Xi-tang once more took the floor. "I've just been getting some notion of why you changed your minds about measuring the land. It seems that you're worried because the bows we plan to use are a fifth of an inch shorter than they were in the past. So you're afraid that your land will seem to be bigger than it really is. And the 'slippery heads' who thought that they might get lower taxes by measuring the land suddenly began to fear that the shorter bow might make taxes go up.

"But now we all know that the measuring is not for the purpose of raising or lowering taxes. It's for the sake of justice. And justice lies not in the bow, but in the heart.

"When we had the fifth of an inch cut off the bow, all we were thinking of was that our bow should match the standard set by the district. Now we're not going to measure all the land, but only the fat and thin. And it's not for the district office but only for our own village records. So this fifth of an inch is a small matter, and you don't need to worry about it. If you like, we can even make the bow a fifth of an inch longer again." This reassuring speech brought to a tranquil end what had started as a stormy meeting, with the peasants' hopes and fears, Wang Xi-tang's apparent desire for vindication, and the need for time to sow cotton all at cross purposes.

Since most of the Party members were new middle peasants and many of them were cadres, they had been well placed for buying up fat land. In the reporting of land that now took place throughout the village, they were zealous in reporting both their own fat land and that of others who were trying to keep it secret.

The branch secretary Wang Shao-zhen was one of the first in the village to report that a plot of his land was fat. After the destruction of feudalism, the land of hardworking, progressive fanshenned peasants like Wang Shao-zhen tended to grow fat from honest sweat. It was these men who reclaimed wasteland, pushed their terraces higher and higher up the hillsides, and cultivated grave sites which had lain fallow for generations. The border-region authorities encouraged such enterprise by granting a period of tax exemption for newly cultivated land. But failure to record increases in the cultivated area had made some land fat.

On March 27, 1948, the measuring teams went to work to set the record straight. The six teams were composed of two calculators (each with an abacus), two or more measurers (with both measuring bow and rope), one recording clerk, and one representative of the poor-peasant league to act as supervisor. In most cases, the people whose land was being measured accompanied the team.

The teams assembled cheerfully outside the village office after breakfast to get their final briefing from the village head Zhao Zhen-fang, who was in charge of all measuring. The measuring bows, inscribed "Land-Measuring Committee of the Ten Mile Inn Village Government," were compared with each other and pronounced identical.

The team which was to measure Wang Shao-zhen's land included Li Bao-wu, the manager of the Fort's oil press who, despite the criticisms which had been made of his management, was still considered a useful man when it came to calculating; a former cloth dealer whose chief qualification was the skill and speed with which he could handle a ruler; and two former struggle objects. Both of the latter had the cloth patches on their backs which struggle objects were required to wear, but their presence on the team indicated that they were now accepted members of society.

The representative of the poor-peasant league who was supervising the team also wore a cloth patch, but his showed that he had won the title of transport hero in carrying grain to the front. Stamped with a red hammer and sickle, it was sewn on his chest rather than his back.

The team plodded across the boulder-strewn dry riverbed. First they intended to measure a plot that had been reported as thin by the white-bearded Wang Yi, father of Wang Wen-sheng. As they walked to the fields on the opposite bank, Wang Yi explained that he had bought the plot jointly with Fu Gao-lin. It should have been divided equally but, the old man said, "Fu Gao-lin was the village head, and I was still peddling buns to make ends meet. So what could I do?"

"Which plot is bigger—his or yours?" asked the oil-press manager, teasing the old man.

Wang Yi smiled and said, "You just measure it; you'll find out."

When they reached the field, most of the team stood hesitating. But the representative of the poor peasant league strode rapidly along the length of the field, then back to the middle, where he stood looking over the lie of the land.

"We'd better take it in three pieces, with three widths and three lengths," he shouted. This was to make allowances for the field's irregular shape.

It was agreed to use the bow first, and then the rope as a check. The former cloth dealer whipped his ruler out from between his shoulder blades, where he had carried it tucked inside his jacket with an inch or two protruding above the collar. He deftly measured the rope, which not only was old enough to be well stretched, but had been painted red at each end so that it could not be tampered with. The measurer announced that the rope was exactly 25 feet long. The team rapidly walked the bow along the length and breadth of the various plots, with

Setting out to measure the land.

A land-measuring team that includes clerks, owners of land, and measurers.

A land-measuring team on the edge of a field.

the leader repeatedly warning them to "go straight, not zigzag" and "right up to the beans." As the figures were called out the two struggle objects wrote them down and the cloth dealer and the oil-press manager manipulated the abacus, clicking the beads back and forth as they multiplied and added.

Wang Yi's share of the plot measured 2 *mu* and 3 *fen*,* Fu Gao-lin's 2 *mu* and 3½ *fen*. The difference amounted to 1/60 acre.

"Well, you didn't get so badly cheated after all, old man," said the team members, smiling.

"Hm, mine was registered as 2.4 *mu*, though," Wang Yi said, "and I hear that he put his own down as only 2 *mu*."

"Yes, he reported that this field was fat," said the team leader. Fu Gao-lin

A land-measuring team with a "bow," or *gong*.

Wang Yi, Wang Wen-sheng's father, watches while his land is being measured.

* A *fen* is one-tenth of a *mu*.

was evidently making an effort to regain the regard of his fellow villagers.

"Wang Shao-zhen reported that his field at the foot of the hill is fat, too," the leader said. "Let's do that one now."

The team trooped off toward it as Wang Yi made his way back across the riverbed, saying, "Anyway, half a *fen* is half a *fen*."

Wang Shao-zhen's field, which was officially recorded as 0.8 *mu* in area, turned out to be 1.3 *mu*—fat, as he had said. As he wrote down the result, one of the struggle objects smiled ironically, as if to say that the people who had led the struggle against him and his class were not such models of virtue.

The team leader came to Wang Shao-zhen's defense. "You can see from the lie of the land that it was just about 0.8 *mu* originally. The whole strip at the western edge, there, has been dug out of the hillside and leveled off. I remember him working on it during the campaign to reclaim wasteland. He sweated plenty. It was the same with that fertile patch in the center, too. There used to be two grave mounds there. He just shoveled them away, spade by spade, while some people"— the leader paused meaningfully—"were talking about how the ghosts would come and spoil the crops."

The land measurement, excluding the first period of discussion and organizing, took up most of two days. It was finished by the evening of March 28, and the work team entered in its diary:

> Some plots of land proved to be smaller and some larger than the records showed, but on the whole there was not much difference. The results of the yield appraisal committee's work was the same: very little difference from the former estimates. Neither result will have a big effect on the work of filling the holes.

But the entire project had served the purpose of bringing the village's growing democratic machinery into use. The masses' true opinions about measurement had been discovered through the people's groups and their representatives. Setting up the teams and committees had given the new cadres experience in organization. Drawing in the former struggle objects as clerks had helped to unify the village. So had the results of the measuring, which virtually ended whatever suspicions the poor peasants still had about the middle peasants. In addition, the Party members had acted as models in reporting fat land and thereby took another step toward regaining leadership in the community.

# —22—

# Removing the Caps and Patches

During the anti-Japanese war some villagers had supplied the enemy with lists of the local Communists and information about guerrilla activities. By 1944 one of the leading collaborators, the landlord Wang Ban-yan, had already been caught; another, Fu Shou-liang, was under suspicion. Through a series of accidents, Old Wen-tang, Ten Mile Inn's honest but somewhat gullible public security officer, came to suspect a large group of villagers of being secret agents. The clever Fu Shou-liang managed to persuade these innocent men to confess and recant rather than risk being convicted. But when they did, the pseudo-spies were asked to name other agents. Ultimately their random responses implicated about seventy villagers and wove a web of such confusion that no one could now unravel it.

The work team did not propose to reinvestigate the affair of the secret agents—to decide who had been ringleaders and who had been led astray, duped, or framed. A detailed analysis of individual guilt and innocence would have led the campaign into the past instead of the future. But it was time to remove the "secret-agent caps"—the stigma of treachery—from the villagers who had been entangled in the affair, as well as to take the patches off the struggle objects who had changed their class by laboring.

Leng Bing, who had almost finished the education of the Party members, was assigned to the case of the "cap wearers." Something had to be done to clear the air and ensure that those who felt they had suffered an injustice should no longer brood over it. Cases of genuine injustice had to be set right, but justice was not to be interpreted as an eye for an eye. The objective was to wipe out the past stigma and encourage people who now supported the democratic reforms to play a useful part in village life.

Leng began by looking into the main facts of the case. He divided this task into three stages. First he talked with a number of the persons

A "struggle object" with a cloth patch on his back.

concerned, including two who had to be summoned from outside the village. One was Old Wen-tang, who had been the public security officer then and who was now a district cadre. The other was Wang Ze-yin, who had been secretary of the village Party branch in 1944 and who was now a cadre in a government-run enterprise in the county town.

From these two and a dozen other peasants Leng gradually pieced together a story of treachery, both real and imagined, at a time when only the staunchest had faith in the final victory of the Communist-led resistance against the Japanese. Gradually he saw the outlines of the intrigue woven

Part of a land-measuring team. A member of a "struggle object" family wears a patch on his back.

by the former Guomindang village head and undercover agent Fu Shou-liang in an effort to save himself and crush his rivals.

In the second stage of his work Leng arranged a meeting of half a dozen cadres, past and present: the former to throw light on what had happened, the latter to gain the understanding of it which they needed in order to administer the village efficiently.

To begin the meeting Old Wen-tang was asked to summarize what had happened. As he explained, it became clear that honest and well-meaning cadres like him had been concerned mainly with safeguarding the village at a time of great pressure, for there had been two years of famine, and a Japanese mopping-up operation was under way. It was also clear that Old Wen-tang had been no match in wits for the wily Fu Shou-liang.

Leng Bing then gave his analysis of the motives, interests, and relationships of the principal people involved. Further details were supplied by others at the meeting, and Leng went on to describe the approach which seemed most useful now, four years later. "We can't go on hearsay," he said. "We must look only at what was witnessed and proved. We had proof of the treachery of Wang Ban-yan and his clique. We know that Fu Shou-liang was guilty, and that a number of others were to blame for rumor mongering and false accusations. But in most cases there was no proof of actual treachery. It's clear that mistakes were made, and this should be admitted. Anyway, now it's time to take off the secret-agent caps. And if any questions of this sort crop up in the future, they must be referred to the higher authorities."

In the third stage of his work on the secret-agent affair, Leng called a meeting of all seventy cap wearers. Once more he emphasized that the approach to the problem should be one of healing, not of reopening old wounds. Although he admitted that mistakes had been made and injustice done, he did not go to the opposite extreme of absolving everyone who was present. Some of them undoubtedly were guilty of some of the charges. But now the thing for them to do was to examine themselves objectively. Those who were innocent would be cleared once and for all, and those who were not would serve as a lesson to everyone, including themselves.

"We want you to say whether you think that your cap was a real one or not," Leng concluded.

During the meeting more than twenty of the cap wearers spoke, some at length, others in a few words. Some showed great intensity of feeling, others composure and even humor. A number of these people had been classed as struggle objects in the Feudal Tails Campaign, so that they had long been excluded from large public gatherings. To them the meeting had some aspects of a festive social occasion. Quite a few relished the opportunity to spin a good yarn, all the more entertaining because they themselves were central figures. Little by little as they talked, the atmosphere cleared. Details which had remained hidden for years were brought to light; tongues which had been tied by fear or shame were loosened. The weight of the invisible caps which they had worn for so long became lighter and lighter as some of the best storytellers of the village got into their stride.

Though the meeting had taken on the air of a successful party, there were occasional sour notes as some of the people who were deeply implicated tried to identify themselves with the innocent. Leng Bing accordingly closed with an expression of warning as well as of promise.

"Don't forget that there were genuine secret agents in this case, and that there were people who accused the innocent. I hope that those who collaborated with the enemy and those who implicated the blameless will face up to what they have done.

"Almost all of you feel some sort of grievance, and it's right that you should reveal it. So tomorrow we'll have a village meeting, and the caps will be publicly taken off."

The village meeting the next day, March 30, dealt not only with the secret-agent caps but with the third and final classification. The weather was gray and chilly, the mood of the people serious as the temple courtyard filled. The meeting was conducted with efficiency, for every family in the village had been placed on one of six lists that were carefully defined according to decisions made at the two previous classifications. These lists contained, on the one hand, the groups of cases which were the simplest and most routine, and on the other, the groups which were most complex and promised to be of most educational value. By reading out and disposing of each list in turn, it was possible to hurry through the simplest cases and devote the time to the complex ones.

The two groups on which most of the discussion was focused consisted of struggle objects. One list contained the former landlords and rich peasants; the other, members of the basic masses who had been incorrectly struggled against. And as the crowd gave their opinions, face-saving no longer held them back, and personal prejudices did not overwhelm their judgment.

For instance, during the discussion of the former rich peasant and heroin dealer Wang Ying-xiang, someone pointed out that he was suspected of having been a member of the subversive Landlords' Back

Home Corps, a Guomindang organization. But an old peasant declared, "It doesn't matter whether he was in the corps or not. And it doesn't matter what sort of person he used to be, or what he's like now. That's got nothing to do with his class. It's his labor that counts."

This view received general support. Although the peasants still hated Wang Ying-xiang, they agreed that he was no longer a rich peasant, for it had been more than three years since he had depended primarily on hired labor for farming his land. He was finally classed as a peddler-trader. His dealings had required more capital than an ordinary peddler needed, for his secondhand clothes business had been only a cover for trafficking in heroin. But he had no hired assistants; he even transported his goods on his own shoulders with a carrying pole.

In contrast, the case of a former landlord was considered complex because, as someone at the meeting pointed out, "He never carried things on his shoulders; he used a bicycle." To this speaker the ownership of such a comfortable means of transportation branded him as something of a parasite. But it was finally agreed that he was an exploiter, not because of the bicycle, but because he hired labor. After a long and complicated discussion he was classified as a trader.

Both of these struggle objects had changed their class by laboring for a stipulated period—the former, for the three years required of a rich peasant; the latter, for the five years required of a landlord. In the end the villagers decided that only two of former members of the exploiting classes in Ten Mile Inn had failed to change their class, and these two were in the process of doing so.

By lunchtime only a handful of exceptionally difficult cases remained, and it was decided to refer these to the joint committee of the poor-peasant league, the peasant union, and the village government. (The committee disposed of them at a meeting two days later.) To all intents and purposes, the classification was finished at last. As the work team had prophesied when they first came to Ten Mile Inn, its result was not to split the village apart but to draw it together. The overwhelming majority of the people had demonstrated to their own satisfaction that they belonged to one family—that of the basic masses. In the whole village only two families remained who still belonged to feudal classes.

Of the remaining eighty-two out of a total of eighty-four families who had been struggled against (rightly or wrongly), fifty-seven were now classed as old middle peasants, seven as new middle peasants, and sixteen as poor peasants. Wang Ying-xiang, the former dealer in heroin and secondhand clothes, was a peddler-trader, while one family was labeled "undecided on account of historical complexity."

The final results for the whole village were as follows:

| CLASS | NUMBER OF FAMILIES |
|---|---|
| Poor peasants | 140 |
| New middle peasants | 125 |
| Old middle peasants (4 of these were well-to-do middle peasants) | 148 |
| Worker | 1 |
| Handicraft workers | 2 |
| Peddler-trader | 1 |
| Old-style rich peasant | 1 |
| Managing landlord | 1 |
| Unclassified | 1 |
| TOTAL | 420 |

In the afternoon the meeting was devoted to one-fifth of the families of Ten Mile Inn: those who had been struggled against, rightly or wrongly, and those who had had secret-agent caps, deserved or undeserved, placed upon their heads. Some injustice had been done, and Wang Xi-tang, who was village head during the Feudal Tails Campaign, accepted a good share of responsibility for the mistakes. In reviewing the various campaigns, he showed where the fault had been his, where others (in some cases his superiors) had been to blame, and where injustice had been a product of objective conditions.

"When someone suggested tracing families back for three generations to decide whether they were feudal tails, I wasn't worried," said Wang, "because I myself wouldn't have been a struggle object unless we'd gone back four!" He went on, "Of course tracing back three generations was all wrong, because few families have been poor for that long at a stretch. If a man's parents are poor, he usually can't afford to marry and so has no children.

"I made a lot of mistakes in the past," Wang Xi-tang concluded. "Now you have the right to speak. However serious the mistakes you think I made are, don't hesitate to point them out. Everybody is here— the work team comrades, the struggle objects, the masses—and all of you should give me your advice. If you don't, harm will be done again in the future.

"But there's one thing I don't want to make any bones about. It was right to struggle against the landlords and rich peasants: that's the aim of our Communist Party. What was wrong was to struggle against simple-and-honest peasants and to grade poor and middle peasants as struggle objects.

"But the reason some of them were struggled against was that they did harm others. They should examine their own conduct. They may think that the struggle was entirely bad, but it had some good in it too, even when it was wrong. It was a good education. Whoever was struggled against must have had something bad about him or some defects. If he hadn't, he wouldn't have been struggled against. From now on, those who don't follow the people but still try to injure and exploit them will be crushed."

Wang Xi-tang did not want any of the struggle objects to feel that because less than 25 percent of their income had been derived from usury and exploitation, there had been nothing wrong with their conduct. If they thought this, they might bear a grudge against their fellow villagers. He therefore dealt with the past in order to reject its standards, denounce its methods of self-enrichment, and praise the cooperative methods which the reforms had made possible.

When Wang had finished, the meeting was thrown open to discussion. After a few moments of fermentation an old man sitting on a large stone in the middle of the crowd muttered, as much to himself as to the crowd, "As long as there are struggles, there have to be mistakes. It can't be helped. If you're always afraid of making a mistake, you can never dig deep into the soil. All you can do is scratch the surface."

"That's just how it is," said one of his neighbors. "Sometimes the mistakes are the fault of those at the top, sometimes our own cadres are to blame, sometimes it's the people. The thing is to do things as well as we can from now on."

"At the beginning I myself took part in the struggles along with the rest of you," said one of the struggle objects, "and I got my share of the fruits. Then it came to checking back three generations, and I was cut off from you. I no longer belonged to the masses. My heart was heavy, but now that the masses want me again, I'll do my best to serve the people."

There were some murmurs of approval at this, but Wang Xi-tang was determined not to let things slip by just to avoid unpleasantness. He turned to the man and said, "It's true that you came from a poor-peasant home. But you left the home of the masses and moved in among the landlords and rich peasants. You cut yourself off from the masses—you know that. You used to set off to the east with your donkeys—to transport coal, you said. And I used to climb onto your roof at night to watch you, to see what you were up to. Why did I do that? You know! It was because you were in touch with the enemy.

"Think it over for yourself. Haven't you learned a good lesson? So I say to you now: Never again set your backside down on the seats of the landlords and rich peasants. Sit firmly among the masses. It wasn't we who drove you out of the family. You cut yourself off and harmed the people. That's why you were struggled against."

The man said nothing.

After a pause Wang Xi-tang went on, "There's another mistake that we made in the past. That was to make the graded families wear patches. Wherever they went, people watched them and whispered, 'Look; a struggle object.' Wearing patches cut them off from the people. The patches were only pieces of white cloth, but they were heavy loads.

"Although the patches weren't my idea, I must accept some of the responsibility for them. So now I won't delay any longer. It's time to take the patches off. Do you want to take them off?" he asked the patch wearers.

From all over the courtyard there were cries of "Yes, yes, we do," and hands were raised to show agreement.

"Is it right that the patches should be taken off?" Wang Xi-tang asked the audience. "If you agree, raise your hands." Hands were raised, agreement was shouted, heads were nodded. No one in the courtyard objected.

"Then take the patches off and pass them up here," said Wang Xi-tang.

The patches were ripped off. Some were passed forward from hand to hand; others were screwed up and flung toward the platform in a dramatic gesture of riddance.

When the hubbub had died down, Wang said, "Now anyone who wishes may say what is in his heart."

One of those who spoke first was the son and onetime accomplice of a villager who acted as middleman for Guomindang Commander Huang who had dealt ruthlessly with the villagers. The son himself had been notorious in the village as one of eight young toughs who had seized or smashed property, beat and tortured people on the commander's behalf.

"My patch is still new," he said, "I hardly wore it. I preferred not to go beyond my threshold rather than show myself with it. Written on it underneath my name are the words, 'Underminer. First Grade.' It almost killed me."

He summarized his past life, acknowledging the harm he had done to the people and admitting that he had joined the Eighth Route Army in hopes of protecting himself and his family from the anger of the people. But the political education he received in the army had made him regret his past behavior and truly want to serve the people. During one of the reform movements, his commanding officer had ordered him to go home and "bow his head before the people."

"When I came back," he said, "I wanted to repent, but the masses would have nothing to do with me. I was isolated. So I was forced to think more and more about what I had done, and I began to realize that I had been a criminal.

"I shut myself up in my room and thought, 'This is the end of everything.' But now I find that the people of Ten Mile Inn still want me. I feel like a prisoner who has suddenly been set free. I want you all to criticize me, to point out my failings.

"Some of you may be afraid that eventually I'll seek revenge against the villagers who killed my father. There's no need to worry. I swear that nothing of the sort will ever occur."

This speech made a deep impression on the crowd, but they still received it with some caution. Many of them had suffered personally at the hands of him or his father, and they wondered whether his statement could be taken at face value.

Others who knew how energetically he had worked at plowing for the soldiers' families felt confident of his sincerity. But some of the villagers reserved judgment, whispering to each other, "Well, let's see if he can reform himself."

Wang Xi-tang had no doubts about the future, though he was not prepared to gloss over the past. "He has stated his case very clearly," Wang said, and then turned to the man himself to add, "All the same, you had better examine yourself again and again. I have the records of your case, and I'll hand them over to you to study." As a token that bygones were really bygones, all the written evidence of the collaborator's misdeeds was to be given to him.

Wiping the slate was the keynote for the rest of the meeting. "Whether or not you had to wear a patch in the past, now is the time for all of you to take your place in your proper class," said Wang Xi-tang. "From now on all of us belong to the laboring classes. We're all of one family and can talk together openly and freely as brothers and sisters, fathers and uncles, mothers and aunts."

One more task remained: to take off the secret-agent caps. Old Wen-tang, who had been public security officer at the time of the case, now rose to speak. He admitted that he had not had a clear understanding of the complicated relationships between the different cliques of village cadres at the time. He had fallen for the tricks of Fu Shou-liang. And he admitted too that he had brought pressure to bear upon the suspects, so that in the end innocent and guilty alike wrote out confessions.

"I called them all together for a meeting and said, 'You must admit it frankly if you have been led astray by that fellow.' At first the people kept silent; time passed without a word. It was getting late, and they began to feel that they had to do something or I wouldn't let them go home. So they told lies and put their confessions into writing, and from that day to this they have been wearing secret-agent caps. Yet it was only a few people like Fu Shou-liang and Wang Ban-yan who were really guilty.

"In my opinion, it's time for all the caps to be taken off."

Life was very different in Ten Mile Inn now from what it had been at the time of the secret agents' case. In 1944 the famine had left the villagers destitute and starving. The military situation was desperate, and it looked as if the Japanese might win the war. Now the Japanese were gone, and the Guomindang, despite American backing, was losing battle after battle. The economy was more prosperous than it had ever been before, and in a few days the remaining "holes" in Ten Mile Inn were to be filled up.

So there was a festive atmosphere in the courtyard when the team member Leng Bing began to read the names of those who were now considered cleared. The crowd chuckled when he came to the names of people who were obviously innocent, and the chuckles grew to loud laughter as the list went on and on.

"Now everything has been made clear, and all the caps are off," Leng Bing said, "so there's nothing to worry about. But remember that some of those whose names were on the list—even the innocent ones— are not faultless. In particular, some of them have a habit of talking recklessly about other people. That was one of the reasons why the mistakes were made.

"Another reason is that Fu Shou-liang knew of the differences among the cadres at the time, especially between the old and the new ones. And he and his clique tried to exaggerate the difficulties, to split their unity. So the people suffered.

"How was it that he could do this? How was it that such a thing as the secret agents' case ever came about?

"We know that the Guomindang were sending secret agents into our Liberated Areas; that's how it was possible. If it had not been for the Guomindang, there would never have been such a case.

"And remember, it's the same today. The Guomindang are still trying to smuggle in their agents. So we must all be on the lookout— both the Communists and the masses. And if we find some evidence we must report it to the government, and it will be settled by the proper authorities." On this call for vigilance the meeting was adjourned.

# —23—

# Model Housewives
# Form a Committee

Things were not going so well with the women of the village. In other parts of the Liberated Areas, women occupied positions in every type of political and administrative body, from the Central Committee down to village government. But in Ten Mile Inn not a single one had been elected to the village congress or the new village government.

The women of Ten Mile Inn had once held the Wu An County record for spinning and weaving. Such an achievement usually created the conditions for rapid social and political advances, but at that point the Feudal Tails Campaign had operated as a check on women's progress. The most active and able members of the local women's association had been old middle peasants, and they were forced to resign as part of the campaign's measures against this class. Leaderless, the women let the association decline. They withdrew into their own domestic concerns, and now they seemed permanently bowed under the weight of feudal tradition.

The work team had come to the village unprepared for this local situation. As they visited the poor peasants in the first week, they did not try to mobilize the women directly, but waited for them to be drawn into activities through their menfolk. And at the time this course seemed to be effective, for the women joined the poor-peasant groups in each section and took part in the classification. Eighty became members of the poor-peasant league, and four were elected to the committee. These women then recruited others for the peasant union so efficiently that it had over three hundred women members, and three women were elected to the union's committee.

Yet the women were elected not on the basis of their political activity but according to their feudal virtues of gentleness, obedience, and industriousness. Furthermore, having voted the women into office, the men seemed to forget all about them. Often the women on the committees were not told about meetings, and their absence was not even noticed. And far from resenting this neglect, the women were glad to have the time free for their housework.

When the peasant union was being organized, Wang Xiang, the former head of the women's association, was severely criticized for her aggressive behavior and was made to undergo a waiting period until she showed signs of reform. Her reverses, together with the destructive criticism directed toward the cadres who had been most active in the past, made a powerful negative impression on the women committee members in Ten Mile Inn. These gentle homebodies became convinced that public inactivity was a virtue.

In the middle of March Zhang Pan-shi, the work team's supervisor on the Party Bureau, said, "It's not enough simply to recruit women into the various organizations. What we've got to do is make them active. We didn't pay enough attention to this at the beginning, and now we need to make up for lost time."

The team assigned Wu Fang, its woman member, to the task of mobilizing the women. She began to hold preliminary meetings in each section with women members of the peasant union to make plans for organizing a women's department. The large meeting which would formally inaugurate the new department was held on March 27. Though it was scheduled for the early afternoon, it did not actually begin until four o'clock. Even then, only 150 of the union's 300 women members had showed up.

Of the three women on the peasant-union committee, Wu Fang could not persuade a single one to preside. When they had been elected, no one had mentioned that they would have to run meetings. The woman who finally consented to take the chair was the reserve committee member, Duan Fu-zi. A small, slight woman of thirty-five with considerable poise, she opened the meeting in the loudest voice she could muster, though she could hardly be heard at the back of the crowd.

In the fashion she had learned from the work team, Duan Fu-zi began with a question. "Why are we holding this meeting?"

"To elect our committee," replied the women who were sitting near the front.

Duan Fu-zi briefly described the functions of the new committee and how it was to be elected.

Then the team member Wu Fang spoke. "Up to now, the women of Ten Mile Inn have not played their part in running the house. From now on you are going to run the house together with the men.

"In the past you were organized into groups, weren't you? What did these groups do?"

Wu Fang, a woman member of the work team.

Women winding yarn onto frames during a meeting.

"Weaving and spinning and rear service," the former group heads replied.

"And besides that, what did you do?"

"Besides that? Nothing."

"That's just the point," said Wu Fang. "The women worked, but they didn't take part in running the house. From now on, things are going to be different. Women have the right to own property. Each will have her own share of land. And women have the right to speak. Have you the courage to speak?"

There was a general response of "We have," but it was not made with much conviction. Wu Fang pointed out that the women needed to have a strong organization so that they would have the courage to speak out.

The crowd agreed that the committee of the peasant-union women's department should consist of nine women, including the three women members of the peasant-union committee. Of the six to be elected, there should be four from the lower village—one from each section—and two from the Fort.

Wu Fang said, "I think we should use the same four qualifications which were required in electing members to the peasant-union committee. So we should choose women who work hard, who are helpful and willing to serve others, and who do not nurse prejudices, spread scandal, or form cliques. And we don't want those who are immoral. Everyone should speak out frankly about the candidates' faults and virtues, without any face-saving. Then we can choose the best of the best."

The meeting broke into small groups to ferment over the nomination of candidates. The Fort group gathered around Chen Chui-de, who sat nursing her two-year-old son. As a member of the poor-peasant league committee, she would have been assigned to the new committee along with the three women members of the peasant union committee, but she explained that she was about to resign from all such activity because she was pregnant again. She would not have time or energy to help lead a women's organization.

The other Fort women agreed that members with young children to look after could hardly be expected to play a leading part in outside activities. "Better give the job to some of the young ones who've just got married and haven't any children," one woman said.

Another added, "Yes, the ones who live with their mothers-in-law and can be spared from work around the house." Times were changing, for in the old days it was taken for granted that a young bride should act as the drudge of her mother-in-law. Now the mother-in-law was looked to as a source of help for her daughter-in-law.

As the discussion went on, it was household duties that became the focus of attention. Little by little the four qualifications which Wu Fang had listed gave way to the practical problem of who could spare the time.

When it came to the election, the Fort's two successful candidates were both young brides. One was the twenty-two-year-old Wang Xi-ling, whose demure face and quiet manner contrasted with her emerald green trousers and crimson jacket. The other was Su Wei-chun, a pink-clad nineteen-year-old who was married to the well-to-do middle peasant Fu Wei-shan. When Su Wei-chun found that she had been elected, she was so excited that her hands fluttered, revealing six glittering silver rings and many jangling bracelets.

The women who were elected from the lower village were not quite so young. Yang Kui-de was twenty-five and had brought her two-year-old son to the meeting. The soldier's wife Li Yu-heng was also in her twenties. Like Su Wei-chun, she chattered and laughed with her neighbors rather than settling down quietly to spin or sew. The third successful candidate was a woman in her thirties with four small children, while the fourth was Jin Tang-de, a motherly soul of fifty with a teen-aged son.

Next the meeting discussed the admission of new members. A number of names were proposed and accepted with little or no debate, when suddenly a quarrel broke out.

A woman from the south-end section proposed three women from her neighborhood for membership, and a hubbub began among the Fort women. One of them shouted, "Those three! Why, they all used to be concubines of Old Moneybags!"

The former husbands of the three had been struggle objects, but now the women were divorced and remarried to men from the basic masses. Instead of taking up the case of each woman separately to decide what her position in her former husband's household had been —whether she had been an exploiter or among the exploited—the crowd fell to bickering. Some accused the south-end women of trying to smuggle undesirables into the union, and soon the major topic of discussion was the shortcomings of the south-end section.

One of the Fort women said to a group of her neighbors, "They're all a lazy, extravagant bunch down there. As soon as a cake peddler starts hawking down by the South Gate, they come flocking out of their houses and buy him out in no time."

Other groups were gossiping along similar lines. So, since it was time for the women to start preparing supper anyhow, Wu Fang brought the meeting to an end. In closing she pointed out the harmful effects of factionalism, but it was clear that the roots of the trouble were too deep to be dug up on the spot. Eliminating factionalism would have to be one of the urgent tasks of the newly elected committee.

The committee held its first meeting the following day in the home of Zhi Di-zi, who was known throughout Ten Mile Inn as a model daughter-in-law. Unfortunately, a model daughter-in-law never expressed her own opinions in the presence of her mother-in-law. And since Zhi Di-zi's mother-in-law sat spinning industriously on the *kang* in the room where the meeting was held, Di-zi never uttered a word even though she was a committee member of both the peasant union and its women's department. Instead she went back and forth from one room to the other, from the house to the courtyard, busying herself with household tasks. So, she not only contributed nothing to the meeting but hardly knew what it was about.

The house was very different from those of the poor. The solid, square, varnished table opposite the door was flanked by equally solid straight-backed varnished armchairs. Over the table hung a mirror in which the courtyard was reflected. According to the old superstition, a devil coming in the door would see his own reflection, and flee in terror. On the table stood two large porcelain vases with a blue-and-white design of birds and flowers. These served as storing places for keys, labor-exchange tickets, and accounts. The *kang*, built under a large, latticed south window, filled one end of the room. It held two spinning wheels, a big bundle of raw cotton, and a wicker basket full of bobbins. Zhi Di-zi and her mother-in-law were both expert spinners, and this *kang* was their workshop.

For the time being, however, the *kang* had become a meeting place. The women committee members crowded onto it and exchanged names and identities, because a number of them did not know each other. For example, none of the women from the lower village knew nineteen-year-old Su Wei-chun of the Fort. But after she had mentioned the various male members of her young husband's family and of her own, there were polite murmurs of "Oh yes, of course."

The women seemed rather apologetic about having been elected to the committee. All of them modestly claimed to be unsuitable and enumerated the difficulties which faced them. Heng-zi, a young wife of a soldier serving at the front, said, "Those of you who have a man in your family are all right. You've got someone to see you home if a meeting's held at night. But there's no man in my house, and I live on the edge of the village. It's going to be an awful nuisance for me to go back and forth to meetings." The other women murmured sympathetically.

Another woman said, "I don't know how I'm going to manage with those four kids of mine. The two older ones fight each other, and so do the two younger ones. I can't leave the house for a moment without something happening. I wonder what they're up to now."

The fifty-year-old woman, Jin Tang-de, said, "My son doesn't really know how to feed the donkey properly, and I have to see to it myself."

Sheng Xin-ai, the wife of the district cadre Wang Chen-chi, had to keep her eye on her two-year-old daughter, who was playing in the courtyard. She said, "I always used to go to women's meetings regularly and tried to make progress. But I'm afraid I'm still too backward to be a member of the committee. Those two mischievous kids of mine hold me back. And what with the boss away at the district headquarters most of the time, and his old mother to look after, I never have a moment to spare."

The nineteen-year-old Su Wei-chun laughed and exclaimed, "Imagine electing me a cadre—I can't believe it! I haven't got any problems like the rest of you. Except that there's something wrong with my back." Whatever she was suffering from, she looked the picture of health.

The other committee member from the Fort, the twenty-two-year-old Wang Xi-ling, said, "I'm too young. We young people can't understand all these complicated village affairs. I'm worried for fear I'll do things wrong."

Song Ting-de said, "My problem is that I can't speak in front of a crowd. If there are more than ten people, my face goes red."

A young woman who had been sitting silently at the back of the *kang* winding thread onto bobbins said, "If the meal isn't ready when my husband gets back from the fields, he's furious. That's my chief problem."

Since all the conversation had been about the difficulties in the way of holding office, Wu Fang began by asking, "Can these problems be overcome?"

There was a general chorus of "Yes." Various suggestions were made about how this could be done. Sheng Xin-ai said to the quiet young woman who feared her husband's temper when the meal was late, "Most of the men have begun to change their ideas now. And our new committee can reason with those who haven't."

The fifty-year-old woman said, "I don't know why you young people are worrying about not being able to handle affairs. You're not too old to learn to read."

Someone pointed to the gay young Wei-chun and said, "She knows a lot of characters already."

The latter laughed, half pleased, half embarrassed. She said modestly, "I really know only a few." Still, it made an impression on the women that one of them could read a little.

Song Ting-de said to the women in general, "I don't think you have to worry too much about how much work there'll be. We'll have a lot of group heads who can do it."

Wu Fang agreed, and added, "Some of you are singlehanded in the house and all of you are busy, but I don't think you need to worry about not having time for your new tasks. Of course, we'll be rather busy while we're just beginning to organize. But once we get things going, we won't need to spend so much time on meetings."

Wei-chun, bubbling with enthusiasm, echoed Wu Fang almost word for word. And most of the other women nodded their agreement. One said, "Even if we're not much good at the job in the beginning, we can talk things over among ourselves and help each other out."

Wu Fang asked, "What did you think about yesterday's meeting?"

"Who on earth are those women that all the fuss was about?" someone asked.

The soldier's wife, Heng-zi, who lived in the south end, replied, "They're from the highlands," and added apologetically, "They are a rather disagreeable lot."

"They claimed to be poor-peasant women," Yang Kui-de said. "If it hadn't been for someone in the Fort who told the truth about their shady past, they might have gotten away with it."

Heng-zi, feeling she was being criticized, replied, "Well, after all, they've worked hard all this year."

"One year!" someone exclaimed. "Landlords have to labor five years and rich peasants three in order to change their class."

However, the committeewomen handled this upsurge of factionalism themselves. "We've got to unite if we're going to get on with our job," said Song Ting-de. "We in this group shouldn't blame each other."

Heng-zi added, "If we have any criticism of each other, let's just speak straight out. We don't want any misunderstandings among ourselves."

Everyone endorsed this view, but the matter of the three ex-concubines was dropped.

The new committee members were not too clear about what they ought to do, and Wu Fang suggested that they elect a chairman and two vice-chairmen to lead the work.

In the election which followed, Song Ting-de received the most votes and became chairman of the women's committee. Zhi Di-zi and Su Wei-chun, who came second and third, were vice-chairmen, the former in charge of work in the Street and the latter in the Fort.

The committee then discussed the internal organization of the women's department. They decided that all the women members should be divided on a voluntary basis into small mutual-aid groups of about ten members each. The formation of these groups was to be the first task of the committee members, each of whom was to be responsible for organizing the women in her own section of the village.

When these plans were completed, Wu Fang said, "Up to now,

women haven't taken a very active part in the campaign, so we must begin immediately."

She was interrupted by the soldier's wife Heng-zi, who had strong feelings on the subject. "How can we take an active part when the men won't even tell us when they're having a meeting, where it's being held, or what they're going to talk about?"

Wu Fang was not prepared for such an outburst. The whole tone of the work team's campaign had been the need for unity among the masses.

Wu Fang, fearing disunity between the men and the women, said, "Let's not start blaming the men for the way things are. We've got our own organization, and we can arrange to have a joint meeting with the committee members of the peasant union, the poor-peasant league, and the village government to discuss the work we are to do in the future."

Sheng Xin-ai immediately responded to this plea for unity, saying, "From now on we women must do our best to get along well with the men."

Nevertheless, Heng-zi had touched upon a genuine problem which had been glossed over in the urge for unity. The peasant women were no longer oppressed by landlords or rich peasants; and young wives, though like Zhi Di-zi they might be extremely respectful to their mothers-in-law, were no longer oppressed by them.

But even the most politically advanced men still had not overcome their feeling of superiority to women. It was this which had made them at first pooh-pooh the suggestion that the women should have separate poor-peasant groups, this which made them interrupt women speaking at meetings, this which had made the election of women committee members something of a formality. There were also still some cases of wife beating, though they were rare. In the main, outright oppression of women had been ended, but both men and women had feudal attitudes to overcome. "If the women take an active part in these adjustment meetings," Wu Fang said, "and come out with their opinions frankly, they'll soon convince the men that they're capable of sharing the job of running the house."

The meeting was adjourned, and that afternoon the new committee-women started to visit the women in their own sections to persuade them to organize and play their part in the rest of the campaign.

# —24—

# Finding the Holes
# and Some Filling

March 24–April 3

In a poor village such as Ten Mile Inn, finding the filling for the holes was no easy matter. Besides the remaining poor peasants who still had to fanshen, the handful of former landlords and rich peasants who had been "struggled to the ground" were now entitled to a fair share of the land. Furthermore, over sixty of the struggle-object families (most of them middle peasants) who should never have been struggled against at all now had to be given some compensation. Somewhere, somehow, a greater quantity or better quality of land had to be found for all three of these groups in Ten Mile Inn. Otherwise their productive capacity would not be properly utilized, and their average annual yield would not meet the equitable standard which the agrarian law demanded.

There were no longer any landlord or rich-peasant landholdings to draw upon. In fact, the members of these former exploiting classes now had a lower average yield than the poor peasants. The bulk of whatever surplus land remained was in the hands of hardworking middle peasants. And the Party made it clear that the interests of the middle peasants were not to be forcibly encroached upon.

The villagers owned just over 4,500 *mu* of farmland, with a total yield of just over 4,300 *dan*. In a population of 1,427, the average landholding was 3.2 *mu* and the average yield was 3 *dan* per person. The actual distribution per head according to class was somewhat different:

|  | Old middle peasants | New middle peasants | Poor peasants | Former landlords and rich peasants |
|---|---|---|---|---|
| Area per person | 3.52 *mu* | 3.07 *mu* | 2.72 *mu* | 1.80 *mu* |
| Yield per person | 3.44 *dan* | 2.87 *dan* | 2.51 *dan* | 1.66 *dan* |

As this table shows, only the old middle peasants were above the village average—by roughly 16 percent in land area and 13 percent in yield. Only about one-third of the families in the village were old middle peasants, however, and on the whole the land was equally distributed among them. This meant that very few old middle peasants were sufficiently above the village average to be genuine "mounds" that might supply filling for the holes. Thus compared with the number of holes, the mounds were few and small.

As the nature of the problem became increasingly clear, the members of the work team disagreed on what course to follow. Some believed that Ten Mile Inn should copy Huang Family Village in North Shanxi, where the poor peasants had obtained a share of land above the average. The *People's Daily* had just published a detailed account of the Huang Family Village campaign, together with Mao Ze-dong's recommendation that the case be studied carefully.

No, said other members of the team, Ten Mile Inn should not copy that model, because there had been holdings of landlords and rich peasants available for distribution in Huang Family Village. By drawing on them it had been possible to bring the poor peasants' land up above the village average without making the middle peasants forfeit a single *mu*. But in Ten Mile Inn many middle peasants would have to give up land simply to achieve equality. The entire team finally agreed that raising the village poor peasants' holdings above average would be a deviation to the left.

Some members then swung to the opposite extreme. The best way to be sure of not encroaching on the middle peasants' interests, they declared, was not to ask them to give up any land at all. There was some land that belonged to the village and the county, and some whose owners had left home years ago or had died without heirs. Only these plots should be used to fill the holes.

Under the guidance of the team leader Lou Lin, this approach too was rejected. Accepting nothing at all from the middle peasants and relying entirely on obviously inadequate sources was unrealistic and unprincipled. In the long run this would not lead to unity, because it would leave the poor peasants unfanshenned and so merely postpone the day of reckoning.

Finally Lou Lin himself put forward a proposal. The aim in filling the holes, he suggested, should not be to bring the "hole" families up to the average area and yield of the entire village, but up to the average of the village *excluding* the old middle peasants. This worked out at about 2.72 *dan* per year—less than 3 *dou*\* below the village average.

This proposal was accepted. "It's true that we have to cement the unity of the poor and middle peasants," Lou Lin said. "But there's no such thing as absolute unity. We have to combine unity with struggle. This applies to unity with the middle peasants, too. But struggle with them is not like the struggle against the landlords; it's among members of the same family." The objective of the struggle, he pointed out, was to combat the pettiness and narrow-mindedness which was the natural tendency of the small producer.

Lou Lin drove home to the team that problems in people's ways of thinking and feeling had to be correctly solved if the process of filling the holes was to be successful.

Having straightened out its own ideas on the subject of hole filling, the work team was ready not to do the job itself, but to offer guidance. The actual finding and filling of the holes was to be undertaken by the masses under the leadership of a joint committee of the poor-peasant league, the peasant union, and the village government.

The new village leaders, like the work team members, had ideological problems to solve. One of the most persistent was the tendency toward absolute equalitarianism, which was deeply ingrained in the peasants' nature.

During the discussion on how to make the land adjustment, the chairman of the poor-peasant league, Li Bao-yu, proposed: "The poor and middle peasants are all members of one family, aren't they? So we ought to make the adjustment in the same way that two brothers divide their inheritance equally."

This proposal appealed to a number of peasants. It seemed not only to smack of homely wisdom but to stress the all-important principle of unity. Lou Lin, however, was quick to put his finger on a flaw.

"When brothers divide an inheritance," he pointed out, "they go over it item by item—the land, the housing, the animals, and the implements. Everything is divided equally. But we don't want to take all the land, houses, animals, and implements in Ten Mile Inn and put them into a pool and divide them equally. If we did, everything would be at sixes and sevens. Production would come to a standstill for a long

\* One *dou* was one-tenth of a *dan*, thus only ten *jin* or eleven pounds.

time, and we'd end up with confusion instead of unity. Instead of helping the Liberation Army, we'd be helping the enemy."

In his seemingly harmless proposal, Li Bao-yu had raised a question of basic importance to the entire campaign. Was the adjustment for the sake of abstract justice—of absolute equality? This question, Lou Lin pointed out, arose from the narrow outlook of the small peasant producer. He and other members of the work team had to make it clear that the purpose of the adjustment was not to secure equality for its own sake. It was to increase the over-all production of the village by drawing everyone with the power and the will to work into the most fruitful employment that the existing economy allowed. At the same time, the adjustment involved more than economics. It had to lay a solid foundation on which all classes in the village could be unified behind the goals of increasing production and winning the war. The work team had to focus the peasants' vision not only on immediate economic ends in Ten Mile Inn, but also on long-term national objectives.

The team set about combatting any tendency to return to each of the middle peasants who had been unjustly struggled against the exact plot, house, tools, or garments that he had lost. But they explained that he did have to be given assistance in solving his current production problems and that the end result might be that he received either a little more or a little less than he had originally lost.

Similarly, those who had obtained more than a fair share of the struggle fruits were not to be forced to "cough up what they've swallowed," as some peasants demanded. They might, however, be urged to offer back part or all of their surplus. But here again, the effect of such an action upon their subsequent ability to produce had to be carefully considered.

Once the work team had stated all its arguments against absolute equality, the joint committee agreed that the standard for filling the holes should be the average of the village—excluding the old middle peasants.

The next task was to work out a method for determining who fell below this standard. The guiding principle, it was agreed, should be the process of self-report and public appraisal which had been successfully used for classification. The committee broke the procedure into steps:

1. Each of the people's groups would call a meeting of its dozen or so families. Anyone at the meeting could declare himself a "hole." The names of the self-reported holes would be given to the leaders of each section.

2. The sections would meet and discuss each name on its list, accepting, rejecting, or modifying the self-reports according to public appraisal.

3. The modified lists would be passed on to the poor-peasant league, which would appraise them from an over-all village viewpoint.

4. The results of the league's appraisal would be posted for the whole village to check.

5. The thirty-one members of the village people's congress would have informal talks with the families they represented in order to gather their opinions on the posted results.

6. Finally, the congress would meet with the joint committee in order to express the general views of the villagers and to sanction the official list of holes.

These six steps were approved by the people at the village meeting on March 25. Wang Xi-tang then gave a little homely advice on the need to be reasonable and realistic in both self-report and appraisal.

"If a person says he hasn't got a donkey, then we can consider whether he really needs one or not. But of course it's no good saying one hasn't got a horse. As the old saying goes:

> "A melon can't be round as a ball.
> No one man can expect to have all.

"The important thing is to be realistic, to report and appraise according to the concrete situation. And we must be just. We must consider others in the same way we consider ourselves, and we must educate others and educate ourselves.

"For example, some of us work hard from dawn to dusk carrying buckets full of dung. Others just hang around the streets with a basket and a fork hoping they'll run across an odd bit of manure here and there. Trying to look busy, they even take their basket and fork to the fair with them, but really all they're out for is fun. They even buy cakes at the fair.

"So if this sort of man thinks he's a hole just because someone else who works hard gets a better crop, then what he really needs is not to have his hole filled up. He needs to have his ideas straightened out."

The next morning the thirty-one people's groups met so that their members could make self-reports. As usual, the six groups of the Fort gathered in the former home of the ex-rich peasant Fu Xin. One group settled inside the spacious hall, another on the porch at the top of the steps, and the rest went into four separate huddles out in the sunny courtyard. Each group had its clerk, who wrote down the details given by everyone who reported himself to be a hole.

One man complained of too small a house; another of exceptionally poor land which he wanted to change for something better. One said he lacked a plow; another a seeder. Some reported their needs forthrightly. Others were shy and hesitant and had to be urged with such encouragements as, "Of course you're a hole. The only decent tool you've got is that hoe," or "You should say so if you haven't got a house of your own. The one you live in belongs to your second uncle, doesn't it?"

Apart from remarks like these, there was no discussion, though the peasants listened very carefully to what everyone had to report.

Fu Zhi, who had once worked as a clerk and who was fond of donning his spectacles and reading the newspaper aloud to his neighbors, was suffering from toothache this morning. He had a large towel wrapped round his jaw so that his muttered report could hardly be heard.

"Hasn't he got half a donkey?" someone asked. Fu Zhi recovered his voice and announced in strong, clear tones that he certainly had not.

Fu Bian-de, who had overcome his old shyness sufficiently to establish himself as one of the Fort's new poor-peasant activists, was tongue-tied once more. He did mumble something in an aside to the recording clerk about lacking tools and a water crock, but did not mention his shortage of land for fear of being thought selfish. Some of his group chafed him and called out, "Speak up, Bian-de. We can't hear a word. What are you whispering for? You haven't got toothache, have you?" There was a burst of laughter, for Bian-de had hardly a tooth in his head.

With all six groups meeting at once, the self-reports of the entire Fort were made in less than half an hour. As each of the groups finished, the members sauntered into the meeting hall. There they squatted on stools and bricks to wait for the public appraisal by the whole section. When the time came, there were about sixty men and thirty women—the women, as usual, all sitting together.

One by one the names of the self-reported holes were read out and discussed, with the holes themselves stating their needs. First came land and housing, then animals, tools, clothing, and grain. Some of the holes gave details of their debts.

Many of the statements were simple and straightforward and after a brief period of fermentation they were passed with little comment. For instance, the spokesman of a fermentation group said about one man, "He ought to be supplied with farm tools, all right, but the question of a donkey will have to wait. The poor-peasant league can take that up." Another spokesman said, "He works all the year round, so he ought to be able to buy some of his tools himself. But he should be 'filled' with a house." The women agreed that he was entitled to a house, and with that the case was dropped.

The case of the seventy-four-year-old Li Li-zi was not so simple. Since the only males in the household were Li and a teen-age grandson, the family was short of labor power. As one villager put it, "The young'un's too young and the old'un's too old." Now the old man announced, "The only thing I have to say is that I'm a thousand *yuan* in debt, and—well, I could do with a bit more grain in my bin."

"What?" called one of his neighbors. "How much did you harvest last autumn?"

"He's no hole!" shouted a young man.

The old man was unperturbed. He took a noisy suck at the mouth-piece of his long-stemmed pipe and chuckled. "That's exactly what I said myself; I'm no hole. But in our group they kept on saying, 'Speak out, say what's on your mind,' and the group leader said, 'Granddad, if there's anything you need, just say so.' Well, who couldn't do with a bit more grain in his bin, eh?" And the old man looked around smiling, his face a mass of wrinkles and whiskers.

Next came the case of Li Meng-xian, who was hardly known to many at the meeting, for he had left Ten Mile Inn seventeen years before as a penniless refugee. Since then he had eked out a living as a potter and a cultivator of stony hillside land in the mountains of Shanxi Province. When he heard that according to the agrarian law, he might receive his share of land either where he was living or back in his native village, he decided to return to Ten Mile Inn.

There was more than the usual amount of fermentation over Li Meng-xian's case, and many sideways glances were directed at the white-haired old man. The first of the spokesmen seemed to echo the thoughts of all.

"We can't say he isn't a hole. Still, we think he may have something up there in the highlands, and we'd like him to tell us the facts."

"That's right," said another. "We don't want to be subjective."

Li Meng-xian now rose to his feet. His seventeen years in Shanxi had not only turned his hair white but also given him a Shanxi highland accent with clipped, nasal endings to his words. Some of the children giggled as he said, "I've got 2 *mu* of land up there, and a bit of a house. But I can't bring them here on my shoulders. All I've got besides that is a plow and a hoe."

"Still, you could bring a letter here. You should get your village head in Shanxi to write one to ours. That's the regulation."

"We could get Old Zhao to write them a letter and ask for the details," someone suggested.

"Why should we write a letter? We don't want to go searching all over the highlands for holes to fill," said someone else.

But the general feeling was that as a native of Ten Mile Inn, Li Meng-xian was entitled to receive his share in the village, as long as he did not receive it somewhere else as well. It was finally agreed that Zhao Zhen-fang ought to write an official letter to Li Meng-xian's adopted village in Shanxi to straighten things out.

One old woman was not too clear on the subject under discussion, but she did understand that people were stating their needs and troubles and having some solutions suggested. She was the mother of the first man in Ten Mile Inn to volunteer for the Eighth Route Army. Now she said, "I'm not in need of anything. I get my land plowed for me and everything else. The one thing I want is to have my boy come home again." And tears trickled down her lined face.

The young wife of a more recent volunteer tried to comfort her. "Don't carry on like that, auntie. He'll come back someday. You must remember whose fault it is that he's gone away instead of staying at home to enjoy a peaceful life. It's Old Jiang's fault; hate Jiang Jie-shi for it. Don't weep."

Other cases followed, some of them confirmed as genuine holes, some dismissed as false, until at last every name on the lists had been discussed. When the results of the meetings in all five sections were totaled by the joint committee, they found that over 200 *mu* of land would be needed to fill the holes which had been accepted as genuine. This was less than 4½ percent of all the cultivated land in the village, but the members of the joint committee considered it a frightening amount. They were afraid that if the figure were to leak out, the middle peasants would panic. To avoid this they decided that the figure should be kept a secret and that when the poor-peasant league went over the sections' lists of holes, it would have to apply stricter standards than the sections had done. In preparation, some of the league committee members were sent out to make discreet investigations of the self-reported holes which seemed most questionable.

The formal appraisal by the poor-peasant league started on the evening of March 28 and continued the following morning. The evening session was a stormy one. Though the team members tried to stay in the background, Li Bao-yu, who was acting as chairman, had to ask their help in keeping order. Nevertheless, the evening and morning meetings together weeded out a number of families which the sections had passed as holes. Some of these were cases relating to the purchase of draft animals, a transaction which the families had described as debts, but which were essentially an investment.

The league found that some of the genuine holes were the result of complicated family relationships. A youth of nineteen, for example, complained that he could not get along with his domineering father. He wanted to set up a home of his own, which meant that he needed land, a room, and tools. His request was referred to the poor-peasant league committee.

A younger teen-ager who said that he too wanted to be independent was laughingly told to wait his turn. "All I want is a pick and hoe," he insisted, and when some of the crowd laughed again, he burst into tears. Others tried to comfort him. One man explained, "It's his brother-in-law's fault. He always takes advantage of the kid because he's an orphan." The boy was promised that his problem would be solved, and gradually his sobbing ceased.

The league committee members had problems of their own to solve, but they were embarrassed when their own cases as self-reported holes came up for consideration. Li Bao-yu, who was chairman of the league, said, "My family isn't always badly off, but sometimes it is. It depends on how much house repairing there is for me to do. So if you think I'm not a hole, that's all right. But if you think I am one— well, it will be a great help."

"They have a new baby. Better give them a bit more land. Make it 2 *mu*," someone suggested.

Later when the league turned to the case of the village head, Zhao Zhen-fang, that modest man was speechless from embarrassment. Li Bao-yu, who was his neighbor, came to his rescue. "At our section meeting," he reported, "some people thought that the village head ought to get 4 *mu*; others said 3 would be enough."

"Give him 3½," someone suggested, and the crowd agreed.

The village's vice-head, Wang Wen-sheng, was probably the worst off of all the new poor-peasant cadres, but he received no such neighborly aid. He had not even reported himself as a hole at his section meeting; he was too concerned to avoid any suspicion that he was using his office for personal gain.

Before the meeting was over, the problem of equalitarianism cropped up. For example, some people maintained that because a certain peasant and his family were good workers and had managed to prosper by laboring for others in their mutual-aid group, they didn't need as much land as other families. With their good labor power they could get along all right just as they had been doing. The tendency to penalize those with more or better than average labor power was a form of equalitarianism which the Party had specifically condemned. And the work team had been so successful in driving this point home that the league refused to put this peasant and his sons at a disadvantage that stemmed from their hard work.

"Why should they have to spend their lives as short-term laborers just because they're hard workers?" asked one man. "Aren't they ever to have a chance to fanshen?"

It was agreed that they should be given an extra 2 *mu* of land.

When all the cases had been taken up, a total of 130 *mu* had been tentatively assigned, as opposed to the 200 *mu* originally requested by the different sections. Half of the holes were unfanshenned poor peasants; the other half were former struggle objects.

In pruning down the sections' estimate of land, the league had succeeded in weeding out a number of "false holes." But it had not sought out the genuine holes who had failed to report their needs—as in the case of Wang Wen-sheng. Such a failure to report was a serious weakness, for a basic aim of the adjustment was to provide a solution to the production problems of the poor peasants. So after the results of the poor-peasant league meetings had been posted, members of the work team and of the joint committee paid visits to families which seemed to be holes but had not reported themselves. They explained that this was to be the last chance—the final distribution of land to the tillers. At Lou Lin's suggestion, an extra 50 *mu* of land was added to the estimates in order to cover these cases.

The visits were partly successful; a few families were persuaded to report to their people's group representatives, who would take up these cases at the coming meetings of the village congress. The procedure would be a significant step in the development of the village's democratic machinery, for it was important that the new congress should establish its rightful position in the eyes of the masses and of the cadres. As Lou Lin had put it. "The new cadres must learn how to use the strength of the people by drawing on the people's congress representatives. It is these representatives who can best voice the people's interests, so it is essential for the cadres to learn how to utilize them."

After gathering the opinions of all the families in their people's groups, the thirty-one representatives who formed the village people's congress met with the joint committee on the afternoon of April 2 and the morning of April 3. The two bodies made the final decisions regarding the list of holes. Though the meeting was officially empowered, it was anything but formal. It was held outdoors in the long, narrow courtyard of the new village government offices.

Prompted by a clerk, the village vice-head Wang Wen-sheng called out a name from the list of holes. A second clerk read out the name, size, and yield of each plot owned by the family: "1.3 *mu* Green Cliff Field, yield, 1.5 *dan*; 1.9 *mu* Swallow Gully Field, yield, 1 *dan*; 2 *mu* Gravel Cliff Field, yield, 1.1 *dan*," and so on. Then with a click-clack of the abacus, a third clerk made the necessary calculations and reported the family's area and yield per head. Next the meeting discussed how much land was needed to fill this particular hole.

Sometimes recriminations broke out between representatives. One man questioned a statement made by the young oil-press worker, Fu Chan-ting, one of the Fort representatives. Chan-ting had been criticized before for his hot temper, and he knew that he ought to answer the question objectively, but it went against the grain.

"I'm very glad to accept your criticism," he said in angry tones. "I'm the group's representative, and if I haven't put their opinions properly you're very welcome to mention it."

The discord was soon smoothed away, and in a short time Fu Chan-ting was his usual smiling self. But it was part of a wider problem which the work team had already noticed. This was that some of the representatives, instead of expressing their groups' opinions, used their posts to publicize their own views and advance their own interests. There was no evidence that Fu Chan-ting was guilty, but the fact that he had been questioned was a sign of the growing vigilance against such conduct.

This incident also reflected the factionalism which still existed between representatives from different parts of the village—the Fort and the Street, the north and south ends of the lower village, and so on. In this respect the congress was inclined to be backward in comparison with the poor-peasant league.

Among the congress representatives, on the other hand, there were both new and old middle peasants, and the latter in particular revealed a more ingrained individualism than the poor peasants.

During the occasional factional outbursts and other tense moments in the discussion, Wu Fang, the woman team member, found it hard to remain a bystander. More than once she threw herself into the discussion to expose representatives that she believed were trying to serve their own interests rather than those of their groups. Lou Lin, on the other hand, let the flare-ups burn themselves out and then quietly contributed a few words on the responsibilities of the group representatives and of the village people's congress.

When the two sessions of the meeting had ended, however, it was evident that problems of factionalism and self-seeking by the newly elected cadres still remained to be solved. For example, the middle peasants who had sought compensation for debts incurred in buying draft animals were motivated by self-interest. And some of the middle peasants who claimed to be holes had only recently sold part of their land, fearing they might lose it if the impending campaign was directed against the middle peasants. Though they had reduced their average landholdings, they had certainly not made themselves holes.

On the other hand, in the stormy discussions produced by exposure of these false holes, the peasants were shedding their lifelong habits of face-saving. And here the village Party members played an outstanding part. In the west-central section, for instance, Wang Shao-zhen had exposed a middle peasant who tried to pass himself off as a hole because he had just gone into debt by investing in a donkey. When everyone else stayed silent, the branch secretary had said, "There are lots of people who don't own a donkey at all. Shall we allow them all to register the price of one?" There was an outburst of approval for this pointed question, and other members of the section became chary of making false reports. In another case, the Communist Wang Xi-tang exposed his own brother for trying to get his house exchanged for a better one, when it was in fact adequate compared with a number of others.

The entire hole-finding phase of the adjustment had two major characteristics. One was that poor peasants failed to report all their holes, partly for fear of conflict with the middle peasants, and partly because a number of them were skeptical of the outcome. They had not fanshenned in previous campaigns, and now they assumed that they would be given inferior land which would demand so much labor and fertilizer that it would hardly be worthwhile to farm.

The second outstanding characteristic of adjustment was that middle peasants on the other hand tended to exaggerate the extent of their holes. This was partly from selfishness and partly from misunderstanding. And without a clear knowledge of the situation in Ten Mile Inn, it was only natural to say, as old Li Li-zi had done, "Who couldn't do with a bit more grain in his bin?"

Nevertheless, some people really did need a bit more. By the time the false holes had been weeded out and the unreported genuine ones discovered, it was clear that more land was still needed. Where was it to be found?

# —25—

# More Earth to
# Fill the Holes

## April 2

Lou Lin himself directed the search for earth to fill the holes, and the joint committee named the able and experienced Wang Xi-tang to supervise its work in this delicate task. To begin with, fifteen of the Party members had offered the village almost 30 *mu* of land—all they had gained in the early struggles. In addition, they wanted to return all the housing and movable property they had received as struggle fruits. As their education had proceeded, the village Communists had become increasingly aware that by buying up a considerable share of the fruits, they had made it impossible for many of the poor peasants to fanshen. Now they were anxious to make amends.

Soon the search for land turned up another 60 *mu*. Some was public property owned by the county or district; some had been set aside in the past as cemetery plots; some had been left behind by emigrants who had not been heard of for years; and some had belonged to people who died without heirs. (Traditionally, "heirless" land was appropriated by anyone who paid for a person's funeral, since this was the accepted duty of an heir.)

Even assuming that the entire 30 *mu* offered by the Party members was acceptable (an unlikely possibility, for many of them would then be holes), this together with the 60 *mu* from other sources left another 80 or 90 *mu* to be found.

The only other source to draw on was the middle peasants, who were well above the village average annual yield per head. But nothing could be taken from them by force; it must be offered of their own free will. They were not to be regarded as struggle objects, and even the term "mound" was not to be applied to them. The "surplus" middle peasants were simply brothers from whom aid might be sought. Nevertheless, a well-planned campaign was to be launched to ensure that the greatest possible number of those with a surplus would volunteer contributions.

The first group to be called on would be people who had over-fanshenned. No one was to be put into this category, however, whose family did not have an average yield per head of 3.1 *dan* or more. (The average for all classes in the village, excluding the old middle peasants, was 2.72 *dan*.)

The second group to be called on would be people who had taken over "heirless" land. But they would not be asked to contribute if giving up the land brought them down to the level of holes. In fact, they were to be allowed a certain margin; they were not expected to offer any land if doing so brought them down below an average yield of 2.8 *dan*.

Finally, the straightforward surplus middle peasants, whose fortunate position was due neither to having overfanshenned nor to holding heirless land, were not to be called on unless their average yield was at least one-third above 2.72 *dan*. In other words, they had to have more than 3.6 *dan* per head before being asked to offer any land.

The peasant-union members in each section called a series of meetings to mobilize the three types of potential donors. At the Fort's meeting on April 2, about eighty men and forty women crowded into the meeting hall. The team members, the genial Geng Xi and Zhang, the district cadre, were present but took no active part. The chairmanship of the meeting was shared by two poor peasants—the young oil-press worker Fu Chan-ting and the young but toothless Fu Bian-de—and one new middle peasant, the Party member Li Bao-en, who had suffered so bitterly during the famine of 1942.

Since his wife was busy making shoes, Li Bao-en held his youngest child in his arms as he called the meeting to order. He made it clear that the land was to be given voluntarily—that the search for earth to fill the holes was in no sense a struggle. He defined the three categories of people who would be called on and stated what their minimum yield should be. Finally he asked for volunteers.

The intensive self-examination and severe criticism that Li Bao-en had undergone during the period of education had sapped his self-confidence, so that his remarks were a mechanical repetition of the regulations rather than an inspiring appeal. But even so there was a ready response: the new middle peasant Li Qi-min immediately rose to make an offer of land.

Thumbing through the pile of land records in front of him, the clerk of the meeting found Li Qi-min's name and read out the names of his fields and the details of his economic situation. A moment's clicking on the abacus revealed that the average yield for each member of the family was 3.74 *dan*.

At first, opinion on the offer was divided. Some said that the offer was suitable because the family's yield was above the 3.6 *dan* standard set. Others pointed out that Li Qi-min had not acquired his land by getting an unfair share of the struggle fruits. He had bought it with the proceeds from his own industry and thrift after the Eighth Route Army came. Besides, as one man said, he was only a fraction above the standard, "and if we took his whole surplus, it would come to only half a *mu*." In the end, the sense of the meeting was that those who had acquired their surplus land through the struggles or through inheritance should contribute earth to the holes first. So for the time being, the offer of the industrious new middle peasant was turned down.

The next offer was from the former rich peasant (now an old middle peasant) Fu Xin, once the owner of the building in which the meeting was held. Evidently he felt that it would be best to make himself inconspicuous, so he whispered his offer to Li Bao-en. But the chairman insisted that he speak up.

"Well," he said, "I'd like to offer my North Pond plot. It's 2.2 *mu*." There was no need for him to add that it was fertile land; everybody knew. Somehow Fu Xin had managed to hold onto good land in spite of all the struggles.

"How much land have you got altogether? What's your total yield?" the crowd asked.

The clerk consulted the records. There were nine people in Fu Xin's family, and the total holding was 27.3 *mu*. The average yield per *mu* being exceptionally high, the total came to 29.15 *dan*, an average yield per head of 3.24 *dan*. And since the land was uniformly good, the production costs and expenditure of labor were low. The family was decidedly prosperous by local standards.

Nevertheless, the principle was that except in the case of those who had overfanshenned or held heirless land, only those with an average yield of 3.6 *dan* per head should give any up. So at first most of the spokesmen favored turning the offer down. But Fu Xin insisted, evidently intent on winning approval of the people who controlled the new society. Convinced of his determination, the crowd accepted the land.

An excited buzz of talk filled the room. Fu Chan-ting rose to his feet and walked here and there among the crowd, calling, "Come on, who's next to offer land? Who's next?"

The seventy-four-year-old Li Li-zi, who had wrongly reported himself as a hole not long before, now offered a plot of 5.3 *mu*. The people accepted only 1.8 *mu* of it, which left him at just the required standard.

At last, in spite of the social approval that accompanied offers of land, they began to taper off. When no more were forthcoming, people began eyeing each other as if they were looking to see who had more land than he needed.

Some peasants with a surplus were conspicuous by their absence. For instance, Duan Shou-yu, whose holdings were well above average, was nowhere to be seen. Earlier he had been nominated by the Fort as a candidate for the new peasant-union committee, but at the election meeting he had been criticized for putting his own interests above those of the village. He had come out toward the bottom in the voting. Now, reluctant to offer any surplus land and eager to avoid criticism for his selfishness, he had chosen to go off on a coal-carrying expedition.

But Li Wei-cheng, the prosperous owner of the Fort's fine meeting hall, had put in an appearance. His family averaged 4.5 *dan* per head, besides owning a good strong mule, and expectant eyes were being turned toward him. At last he rose to speak.

"All of us agree that labor is the main thing in deciding whether a man is entitled to his land or not. And I think everyone here knows the story of my land. My third brother used to spend as much as a silver *yuan* a day on heroin. In the end he mortgaged every scrap of his land for 270 *yuan*. And when all that was used up, he went off to Shanxi; nobody's heard of him since.

"I redeemed his land with the sweat of my brow. For years I worked and saved in Manchuria until I could scrape together enough to pay off the mortgage."

Clearly Li Wei-cheng did not want to give up the land. But it was obvious that with a little urging he would offer some of his surplus plots. Bearing in mind the principle that gifts must be voluntary, Li Bao-en suggested that discussion on this case be put aside. If enough land was offered by more enthusiastic givers, there was no need to embarrass one so halfhearted. If there was a shortage of land in the end, Li Wei-cheng's case could be reopened.

Among the holders of heirless land, some volunteered it readily; others could hardly bring themselves to, even though they had no genuine claim to it.

Li Xin, for example, had gained possession of 1.6 *mu* after paying for the burial of the former owner, an old woman who was a distant relative. He gave the land up soon after the meeting opened. In contrast, Fu Wei-shan, another peasant who was in the same situation, kept putting off the fateful moment. When further delay seemed impossible, he rose reluctantly to his feet. He talked about his yield, landholdings, and general economic situation for several minutes, then started to sit down, mumbling something about the people making whatever decision they thought fit. Li Bao-en feared that if things were left this way, the man might complain afterwards that his gift had not been voluntary. Li therefore called on Fu Wei-shan for a straightforward proposal.

Unable to evade any longer, Fu said, "None of my own land is any good for wheat. So what I'd like to do is to give up 2 *mu* of my own land which isn't so good and keep the heirless land." If he contributed his 5 *mu* of heirless land, his family would fall below the 2.8 *dan* minimum and become a hole. Yet if he kept it, they would average 3.5 *dan* per head—well above the average. He compared his case with that of Li Wei-cheng, which had been put on one side.

"The land that Li Wei-cheng redeemed after his brother's death wasn't counted as heirless, was it?" he asked. "So why should this 5 *mu* that belonged to my uncle?" The uncle had died many years before and left the land to his son. Then the son had died, and Fu Wei-shan had paid for his burial and held the land ever since.

The discussion which followed focused on a point which Fu Wei-shan had obscured: although it was true that Li Wei-cheng had acquired his brother's land without being his descendant, he had acquired it at the heavy cost of his own labor.

Fu Wei-shan grudgingly admitted that the two cases were not quite the same, and he agreed that he ought to give up his heirless land. To avoid making him into a hole, the people suggested that he should give up only 3 *mu* of it, and that his ownership of the remaining two should be legally confirmed.

But Fu Wei-shan's case did not end there, as he discovered when the meeting adjourned for lunch. He had recently married Su Wei-chun, the lively and attractive nineteen-year-old who had just been elected head of the women's committee in the Fort. Now she felt humiliated that her husband should have been so miserly about giving up their heirless land. She had not criticized her husband in public, but back in their own courtyard she gave him a piece of her mind.

The result was that the moment the afternoon session started, Fu was on his feet offering the remaining 2 *mu* of heirless land. But the people stood by the morning's decision, pointing out that it was no use making the family a hole.

The meetings in Fort and Street went on for the whole day. In some cases land was contributed only after a long conflict in the mind of the giver or among the members of his family. In others the offer was made unhesitatingly and with good grace.

Some donors set special conditions. The widow Xin Ai-zi, who lacked labor power, offered three plots of land, two of them with no strings attached, but the third was grave-site land, however, and she asked that it be distributed to some poor member of her own clan.

Wang Cheng-yi, a man of sixty or so, also made a conditional gift. "I'd like to give something," he said, "but I want it to be that plot up on the Yangyi Plateau. I'm getting on a bit now, and I find it a hard climb."

One old middle peasant, after weighing the matter with infinite care, had decided that by giving up a certain plot he wouldn't lose too much, for he would be cutting down on his labor costs as well as on taxes. "I suppose I could just about spare that plot of land," he said, with his enthusiasm well under control, "but of course I'd have to cut down the cedrela tree. It's a valuable piece of timber."

One of the young poor peasants said angrily, "Those old middle peasants! What a calculating bunch they are! So stingy they'd cut down a single tree no bigger around than your thumb."

"Pipe down," growled an older man beside him. "What are you trying to do, start trouble?"

Another old middle peasant helped smooth things out. He had been one of the first in his section to offer land; now he said, "I forgot to make clear when I offered my land that the trees go with it." There was a burst of clapping. It was clear that the majority of the poor peasants wanted to display their unity with the middle peasants.

The same old middle peasant then made a suggestion. "I think we should come to a definite arrangement about trees. We shouldn't cut down any that bear fruit, or any that are smaller around than this." He held up his hands with the thumbs and the index fingers touching, and there were murmurs of approval.

Some well-to-do middle peasants with holdings considerably above the average were still not willing to part with their land. One of these was Wang Xi-cai, whose average yield was one of the highest in the village. "I get a pretty fair yield from my land," he said with cautious understatement, "so I suppose you're thinking that I ought to give something. The problem is, I have land but I haven't got a wife. It's hard enough to find a wife even when you've got a decent bit of land," he went on sadly. "If I gave my land away, I'd never find one." With a troubled smile Wang Xi-cai looked around the hall.

"True enough," said a new middle peasant in his thirties. "Wives are harder to come by than land, these days."

The people laughed, and Wang Xi-cai was left with his holdings intact. It was agreed that he had a reasonable case.

Even without him, there proved to be enough donors. By the evening of April 2 all the sections had handed in the lists of their members who had offered land. Thirty-eight peasants were willing to contribute a total area of 116.2 *mu*. Since only about 90 *mu* were needed, Ten Mile Inn had found the earth to fill its holes.

# —26—

# Filling the Holes

## April 3–7

By the time the families that were genuine holes had been agreed upon by the people's congress and a corresponding quantity of earth had been found, the half-month period in April known as Clear-and-Bright was not far off. This was the traditional time for sowing the staple crop of millet. At the very beginning of the campaign the border-region government had promised that whoever was in possession of the land on the first day of Clear-and-Bright would reap the crop. Now it was only a few days away, and the joint committee decided to put aside all business except that of "holes" and "earth." Tools, cloth, clothing, and grain could be distributed later.

On the afternoon of April 3 the joint committee and people's congress met with the holes to arrange the allocations—to decide which piece of earth was to go into which hole. First the five sections met separately in different parts of the temple grounds to make preliminary decisions. The sun beat down so strongly that each section sought some shady recess in the temple courtyards or buildings. The hole families and people's congress representatives of the south-end section sat under the eaves of the entrance pavilion, catching the breeze which blew up the valley and through the open temple gates. The Fort's six representatives and its dozen hole families crowded into one of the small pavilions.

Although the pavilion was used every day by the village school as a classroom, it was still cluttered with incense-burner pedestals, old stone monuments, and even a large, empty coffin. Unperturbed by the unconventional furnishings and the crowd of people, some of the schoolchildren continued to practice writing their characters.

One by one the names were read from the list of holes. The reader was the onetime rich peasant Li Wei-shu, who used to be a schoolteacher. Now that he had been taken back into the village family, the people were glad to make use of his literacy. His manner conveyed a mixture of modesty and satisfaction as he read the names and particulars of everyone on the list, pausing after each to allow discussion.

One of the first names Li Wei-shu came to was his own. In the village records he had no land at all, for he tilled nothing but reclaimed hillside plots, which were not counted. Officially speaking, the former rich peasant's son was thus landless, and it had been recommended that 9 *mu* be given to his family of three.

"He's young, and so's his wife," someone said. "There's no problem of labor. Let's give him some good land and some bad."

"I'm not so concerned about how much land I get," Li Wei-shu broke in, "as about how many pieces it's in. I've got scraps of land on practically every hilltop. Last year I wore myself out going up and down from one plot to the other, and in the end I got no crop worth bothering about."

An elderly peasant, lean and hardened by toil, was unmoved. He looked patronizingly at the scrawny young teacher and said, "That's just what you need to toughen you up."

Another poor peasant could not refrain from driving the lesson home: "Now you know what our lives were like in the past!"

Li Wei-shu nodded, but said nothing.

The villagers agreed that Li Wei-shu ought to receive 3 *mu* of good land with a yield of 1 *dan* per *mu*; 4 *mu* of middling land with a yield of 0.7 *dan* per *mu*, and to toughen him up, 2 *mu* of poor land with a yield of only 0.5 *dan* per *mu*. This would put the household on a sound economic basis as soon as the first harvest from the new land came in, and Li Wei-shu seemed content with the decision.

The south-end section, which was meeting in the temple gateway, was considering the case of the former rich-peasant heroin dealer Wang Ying-xiang. He too had no land, but instead of reclaiming hillside plots as the ex-schoolteacher had done, Wang Ying-xiang had been living off his relatives. It was suggested that he be given 3 *mu* with a total yield of 3 *dan*.

Wang Ying-xiang seemed unsure whether to retain his old disgruntled and defiant manner or to adopt some different attitude. He evidently thought that there was bound to be some catch to the offer. "The land will be no good," he muttered.

There was a chorus of protest: "What do you mean, no good? 3 *mu* yielding 3 *dan*?"

"Of course it will be good land." And so it was, by local standards.

"Well, it will be a long way from the village, and all in scattered plots."

There were smiles at his skepticism, but someone said reassuringly,

"No, no. You'll get some land that's both good and not too far away. Don't be so worried!"

With a cynical scowl on his unshaven face Wang Ying-xiang lapsed into silence. He was eventually given 2.5 *mu* of the best land in the village—Green Cliff Mound—with a total yield of 2.875 *dan*, a little above the minimum standard.

The new vice-head of the village, Wang Wen-sheng, was making the rounds of the section meetings to see how things were going. He happened to be listening at the time, so when the discussion ended he drew Wang Ying-xiang aside to convince him that everything was open and aboveboard. But whether or not he made any impression was impossible to tell from Wang's face.

The preliminary meetings were soon over, and within an hour everything was ready for the all-section meeting. The hole families, together with the people's congress representatives and the members of the joint committee, crowded into one of the lower temple courtyards where there was shade from the sun. Some people sat on the steps or porches of the surrounding buildings; others squatted on bricks in the center of the courtyard. Classes were still going on in one of the adjoining rooms, and the peasant-union chairman Wang Xi-tang made his opening remarks to the chant of lessons recited in youthful voices.

"Everyone must have his class point of view," said Wang Xi-tang, "and his brotherhood point of view. For all the poor are of one family.

"If you aren't satisfied with the decisions that are made, you should say so right away. Don't wait till the meeting's over and then go around grousing.

"Of course all the holes want good land. But good land is scarce; it's poor land that's plentiful. So those who already have some land which is good or close to their homes will have to be satisfied with land which is poor or a long way off. A demand for a plot of good land by a person who already has good land will have to be turned down.

"Every person should compare his own situation with that of other families in the village."

Sitting at two tables in the center of the courtyard, the clerks with their records became the focus of attention when Wang Xi-tang had finished. One of them read a name from the list of holes which had been approved by the congress and the joint committee. A second read from the land records and census sheets the number of people in the family and their present holdings. The first then stated the area of land and yield which had been recommended to fill the hole. A third clerk ran his eye down the list of plots which had been offered until he came to some that seemed suitable. He read out their names, area, and yield, and the representative and committee members voiced their approval or disapproval. This procedure was soon working smoothly.

The meeting was run by Wang Xi-tang, assisted by the village head Zhao Zhen-fang and the poor-peasant league chairman Li Bao-yu. Much of the time the inexperienced Zhao Zhen-fang stood diffidently at Wang Xi-tang's elbow, as if trying to absorb Wang's confident manner. The new village head still looked very much the poor peasant. He was wearing his winter jacket, which was splitting at the seams because he had no wife to mend it.

There was a conspicuous absence of work team members at the meeting. Now and then one of them dropped in to see how things were going, but took no part in the proceedings.

One of the first cases to be considered was that of the poor-peasant oil-press worker, Fu Chan-ting. His section had decided that he should be given a plot with a yield of 1.1 *dan*.

The clerk with the list of patches said, "Here's a 1.9-*mu* plot of Mother Wang's land with a total yield of 1.3 *dan*."

The chairman said, "He should get a 1.1 *dan* yield, so that land would give him two bushels more than we decided."

But there was no field producing exactly 1.1 *dan*. "What's two bushels? Let it pass," was the general verdict.

One clerk jotted down Fu Chan-ting's name opposite the title of the field, while another with the list of holes wrote: "Mother Wang's Land, 1.9 *mu*" opposite Fu's name.

The next case, that of the wounded ex-soldier Zhao Tang-zi, was presented by Wang Xi-tang himself. "Zhao Tang-zi is a retired-and-honorable veteran." This was the phrase applied to former servicemen who had been wounded in action. "We must pay special attention to his needs, for he's weak from shedding blood. We should give him good land nearby, a good house, and enough tools."

No one questioned this statement. Among the general murmuring of "Of course that's right" and "It's only our duty," a concrete suggestion was heard: "Let's give him Green Cliff Mound Field. It's 4.7 *mu* with a yield of 1.17 *dan* a *mu*. And we can add Back o' the Mountain Field, which is 3.4 *mu* with a yield of 0.98 *dan* per *mu*."

This was agreeable to everyone, including Zhao himself. Together with what he already had, it made him decidedly well off by the standards of Ten Mile Inn.

Some cases were extremely complex. Wang Yuan-de, for example, had always bitterly disliked his father, and when his mother died and the father remarried, he found his home unbearable. A division of the family was agreed upon, but the son got no good land from it. He was now a hole, while his father had an annual yield slightly higher than average.

The congress and joint committee proposed that the father give 2 *mu* of land yielding 2.1 *dan* to the son. One of the relatives, however, raised such a storm of protest over the decision that the case was referred to the poor-peasant league committee for investigation.

At the session of April 4, the poor-peasant league chairman Li Bao-yu reported his findings:

"I visited and talked with every member of the family, young and old, men and women, and found out the real state of affairs. Then I talked over the findings with the league committee members and we all agree, now, that it would be a mistake to order the father to give land to his son. We recommend that Wang Yuan-de be given 2 *mu* yielding 2.1 *dan*, but that the land be taken from the patches."

The league's investigation showed that the family was torn by feuds and conflicts, and that a delicate adjustment had been made in which Wang Yuan-de's father and two uncles shared the expense of supporting their aged mother. Her meals were prepared in rotation by the three daughters-in-law. Part of the father's land was in fact the grandmother's old-age allowance, so that if land were taken from the father, the balance would be upset and the problem of the old woman's support would again arise.

The league committee decided that it would be a mistake to insist on the original plan and recommended that Wang Yuan-de be given his land from the village pool, not from his father's holdings. Everyone agreed, and the Wang family's fragile internal arrangements were maintained.

In the case of the newly returned emigrant Li Meng-xian, his section recommended that because he was old, the land given him should be good, and because he was single, it should be near his home so that he could get back and forth to prepare his meals. The section spokesman also pointed out that according to the classification he was a handicraft worker rather than a farmer, for during his seventeen years in Shanxi he had earned his living largely from work in pottery kilns. The section had decided that he could still make something from his craft and so would not need a full share of land.

In the big meeting, however, someone pointed out that under the agrarian law single people could receive a double share of land if it was available. The law made this provision because the basic economic unit of peasant society was the family, and the plight of single people was exceptionally difficult. The meeting finally reached a compromise in which Li was given two plots—one of Mother Wang's land, one of Old Flat Graveyard—which were close to his home in the Fort and which had a total yield of just over 4 *dan*.

The old man had been nervous about coming back home. After all, he did have 2 *mu* up in the highlands, and he was afraid of burning his boats. Now he would receive twice as much as he had left behind, and he would be able to end his days among his boyhood friends. For the rest of the meeting he sat smoking contentedly, the three-year-old grandson of a neighbor on his knees.

As time passed there was less and less good, close land for distribution, and several holes refused to accept what was offered them. When the clerk suggested that Wang Shen-chuan be given a field high up in the hills to fill his 3-*mu* hole, Wang said, "I won't take it. The field I have is high enough as it is." And he stalked angrily toward the door.

The clerk read further down the list and suggested Western Slope Field. But Wang Shen-chuan shook his head, saying, "I don't have enough labor for that." It was clear that he did not want to be bothered with land which was not easy to work.

Someone asked, "Why did you register yourself as a hole, if you don't want land?"

For the moment this case was put aside, but Wang Shen-chuan's attitude seemed to be catching. People began to turn down the land that was offered to them.

After a couple of these refusals the team member Wu Xiang, who had been looking on, warned the villagers, "This isn't going to happen again next year. You'll have to make up your minds now whether you want the land or not. It's your last chance."

The spell was finally broken by the Party member Wang Wen-tang, who was offered a plot in Peach Gully on the outer periphery of the village's land. Far from raising any objection, he agreed readily.

Another Communist bent on setting a good example was the branch secretary Wang Shao-zhen, who had insisted on giving up 2.4 *mu* of good land which he had acquired during a previous campaign. Now his household of six needed 4 *dan* a year to bring them up to standard.

"Since he's a hole," someone said, "it would be better for him to keep that land he gave up."

Wang Shao-zhen protested that he would not take it back, because he set his political reputation above the ownership of land. Yet since his 4-*dan* deficit had to be made up somehow, in the end he agreed to take that field but to allow part of it to be used as a pathway to a neighboring plot. This still left him with a hole, which was finally filled with another 2 *mu*. The conduct of the village Communists, contrast ing as it did with that of the disgruntled minority who rejected what was offered them, helped to reestablish the Party members' prestige.

The task of adjusting landholdings was completed just in time for the spring sowing of millet. Early next morning, people streamed out to their fields to get on with farm work.

When the immediate rush was over, the village government turned to the problem of filling the housing holes. For days the joint committee members and representatives of the people's congress had been gathering information to supplement the village records. The records showed the number of housing "sections" per family, but did not take it into account that a room might contain anything from one section to five or six. Although a family might have a reasonable number of sections, the rooms might not be laid out to ensure proper segregation of the sexes. A mother might have to share a room with her grown-up sons, or a father-in-law with his daughter-in-law.

After investigation, self-report by the holes, and study of the records, it was estimated that 200 sections of housing were required by sixty to seventy families. There were about thirty families whose need was urgent.

During the Feudal Tails Campaign a considerable amount of housing belonging to the struggle objects had been earmarked for distribution to poor peasants. But before that could happen, the border-region government moved into the locality. It needed space for offices: for the South Hebei Bank, for a reception center for students and others newly arrived from the Guomindang areas, for a transit center for old and wounded soldiers being demobilized from the Liberation Army, and for the Liberated Areas Relief Association. So the Ten Mile Inn peasant union had decided to postpone the housing adjustment. Thus the feudal tails, instead of giving up their houses to the poor peasants, gave them up to the border-region government.

This had happened in the spring of 1947. The winter would normally have been the time for repairing old houses and building new ones. But the poor-peasant line had been at its height during the winter of 1947, and peasants with the means to improve their housing were reluctant to do so. They were afraid that another struggle was in the offing, and that all the houses they had built or repaired would be taken away from them. The Ten Mile Inn housing situation had thus gone from bad to worse.

Now in April 1948, when it was time to fill the housing holes, no one knew that by May the Liberation Army would have gained so much territory that the border-region capital would be moved further north. Since they could not foresee that some hundred rooms would soon be vacated, the village cadres and committee members were at their wits' end to find housing. After a long and stormy committee meeting, the village head Zhao Zhen-fang said in despair, "I'd rather have been carrying loads of muck to the fields these last four hours than sitting around on my backside worrying these things out."

Finally on the afternoon of April 6 a meeting was called of all peasants who had surplus housing which they might be willing to offer to fill the holes. And that evening the five sections held meetings at which their members reported on their housing requirements. Some asked for outright allocations, others for exchanges which would give them a more suitable layout of rooms.

The proportion of women present at the section meetings was strikingly high. Obviously they felt deeply concerned about the housing situation, and many of them who were normally reserved plucked up courage to make their own reports of their families' needs.

Difficulties and dissatisfaction were unavoidable; there were too many holes and too few rooms. It proved impossible to suit everyone, and a few of the holes grumbled about the solutions proposed.

Zhao Zhen-fang appeared worried because people were dissatisfied with the way things were run now that he was village head. And he could not lean on the experienced Wang Xi-tang, who was ill.

"We'll never solve all these problems," Zhao sighed. "If only Xi-tang weren't ill, everything would have been worked out all right!"

"It isn't that Wang Xi-tang's so much cleverer than we are," protested Li Bao-yu, whose attitude was not so dependent. "It's the shortage of housing! He'd have a hard time of it too, if he were here."

The vice-head of the village, Wang Wen-sheng, agreed that the housing problem was practically impossible. "All we have to distribute is a little clear soup," he said. "There's nothing solid at all."

Nevertheless, they did succeed in easing the housing situation, which improved further that spring after the border-region government moved. And later, during the next slack farming season, the peasants also began to repair their houses and build new ones.

Meanwhile, to conclude the land adjustment before the Clear-and-Bright season, the clerks of the village office gathered for the last time in the village government premises. These were to be given over for family residences on the following day. In the flicker of oil lamps and with the clicking of half a dozen abacuses, the clerks calculated the results of the adjustment. Working far into the night, they prepared tables that were posted throughout the village so that everyone could see the results. Over 100 families had received land, and roughly 250 *mu* had been distributed.

As far as the new middle peasants were concerned, their standard had changed little. On the one hand, a number of them who had overfanshenned voluntarily returned land which they had received in previous campaigns. On the other hand, a number of them who were holes received land.

Among the 82 struggle-object families who were now accepted as members of the village masses, only 24 had been reduced to the status of holes. Although they made up less than a quarter of all families receiving land in the adjustment, they received almost a third of the plots that were distributed—81.7 *mu*, yielding 78.4 *dan*.

The two remaining landlord and rich-peasant families, though they received the least land in the village, had enough to get along on. They would have been given more, but neither family had the labor to cultivate it.

Finally, the old middle peasants still had a per capita yield above the average for the village. But whereas they had formerly surpassed it by almost five bushels, now they exceeded it by less than three.

The public announcement of these results took place on April 9, 1948. It was a day suitable for a village meeting, for though the rain had stopped at last, the soil was still too soft and sticky to work. The peasants were well satisfied with the weather. "Rain in spring is as precious as oil," they said. The prospect of good crops created a festive atmosphere.

The new ownership of land and houses was jointly proclaimed by the peasant union and the poor-peasant league. Thus the new land rights were publicly confirmed and all old deeds nullified.

"There's bound to be a certain amount of dissatisfaction with the results," said Wang Xi-tang. "That can't be avoided. Even when we go to the fair and buy a leather tiger for our babies, we pick and choose and think afterwards that we might have struck a better bargain. But we've done the job ourselves, all together, so if there's anything wrong, we've only ourselves to blame.

"Now we'll read out the results in full—how much housing and land was needed, where everything came from, and how it was distributed."

As the list was read by the clerk and the full scope of the accomplishment became clear, the crowd's good spirits rose. They reached a peak when Wang Xi-tang announced:

"The land on the list came from various sources: from the county and the village, from emigrant and heirless families. But some of it came from a very special source. This is the land voluntarily given up by our brothers, the middle peasants. Their generosity shows that we laboring people are all of one family, and they have acted toward the poor peasants like elder to younger brothers. Now we'll read out their names, one by one."

As each of the middle-peasant donors was named, there was a burst of clapping.

"This land which the middle peasants have given," concluded Wang Xi-tang, "was earned in the sweat of their brow. They offered it of their own free will to help their poor brothers fanshen. This is a noble deed! In the future, if any of these who offered land should find himself in difficulty, we must help him and look after him."

# —27—

# Making Bygones Bygones

April 9

For three weeks the cases of the former cadres Wang Ke-bin and Fu Gao-lin had been left in abeyance, because they had aroused such intense feeling that the work team decided they were diverting attention from the main task of adjusting land ownership.

Now that the holes had been filled, however, a meeting was held in the temple courtyard to consider their cases. The team member Leng Bing was called upon to speak.

"In talking over the case of Wang Ke-bin," he began, "some people have been saying, 'Better send him to the people's court'—as if that were some sort of punishment. But the people's court is only a place where one can lodge complaints, lay bare the facts, and plead a cause.

"Others have been saying, 'It doesn't make any difference whether we send him to the people's court or keep him here in the village. It's all the same. There's only one aim—to reform him.'

"And some think differently again. They say, 'Let's not send him to the people's court. Keep him here. He'll get the same sort of education both ways. Even if he does go to the court, he'll probably be sent back soon, perhaps after doing some labor service for the county. So we might just as well settle things in our own village and let him do some work for the soldiers' families here.'

"I agree entirely with this last idea. I think that the only purpose of this meeting is to have Wang Ke-bin reform himself.

"Now let him speak for himself." Turning to Wang Ke-bin, who was waiting at the foot of the porch steps, Leng concluded:

"Wang Ke-bin, now the time has come for you to confess your errors before the masses. Be frank, and hold nothing back. The people will be watching you, listening to you. Everything depends upon your attitude."

The last three weeks had changed the tiger Wang Ke-bin. His talks

233

Wang Ke-bin, former village head, reads a confession of past misdeeds. Wang Wen-sheng presides over the meeting.

with the team members, who had questioned him about the accusations which the villagers had made to them in private; the peasants' criticism and his self-criticism at the public meeting; the indignity of sweeping the village street—all these had taxed his endurance and his lifelong attitudes. His hair, streaked with grey, was tousled, his beard unkempt, his face thinner and more deeply lined. He moved forward, nervously trying to straighten several sheets of paper which were blowing in the wind. As he tried to make them out, two deep vertical furrows appeared between his brows. He spoke in a low, hesitant voice.

"I know no characters," he said, "but let me try to read from this draft, which has been written for me by someone else." The statement that he knew no characters was a piece of formal politeness, a show of modesty. In fact, his public display of the art of reading did something to preserve what little was left of his prestige.

Wang Ke-bin's confession, however, was no formality. He listed twenty-five items which, he said, covered "my evil doings of the past."

". . . Item Five . . . He didn't obey me, so I made him 'walk the streets.' [That is, the man had to go through the village with a paper cap on his head and beating a gong to draw attention to his wrongdoing.] Afterwards he fled.

"Item Six . . . He disobeyed my orders, so I had him tied up and hung from a beam."

He read quietly and haltingly, explaining now and then that the writing, not being his own, was difficult to read. There were constant cries from the crowd and from Leng Bing and the chairman, Wang Wen-sheng, that he speak up. But Wang Ke-bin either would not or could not raise his voice, and could not or would not do without his notes. He stumbled on to the end, relating how harshly he had suppressed pilfering of crops during the famine years, and how he had eaten dumplings in the homes of the landlords and rich peasants. He itemized the bribes and "gifts" he had extorted from the people:

"I made 50 *yuan* out of the divorce and marriage of Fu Tien-yin, and 1 foot, 2 inches, of white cloth from the wife of Li Shao-niu.

"How did I do this? To legalize a marriage or divorce, everyone had to come to me to put the official seal on the certificate."

Wang Ke-bin summed up his behavior in the last item on his list: "I abused and struggled against anyone who didn't keep on the right side of me."

As the prospect of winning acceptance in the new life of the village opened up before him, Wang Ke-bin's voice regained something of its old fire. Putting aside his notes for the first time, he said:

"Of my own free will I should like to offer three cows—one full-grown, one heifer, and one calf; also three sections of housing and a mill."

He had already made it clear to the work team that although he was willing to give up three of his four animals, he wanted to keep his packsaddle. Obviously he had no intention of lapsing into inactivity, but planned to devote his energies to production.

He concluded: "And I'd like to offer to do four or five days' labor for the village, cultivating soldiers' land or building up terrace walls.

"From now on I will correct my mistakes. I will not seek revenge against anyone, and I will act according to the wishes of the people. If I don't do this, it will be adding a new crime to the old ones. From now on I'll be simple and honest and follow the masses to the end."

"Have you finished?" asked the village head Zhao Zhen-fang.

"That's all I have to say. I can't think of anything more."

"Then now is the time for anyone to express an opinion."

"From the way you talk," said Li Bao-xu, one of Wang Ke-bin's old rivals, "anyone would think you'd never done anything wrong. Your self-criticism isn't complete by a long shot."

"Mothers! Some people are never satisfied," someone exclaimed. There were mutters of disapproval from various parts of the crowd.

"What point do you have in mind that he's left out?" asked Leng Bing.

Li Bao-xu hesitated. His friend Wang Er-xi, who was sitting beside him and who was also a bitter enemy of Wang Ke-bin, chimed in: "What about my wife? If she'd had no letter from you, she'd never have been granted a divorce by the district."

"It's true I gave her a letter from the village office," said Wang Ke-bin, showing something of his old spirit. "She came to me and asked me to grant her a divorce. I said I couldn't deal with a matter of that sort myself, but that I'd give her a letter to the district and they could handle it. So that's what I did."

"That's a lie," said Li Bao-xu. "It wasn't that way at all."

"How do you know it wasn't?" shouted someone in the crowd, expressing the general lack of sympathy for these old militants who were out to pay off ancient scores against Wang Ke-bin.

"Someone told me," Li Bao-xu said lamely.

"Who told you? What did he say?" came cries from several parts of the courtyard.

"I know something about that," said Fu Gao-lin, who was waiting his turn to make his own confession. "Er-xi's wife went to the district for a divorce and said that he was a puppet soldier.* At the time Er-xi said to me, 'You see the way she carries on; I can't do a thing with her. Better let her go her own way. I don't care, so long as I get a little compensation.' "

"I never got any compensation," shouted Wang Er-xi angrily.

At that Fu Gao-lin rose to his full, imposing height and said, "I handed the money to your mother, and you counted it out in front of me."

"Who can prove it?" asked Wang Er-xi.

The Party member Wang Kui-ming bore out Fu Gao-lin's statement. "He received the money all right, and he put his thumbprint on the receipt."

The crowd shouted at Li Bao-xu, "Pipe down," and "Shut up," and "You're talking a lot of nonsense," as well as some stronger expressions.

As the uproar increased, an extraordinary thing happened. The team leader Lou Lin, who had always remained quietly in the background, strode along the porch to the head of the steps. "There's no place here for those who are after revenge," he shouted in a powerful and commanding voice. "If that's what you want—get out! We want Wang Ke-bin to reform. We want to educate him. Not to blow like a hurricane through the grass."

The whole village was surprised, but most people agreed with what Lou Lin had said.

The hubbub died down. The grudge bearers lapsed into silence, and the rest of the villagers continued discussing Wang Ke-bin's proposals for his punishment.

"Even if he did pay back all the money he grafted, it wouldn't be worth a *jin* of salt today. Better have him give compensation in terms of millet," said the hardheaded animal dealer Li Bao-hui.

There was some discussion of the price of millet when Wang Ke-bin had been in office.

* I.e., he had fought with the Japanese forces against his own people.

"If he coughs up all he swallowed and three cows, three sections of housing, and a mill into the bargain," a peasant said, "he'll become a hole."

"It's not compensation that's most important. It's his reformation."

"The question is, will he be able to reform himself?"

"I think he'll manage all right. He made a pretty good confession."

"And the punishment he suggested was suitable, too."

"Yes, the punishment's all right."

It was Wang Ke-bin himself who rounded off the discussion. "I promise never to seek revenge," he said. "When the struggles were going on, I struggled against all kinds of people. I didn't stop to think whether they were landlords or poor peasants. That's where my wrong-doing lies. From now on I must take a proper class stand and pay attention to the simple-and-honest peasants."

The sun was already sinking as Wang Ke-bin's case came to a close.

Fu Gao-lin was next, but his case was soon disposed of. This was partly because it was growing late, partly because Fu Gao-lin, unlike Wang Ke-bin, had refrained from political activity since he was ousted from office, and partly because he had already paid substantial compensation.

When he was called, he paced to the foot of the porch stairs, turned to the crowd, and asked, "Do you want me to go over all my wrong-doing from beginning to end, or only the points which haven't yet been covered?"

"Just the unsettled business," the crowd replied.

Fu Gao-lin stood with his arms folded across his chest and spoke briefly of his harshness during the famine years, of eating dumplings with the landlords, and of urging the wives of the poor to obtain divorces. On points that he overlooked, he was prompted by people in the crowd or by Leng Bing from the platform.

His list soon came to an end, and he too proposed his own punishment. Because his case had mostly been settled, and because his position in the village was already more secure than that of Wang Ke-bin, the compensation he offered was largely a token admission of past guilt and a gesture of good faith.

"I think I should offer 8 jin of grain and ten days' labor as my punishment," he said. "And whatever criticisms are made of me, I promise not to seek revenge. From now on I'll do nothing wrong; I'll follow the wishes of the poor peasants. And if I don't keep my word, let me be punished by the people."

The crowd accepted his punishment and thus brought to a close the case of Fu Gao-lin—and with it the meeting.

# —28—

# Some Problems of Democratic Leadership

The new cadres of Ten Mile Inn, who were anxious to avoid the authoritarianism for which the old ones had been so sternly criticized, usually did not give orders at all. They hesitated to decide anything, no matter how trivial, without submitting their proposal to a mass meeting of the village. Then if any fault were to be found with it, the responsibility belonged to the masses. Even when a majority of villagers agreed upon a certain course of action, the new cadres usually shelved it if one or two people strongly disagreed. The new men had seen only too well how a handful of people with strongly held views could make things hot later for the cadres.

Closely related to the new cadres' avoidance of responsibility was their failure to delegate work. They were in a perpetual rush with routine jobs. The village head Zhao Zhen-fang carried a stretcher, because the man on rear-service duty could not be found; he led the way in digging out a government truck which was stuck on the muddy village street; he hurried around trying to borrow a quilt to lend a passing soldier for the night, though there was a reception center to deal with this; he even made the paste for posting village government announcements. Zhao Zhen-fang was the busiest man in Ten Mile Inn; he was doing everything except lead.

The village vice-head Wang Wen-sheng was second to Zhao Zhen-fang in popularity but excelled him in ability. Wen-sheng was in close touch with the thoughts and feelings of the villagers, especially in his own south-end section. His neighbors sought him out, because they could count on him as an affable, not too critical listener. But though the villagers confided in him, his knowledge of village affairs was limited, since he had lived away from Ten Mile Inn during his many years as a laborer.

Just as Wang Wen-sheng hated to criticize others, he was easily upset if others criticized him. If ninety-nine out of a hundred people approved of his actions, but one disapproved, he was likely to become demoralized. In the old days this quality had made him popular even with the landlords, for he would work himself to the bone rather than risk criticism from an employer whom he despised. The same quality had long delayed his participation in the fanshen movement. And during land adjustment, when the time came for all families to report whether they considered themselves holes, Wang Wen-sheng kept quiet. Poor as he was, he was still afraid that people might accuse him of taking advantage of his position as a cadre.

It was not surprising that men like Wang Wen-sheng and Zhao Zhen-fang, who were mild and kindly to a fault, should have been elected to office. When some people had raised the question of the candidates' ability and experience, the work team stressed the need for cadres who were simple and honest. The team maintained that these were essential qualities, that the other requirements for leadership could be developed with time.

By concentrating on the *laoshi* the team hoped to bring to light whatever talents still lay hidden among the people. But in fact, the masses did not accept this special emphasis on the *laoshi* without some modifications. Zhao Zhen-fang and Wang Wen-sheng were elected cadres because of their popularity; but it was not the masses who had made them head and vice-head of the village. They had been appointed to those posts by a meeting of all the new cadres together with the committees of the league and union. It is true that the masses approved the appointments, but this was more a confirmation of their opinion that Old Zhao and Old Wang were good fellows than an endorsement of their ability.

In voting for other candidates, the peasants showed that they were taking ability and special qualifications into account: for treasurer they elected a man skilled in finance; to direct rear service, a man with experience in it; to organize defense, an Eighth Route Army veteran; and so on. It did not mean that these men were not honest, but it did not mean that they were simple, either. Everyone agreed, for example, that Wang Xi-tang, who was elected chairman of the peasant union, was honest, but no one could claim that he was simple. So for him the villagers used a different word, *zhengpai*, which meant not simple and honest (*laoshi*) but "upright" or "a man of integrity."

The poor-peasant league chairman Li Bao-yu did not strictly belong to either of these categories. He had been active in village affairs for a number of years as head of mutual-aid group 5, where he carried out his duties competently and with the strong support of the group. But he had accepted without question the age-old view that leadership required skill in political maneuvering—in playing off one faction against another. And he succeeded in developing these arts with too much success to be described as simple and honest.

In addition, Li Bao-yu sometimes exhibited a narrow loyalty to his own north-end section at the expense of the rest of the village. He felt that he had been elected largely through the support of his neighbors and that he therefore had special obligations to them. In assessing the housing holes, for example, he passed a number of doubtful cases because they came from his part of the village.

But Li Bao-yu was willing to learn, and in the opinion of the work team he was the ablest of the three chief cadres. He was not so super-sensitive to criticism as the head and vice-head of the village, and he was willing to shoulder responsibility. He had accepted without protest the thorny problem of directing the appraisal of the housing holes—a task that even Wang Xi-tang had shied away from. Further-more, Li Bao-yu was eager to learn the new methods of leadership. As he said toward the end of the land-adjustment period, "I thought making the adjustment would be very simple—that you just had to open the account book, see who's got good land and who bad, who's got more land and who less, and then just even things out. I didn't know about the method of self-report and public appraisal. I found out a lot from the work team about handling affairs."

As for the women's leaders, they were finding that it was much harder to be model leaders than to be model housewives and daughters-in-law. Chen Chui-de of the Fort, who was a member of the committees of both the poor-peasant league and the women's department of the peasant union, could not put her finger on the difficulties in organizing the women. "They just won't come to meetings, that's all," she said. "You have to call them five or six times."

Wang Chui-de, one of the experienced former women's leaders who had been forced to drop out during the Feudal Tails Campaign, said, "The trouble is that these newly elected women don't know how to single out the main problems. They get sidetracked by all sorts of small things. Of course, it's not altogether their fault. They haven't had a chance to go away on a special training course, as we did when the women's association was first set up. So they just lean on the men and echo what they say, and the men don't understand the women's special problems."

Wang Chui-de had plenty of ideas about how to improve things, but though she had just been taken back as a member of the village family after a year as a feudal tail, she said, "Those of us who think we know what the main problems are still feel uncomfortable about pushing ourselves forward."

The reluctance of both men and women leaders to assume responsibility meant that certain difficulties were bound to arise in the political leadership of the village. The chief of these was the difficulty of dealing with the politically backward militants. The problem was not confined to Ten Mile Inn; it was found throughout the district. Zhang Pan-shi of the Region's Party Bureau wrote to the leaders of the work teams under his direction: "Villagers who persist in harboring petty personal prejudices must be taught to accept the decisions of the majority; otherwise ultrademocracy will result. If they don't mend their ways, they should be warned that they may be expelled from the poor-peasant league or the peasant union."

The militants were not so disruptive in Ten Mile Inn as in some of the other villages. After Lou Lin had come back from a meeting at the Party Bureau headquarters in West Harmony, he told the team members:

"In some of the other villages, the militants have been a great drag on the movement. They've even gone so far as to tie people up and beat them, and the masses are afraid of them. Here they're not such a serious problem, although they do give the new cadres a lot of headaches. They're always wanting to reverse decisions which have already been made and reopen problems which have already been solved.

"The trouble with them is their prejudice against certain individuals. They need to be taught that real militants are those who stand with the people, not those who isolate themselves and are domineering."

During the course of the campaign the work team had learned how the old militants were aligned. There were five leading spirits, not counting Wang Ke-bin, who was no longer one of the leaders now that he had been dealt with by the masses. Besides the aggressive Li Xi-jin and Fu Gao-lin's enemy Zhang Zhang-ho, there were Fu Yu-he of the Fort and Wang Chi-shang and Wang Mi-chuan of the Street. Together these five leaders had a dozen or so active henchmen. Finally there were twenty or thirty rank-and-file followers who trailed along behind the others but took no initiative.

On the whole, it was only the five leaders whom the team considered to be inspired by blind prejudice or personal ambition. Most of the henchmen were like Chi Hua-zhan, who liked to speak his mind regardless of the consequences to himself or to the village. Sometimes what he said was to the point, sometimes it was hearsay; sometimes it was based on wild statements made by the leading militants. Thus on some occasions he advanced village democracy, and on others he obstructed it. Some of the villagers praised Chi Hua-zhan, saying, "He's come out with exactly what I had in mind but was afraid to put in words." In fact, it was generally agreed that his words were "strong as a mountain." Others objected, "His words are powerful, all right, but they're not always true." Still others complained among themselves, not only about Chi Hua-zhan but about the activists in general, "They're always hogging the floor. The rest of us can't get a word in edgewise."

The work team eventually decided that the three types of militants —leaders, henchmen, and rank-and-filers—should receive three different types of treatment. All of them were visited by team members, who criticized them and urged them to reform. In addition, at public meetings the leaders and henchmen were always asked to give evidence supporting any statements that they made. This soon checked their irresponsible talk.

Meanwhile the team members pried away rank-and-file followers by explaining to them the origin and harmful effects of factionalism and the way it was kept alive by small cliques. And the team members asked the followers' sections to ferment over them and their destructive activities. The followers could be reached more effectively by public opinion in small-group fermentation than in big village meetings, where the militant leaders might play a dominating role.

The leaders themselves, however, had to be exposed in public whenever the opportunity arose. This more than anything else helped to detach their followers from them. In one of the meetings to appraise hole families, for example, a clique leader who did not like the way things were going decided to break up the meeting by stalking out with all his followers. But the moment he started to do this, a work team member sharply criticized his attempt to force a decision and called on the rank and file not to cut themselves off from the people. The followers soon quietly sat down again, leaving their leader isolated and confused. Li Bao-yu, who had been chairing the meeting, took heart from this and adopted a firmer manner. And since the meeting was no longer dominated by the handful of militants, the more backward peasants began to speak out.

The team members' private conversations with the militants soon began to take effect. Wang Mi-chuan admitted that he talked carelessly and too much, and that it might be a good idea for him to let others have a chance to speak out. Some members of a south-end clique confessed that their complaints about the local Communists were really directed at one Party member against whom they had a grudge. And after a heart-to-heart talk with the militant who was most conspicuously antagonistic to the local Party branch, Fu Yu-he of the Fort, a team member said, "That young fellow has plenty of good stuff in him. We must find a way to win him over."

Wang Chi-shang, however, was angry that a team member had

privately criticized him. He went to Wang Xi-tang for support against what he felt was undue pressure, but instead of supporting him Wang urged him to mend his ways. Wang Chi-shang left the village in a rage, but soon returned a changed man. Whatever had happened to convert him, he was such a reformed character that by the middle of May he was accepted into both the peasant union and the poor-peasant league.

Unfortunately, the burden of educating the militants fell on the work team. The new village cadres felt that the problem was beyond them. Those who had been cadres before, like Li Bao-en of the Fort, were too chastened by the Party education to assert leadership. The only exception was Wang Xi-tang, who had perfected his own method during his years as village head. As he described it: "When I sense that there's going to be some difficulty at a meeting, I always have a private talk beforehand with any people who are likely to make trouble. I ask them their opinions and try to win them over. My experience is that if this is done, the meeting will be orderly and will turn out all right."

The success of Wang Xi-tang's method, however, depended upon his own prestige, which had been built up by years of painstaking work. The new cadres like Zhao Zhen-fang and Wang Wen-sheng found it natural to lean heavily upon him, and the danger was that he would soon dominate everything. It was essential for the fullest development of democracy in the village to shift responsibility in fact as well as in form onto the new cadres.

The formal handing over of office had been delayed, because it was difficult enough to persuade the new cadres to play a leading role in the adjustment of land and houses. With their diffidence and inexperience, it would have been impossible to load them down at the same time with the routine village administration. As the adjustment drew to a close, however, it was time to install the new cadres in office.

The work team and Wang Xi-tang agreed that there should be an impressive ceremony which would convince the villagers of the importance of the occasion. And on April 9, at the village meeting in which the land and housing adjustment results were announced and the cases of Wang Ke-bin and Fu Gao-lin were dealt with, the new cadres formally took office.

First the old village head, Wang Xi-tang, gave details of the accounts and of public property in hand. Everything testified to the honesty of the outgoing village government. Finally Wang announced, "Now I'll ask the peasant union to hand over."

Everyone sat up with attention. Since the peasant union had been

in charge of the past struggles, the undistributed fruits from the previous campaign were in its keeping. The union's clerk announced that
these were all in order and said, "Now I'll read you the summary we've
drawn up. You won't want to be bothered with all the details."

But one or two of the newly fanshenned peasants, determined to
uphold their rights, shouted, "We don't want a summary; read out
the whole thing!"

The clerk laughed good-naturedly and reached for a pile of account
books on the table. He picked up five thick volumes and waved them
around for all to see. Opening one, he ran his finger down the columns
of a closely written page. The demonstration was convincing; the
crowd laughed and agreed that the summary would be enough.

When it had been read, Wang Xi-tang asked the poor-peasant league
committee, which had spent the whole of the previous day checking
the voluminous accounts, if it had any comment to make. The committee's representative stepped up to the table. "All I can say is that
we went around and saw all the things that were stored in the various
houses. They're there, all right, and everything is just the way the books
tell. Anyone who wants to can go and look for himself."

Armfuls of account books, abacuses, and stationery were now
passed by the old cadres over to the new ones. This was the formal
handing over. The old cadres, shedding their burdens of books and
papers together with the burden of office, were happy to have publicly
established that they had been both painstaking and honest. They
called out cheerfully to the crowd, "Go and have a look at our account
books sometime. You know where everything's stored; see it for
yourselves."

The villagers responded amiably, and soon the whole crowd was
talking and laughing, standing on tiptoe and commenting on the expressions of the men who were accepting their instruments of office.
The new cadres alone seemed to regard the moment as a serious one.
In particular Zhao Zhen-fang had a long face when, with all eyes upon
him, he advanced reluctantly to the center of the porch. As Wang
Xi-tang solemnly handed him the box containing the village head's
seal, there was a burst of clapping. Village power was now in the hands
of the newly elected cadres.

# —29—

# The Party Branch
# Faces the Future

## April 10–14

On the evening of April 10, the day after the final adjustment of land and housing, the Party branch held a meeting to which each section was invited to send delegates. The purpose of the meeting was to complete the unfinished business of analyzing the Party members' shortcomings and distinguishing between the serious and the trivial— between those which affected the mass of the people and those of a personal nature.

The people at the meeting decided that some mistakes of the past had been caused by orders from higher levels of the Party which were not based upon sufficient investigation of local conditions. These orders put the Party cadres into an impossible position where they could obey only by resorting to authoritarian methods. For example, Wang Xi-tang had to use compulsion in mobilizing people for stretcher bearing because Ten Mile Inn was asked to do much more than its share of rear service. In addition, the incorrect struggles conducted during the Feudal Tails Campaign had been due mainly to mistaken instructions from above.

In other cases it was decided that directives could have been carried out if the Party cadres had been given more thorough education by their superiors. One cadre, for example, had been impatient and bad-tempered during the work relief campaign owing to lack of education in the mass line.

Circumstances such as those caused by famine or war had also been responsible for some errors. In particular, difficulties in communications had prevented newly formulated Party policies from reaching the village in time to be promptly acted upon. Finally, there were misdeeds for which the individual Party member himself had to accept full responsibility. Buying an unfair amount of struggle fruits was an example of such individual wrongdoing.

Analyzing the Party members' mistakes in this way had two advantages. It helped the Communists themselves to view things objectively and throw off any remnants of despair about their shortcomings. In addition, it gave the people's delegates a greater understanding of the problems which the Communists had had to face and of what they had accomplished.

The next morning the branch met again, this time alone. The desperation that the Communists had felt only a couple of weeks before, when Wang Xi-tang had wanted them to surrender their weapons for fear that some of them might commit suicide, had disappeared. They were all in high spirits. The experience had been grueling, but one Party member expressed the opinion of many: "The Party stands closer to us than our own fathers and mothers," he said. "In the old days when I was a beggar, my parents handed me a bowl, and all they hoped was that I'd beg enough to keep myself alive. Now the Party has not only freed me from feudal exploitation, but set me on the right path in life."

The branch then took up the question of punishments. The Chinese Communist Party had seven classes of disciplinary action: private advice, private warning, public advice, public warning, dismissal from Party office, probation, and most severe, expulsion. As one old peasant in the village had said, "Expulsion from the Party's like a shot through the heart."

The former branch secretary, Wang Shao-zhen, briefly reviewed

Village meeting of the Communist Party.

his faults and recommended his own punishment. He did not spare himself. "You have criticized me for my serious shortcomings," he said without rancor. "During the four years or so that I was political director, I had people tied up and beaten and detained. I sold a rifle and some bullets and helped my brother in that marriage business of his. I ought to be severely punished by the Party. I suggest that I be put on probation."

The branch divided itself into small groups for discussion. When they reassembled, Wang Shao-zhen's group supported his suggestion, but the others disagreed.

"Our group thinks he made a very good self-criticism, and that all he should receive is public warning," said one spokesman.

"His self-criticism and statement to the people's representatives was the best of all," said another. "Our group thinks that all he deserves is private advice."

"He's very young. He hasn't had much experience. We can't suspend his membership, as he suggests. He ought to receive public advice."

"The people are convinced that he can reform. The trouble is that he wasn't given enough education. He ought to receive private advice."

The branch discussed these punishments until fairly general agreement had been reached. Then there was a vote, which was overwhelmingly in favor of public warning.

The next case taken up was that of the public security officer, Wang Lin-yong, who had been criticized for carrying on an adulterous affair as well as for using his position to bully the villagers.

"Our group thinks he should receive a heavier punishment than Wang Shao-zhen," said one spokesman. "He ought to be put on probation."

"That would mean he already had one leg out of the Party."

"We agree with that. He hasn't shown enough improvement following the Party education."

"Our group's of the same opinion. The branch has discussed his immorality several times and has given him a lot of education on the matter. Though he understands it clearly, he doesn't improve." The fact was that Wang Lin-yong had refused to give up his mistress. "But as it's a matter of personal conduct, we think that public warning would be enough." And public warning was the final decision of the branch.

The case of the militia commander, Wang Chi-yong, went much the same way. His returning from the front on the pretext of having injured his leg was considered a serious matter. So was his tendency toward loose talk. It was first recommended that he be put on probation, because he too had made insufficient progress in his Party education. But in the end the branch decided to recommend public warning.

The remaining branch members were considered more in need of further education than anything else. The former peasant-union chairman Fu Zhang-sou, for instance, was regarded as too recent a Party member to be held fully responsible for his mistakes. Others were pronounced free of serious shortcomings. "Their cases can be dealt with by further criticism and self-criticism inside the branch," Li Bao-en suggested, and the others agreed.

The team member Leng Bing brought this phase of the meeting to a close. "I should like to make a suggestion to Comrade Wang Shao-zhen," he said. "I hope that from now on he will weigh his words more carefully. During this movement to educate the Party members he often talked pessimistically to other comrades. He should not have done so.

"As for Comrade Wang Chi-yong, he has a tendency to form a clique among the cadres. He has not yet shown himself to be entirely frank, and he still hasn't made a completely clean breast of things. I hope he will try hard to overcome his failings in future. The punishment you have chosen for him is light."

However, the branch's decision in the case of Wang Chi-yong, as well as in all the other cases, was not final. It was only a recommendation which had to be ratified by the County Committee, which would study the branch's findings and recommendations along with other relevant material and make the final decision.

The question of the Party's relationship to the other organizations in the village was an important one in Ten Mile Inn. By the end of March there were four main attitudes toward this issue among the villagers.

One view was held mostly by the older people whose memories extended back over many stages of Ten Mile Inn's history. Some could still recall what conditions had been like before 1911 under the decaying Manchu empire, and many had vivid memories of the chaotic rule of the warlords which followed the empire's collapse. Still more remembered the hateful period of the Guomindang. These villagers realized that the enormous improvement in their present lives had been brought about by the Communist Party. They wanted the Communist leadership to continue.

A second group of peasants also recognized that the improvements in their lives had been achieved under the leadership of the Communists; but they felt that it was this very leadership which was now delaying their fanshen. They knew that the Party members had taken too much on themselves in the past instead of drawing the broad masses into the struggle. Now they thought it would be better for the Communists to be deprived of leadership altogether. They felt that the Party members were too able and that the masses would never assert or express themselves so long as the Communists retained a position of leadership. They would have preferred to hand this function over to the poor-peasant league.

Then there was the view of Wang Xi-tang, which, like all his views, attracted supporters. He believed that leadership should be placed in the hands of the peasant union, of which he himself was chairman. This did not mean that he was not loyal to the Party or that he placed his own interests above those of the people. His opinion came from his consciousness of his own superior ability. And Wang Xi-tang was without question the most capable cadre of Ten Mile Inn. As the work team gradually withdrew from the direction of village affairs, it was only natural that more and more responsibility was placed upon Wang's experienced shoulders. Because the peasant-union chairman was such an outstanding person, the union itself seemed to gain in importance. And since the Party branch had been mostly out of action while it was reorganizing its ranks, Wang Xi-tang began to underestimate its role and overestimate that of the organization which he now headed.

The fourth opinion prevalent among the peasants was that the Party, the poor-peasant league, and the peasant union were all on an equal footing. The people who held this view were quite willing to have the Communists join both the league and the union and serve on their committees. In other words, they had no qualms about accepting the leadership of individual Communists.

On the surface, there had seemed to be complete acceptance of Communist leadership in Ten Mile Inn before the work team came. In reality, however, the seeds of the problem already existed and were bound to survive as long as the branch failed to offer leadership based on the mass line. The arousing of the masses to criticize the Party members, and the withdrawal of the branch from an active part in village affairs, had temporarily replaced party branch leadership in the village with work team Communist leadership. But the purpose was to restore Party branch leadership on a better and still more effective level.

The work team had always kept this end in view, but now it seemed that no one else had. The sharp criticism of certain militants had an effect on the masses, and the pressure which the team had put on the Party members deprived them of self-confidence.

Although the Party's members' morale rose steadily during the last two-thirds of the campaign, not all of them had regained their confidence as readily as Wang Xi-tang had done. After the meeting on punishments was over, the branch held another session to discuss, as Leng Bing put it: "How to be good Party members, how to get along with the people, how to learn from them—and how to lead them."

"Well, if you want to get along with people," one member started off, "it seems that the best thing is to do nothing. Look at how long Fu Gao-sheng has managed to be a cadre. He's as active as an ant in a hot pan when there's somebody from the district government here, but when they leave, he does nothing."

"It's the same with Comrade Fu Pei-chang," said Wang Shao-zhen. "He criticized the rest of us more than anyone else during our criticism and self-criticism meetings. He himself had never made any mistakes, because he's never done anything. No activity, no mistakes."

Leng Bing spoke. "I'd like to say something on that point. To be a good Party member is to have a responsible attitude toward the Party and its work and toward the people.

"Is it a good thing when there is no difference between a Party member and other people? No; because to be a Party member means to be active. It means to be an eloquent propagandist, to have an influence on the masses. I hope that those comrades who never speak out will try to do so in the future. It's their responsibility.

"It is especially their responsibility in the Party branch meetings. Unless personal opinions are expressed, there can be no discussion. And without discussion, how can correct decisions be reached? It's the responsibility of every Party member to speak out. And if mistakes are made, every Party member has a share of the responsibility."

The former peasant-union chairman Fu Chang-sou said, "My trouble is that I'm so afraid of making a mistake these days that I've become timid. I feel as if my hands and feet were tied. I'm afraid to move."

"I'm the same," said Li Bao-en. "Sometimes I almost feel it's a stroke of bad luck to have been made a cadre again. Most of the old set of cadres have been thrown on one side, and I'm afraid that the same will happen to this lot in the future. So I feel as if no good can come of being a Communist, because it means you have to be a leader."

Li Bao-en, who had been elected a finance member of the village government, said that the responsibility was making him so nervous that his family life was affected. A peasant had come to his home when he was out and asked to see the village account books. His wife did not know the caller and so said she had no idea where the books were, but her little daughter naïvely pointed them out. The peasant looked through them, tossed them on the table, and left. When Li Bao-en returned, he was so vexed to hear about it that he slapped his child. "She wept bitterly. But I couldn't help it, I was so worried. It's true it was only account books, but it might have been something more important."

Li Bao-en went on to describe an incident during the early stages of the Party education:

"One night there was to be a meeting in the Fort, but I had to attend a Party meeting. I was very careful about my conduct, and I asked leave of Fu Chan-ting, who was chairman of the poor-peasant league group. He told me that I might go but that I should come straight back when that meeting ended, because the Fort meeting was an important one.

"The branch meeting was soon over, and I rushed back to the Fort and into the meeting room. But no one was there, and I tore around the Fort in the dark looking for the meeting place. At last I found a meeting. I slipped in and looked around, only to realize that everyone there was a struggle object. I felt very uncomfortable and hid at the back of the crowd. Nobody said a word to me, and I wondered, 'What's this? Am I now regarded as a struggle object?'

"In the end I decided to leave, but I had a terrible night, full of bad dreams. As soon as dawn broke, I rushed over to Fu Chan-ting's place. In the end I found out that I had gone to the wrong meeting.

"You can see how I felt at that stage of the Party reorganization— so timid I was afraid to do anything."

"Yes, it was a queer time," said Wang Wen-tang. "Nobody would say a word to us. To be a Communist was like being guilty of something. The members of the work team looked at us with searching eyes. We couldn't get close to the people. It was a bitter period. I never had a moment's happiness till the day came when we were allowed to answer the accusations, to say which were right and which wrong. After that I felt happier. And now that we have fixed what was right and what wrong, and whether the fault was our own or someone else's, I feel that the road has been opened up and we can move forward freely."

"When I first heard that the Party members' mistakes were going to be settled according to the people's wishes," said someone else, "I felt very frightened. I said to my wife, 'I've made a lot of mistakes in the past, and the people will never forgive me. Maybe I'll be sent to the people's court. So you and I had better follow different paths in the future. You go your own way, and I'll meet my fate alone.' My wife wept, and I was very unhappy.

"Then all of a sudden things changed. I was asked to examine my conduct more deeply. I confessed my mistakes—and then I was admitted to the peasant union. After that I went into things more deeply still and got everything off my chest."

Leng Bing joined in the discussion. "It's true; during those first twenty days or so there was a heavy pressure on your hearts. That was only in order to ensure deeper self-criticism. Now look at the results— everything has come out well.

"We said at the beginning that no one would suffer an injustice. But at that time the branch members hadn't gone into their conduct deeply. It was only natural that the team should stand by the poor peasants, not the cadres and Party members.

"This did put heavy social pressure on you, but without it you wouldn't have criticized yourselves so well. That means you wouldn't have been given a chance to reform, and the Party could never have been properly reorganized."

"That's true," said Wang Shao-zhen. "Without the pressure there would have been no depth to our self-criticism, and the people would never have dared to speak up."

"And now," Leng continued, "isn't everything falling into line? What else is there to attend to?"

Leng answered his own question: "The great issue still remaining is how to get along with the people. We must study this very carefully. In the past we didn't realize the strength of the masses. We didn't pay enough attention to the demands of the poor peasants." Leng was identifying himself with the branch and the mistakes it had made.

"We didn't sink ourselves deeply in the people. There was a wall between them and us. What was it? It was the so-called militants. Instead of going to the people and finding out their needs, we shut ourselves up in a room and conferred with these so-called militants.

"Of course militants are important. But what is a real militant? Someone who is active among the masses, who moves forward with them, not away from them.

"Why did we make so many mistakes in the past? Because we were cut off from the people. From now on the work will be much easier, because the people themselves are in power. The more active the people are, the more effective the Party branch can be.

"At the same time, we must not be the tails of the people. We must discuss everything reasonably with them, but we have to give them leadership. We should learn from the people and teach them at the same time."

The next topic of discussion was the need for regular meetings of the branch. There was some debate on the merits of meetings of the whole branch compared with meetings of smaller groups. The Party members finally decided that both types would be held regularly on the first and fifteenth days of each month, whether there were special issues to deal with or not.

"The main purpose of the small-group meetings," said Leng Bing, "should be criticism and self-criticism. There was not enough of this in the past. If it's done regularly, mistakes can be dealt with while they're still small and big mistakes can be avoided entirely.

"Another way of catching mistakes early is for the small groups to consider very carefully any complaints made by the masses. And I suggest that every three or four months there should be a special branch meeting to which the masses are invited to send delegates to make criticisms. This will be like a breath of fresh air from the people to the Party members. What do you think?"

The branch agreed and the session closed with the comforting observation from Leng Bing that if these steps were followed, "There will be no need to have a large-scale reorganization and reeducation movement like this every couple of years."

The remaining organizational task for the Party members was the election of branch officers. When the work team had arrived in the village and begun the education of the Party members, the officers had all been relieved of their posts.

Late in March, when fifteen of the branch's twenty-eight members had been admitted to the peasant union, the branch had held an election of officers. At that time the Party members were still shaken by the criticism they had received, and they had the feeling that they ought to elect a new set of men altogether. They also tended to value the candidates who were personally popular and who had made no mistakes. As a result Zhang Zhao-lin, a veteran of the Eighth Route Army, was elected to the post of branch secretary.

As it turned out, however, Zhang Zhao-lin was a failure in that post. One reason was that he did not know the ins and outs of village political life, because he had left to join the army when he was very young and had only recently been demobilized. Another reason was that he had been elected to the village government committee, which took up much of his time and energy. Furthermore, in Leng Bing's opinion Zhang Zhao-lin had less ability and drive than his predecessor, Wang Shao-zhen.

Fu Pei-chang, who was elected a group head, also did an unsatisfactory job. According to the other Party members, "He's always looking upwards"—that is, he took pains to keep on the right side of his superiors. Fu was extremely popular with the people and had been one of the first village Communists to reestablish his prestige, but he had done this by ingratiating himself as a "good fellow" rather than by upholding Party principles.

Since a new election was clearly necessary, the branch was called together for it on April 14. This time the Party members would vote for four group leaders and a branch committee of five, including the secretary—the most important post of all.

Leng Bing said that in voting, the things to take into account were the candidate's "Party age" (length of membership), experience, class standpoint, and ability. Reasons were to accompany each nomination.

The first candidate to be proposed was Wang Shao-zhen. The nominator stressed his experience and the thoroughness of his self-criticism. Then Zhang Zhao-lin and Li Xi-yuan were nominated because "they were not afraid to risk their lives at the front." Someone also nominated Wang Xi-tang, but the others pointed out that he was too busy as chairman of the peasant union. Li Wei-cheng had not been in the Party long enough. Li Song-ting, on the other hand, was nominated as "an old cadre who has been a militiaman for ten years and knows the ropes." Wang Wen-tang, the former hired hand, was proposed because of his experience in struggling against the landlords.

The winners were Li Xi-yuan, who had once led forty Ten Mile Inn militiamen to join the Eighth Route Army; Zhang Zhao-lin, who had served as a finance member of the previous village government; Wang Wen-tang, formerly the propaganda secretary of the branch; and Fu Jin-sheng, a young militiaman.

The position of branch secretary went to the man who had held it before: Wang Shao-zhen. His reelection was in keeping with the spirit of the movement to reorganize the Party ranks: "Cure the sickness to save the patient." Those Communists who had displayed energy and ability, and who had risked their lives to lead the people against the Japanese and against feudalism, were not thrown on the scrap heap. After their education they returned to serve and lead the people better than they had done before.

# —30—

# Distributing
# the Fruits

Absolute equalitarianism, like ultrademocracy in political matters,
is the product of a handicraft and small-peasant economy. The only
difference is that the one manifests itself in material affairs, the
other in political affairs.

—Mao Ze-dong, "Correcting Mistaken Ideas in the Party"
(December 1929). Translated directly from the Chinese.

The seal was still unbroken on the storeroom containing the fruits
that had been dug out of the "air-raid shelters" in the summer of 1947.
Now it was time to open the room and distribute the cloth and clothing
—as well as the millet, maize, and wheat that were being held in the
village granary.

Some of the cloth and clothing had been the property of landlords
in wealthier villages who had hidden it with friends or relatives in
Ten Mile Inn. But most had belonged to middle peasants in Ten Mile
Inn itself and had been taken from them during the excesses of the
Feudal Tails Campaign.

To forestall demands that everything which had been wrongly confiscated should now be returned to its original owner, the work team
and the new leaders of the village agreed to follow two main principles
in making the distribution. First, they would not return to each individual what had been unjustly taken from him but would give to those
in need—to the holes. Second, there would be no absolute equalitarianism; the people whose needs were greatest would receive most.
As in the case of land and housing, holes would be filled with whatever
was available, no matter whether the recipient was a member of the
basic masses, a former landlord or rich peasant, or a middle peasant
who had been wrongly struggled against.

The procedure for distributing the cloth and grain was much the
same as it had been for land and housing. On the morning of April 11

255

the joint committee of the poor-peasant league, the peasant union, and the village government met to discuss how the distribution should be carried out. Each of the thirty-one people's groups met that afternoon, and each family made a report on the amount of clothing and grain it had on hand.

Meanwhile the cloth and clothing were being formally handed over to the newly elected village cadres. In order to save time, this process was combined with a detailed valuation of the goods. The fruits were in the official custody of the village director of production and the chairman of the

Seals on the door of the room where "struggle fruits" taken from the landlords were left until distribution.

peasant union, and it was they who unlocked the storeroom and broke the seal on the door. Everything inside was as orderly as a stock room in a department store. The goods were piled tidily on shelves, each bundle neatly tied up in a piece of cloth and labeled with the name of the original owner or air-raid shelter.

The bundles—forty-two in all—were taken out into the courtyard

"Struggle fruits" on display in the old temple courtyard, awaiting distribution.

and placed on reed mats. There they were opened one by one and checked against the village government's records. As each bundle was pronounced correct, it was considered to be formally handed over by the old cadres to the new.

At the end of the courtyard where the checking was in progress, there was an atmosphere of quiet concentration. But the other end was filled with lively chatter and bursts of laughter. There each article was held up and examined by a group of expert valuers, who priced and tagged it. Fancy bedspreads, gaily colored women's jackets and trousers, scarlet cloth for babies' clothes, pairs of shoes, and handfuls of trinkets were soon heaped on reed mats all over the courtyard. The constant click of the abacus, the calling of prices to the clerks who were recording everything, and the chatter of the onlookers transformed the courtyard into a miniature marketplace.

The half-dozen valuers had been chosen because of their business experience. The village clerk Wang Fu-xin, for instance, had worked for a cloth dealer in the neighboring county of Shixian and was accepted as the authority on homespun goods. Fu Chou-kui had once had a small cloth business of his own in the city of Jixian in south Hebei. After the land reform he had come home to resume the life of a peasant, but he seemed to enjoy working at his old trade for an afternoon. He kept a wooden ruler stuck inside his collar down the back of his neck, and every now and then whipped it out smartly to measure a piece of cloth with the deft movements of an expert.

"This is from Tokyo," he said authoritatively, holding up a piece of silk. "Better price it at 20 *fen* a foot," and, "This piece is first-class Shanghai dye. You could wear that silk till it was in rags, and the color would never fade. It's well worth 18 *fen* a foot.

"You see this stuff?" he said, picking up some material which looked very similar. "It's mixed with hemp. Made in Hankou."

Laughing, the vice-head of the village picked up a landlord's silk suit. After tucking the trousers into the waist of his own pair, which were made of heavy homespun, he draped the short jacket over his shoulders and swaggered officiously about the courtyard.

"This stuff was all right for the Old Moneybags," one man said, "but it's no use to us."

What everyone wanted was good, strong homespun, for silk and satin were too fragile. So was factory-made cloth, which was regarded as suitable only for women because it could not stand the wear and tear demanded of men's clothing.

For the same reason leather shoes were not popular. "Those things are all right for intellectuals," said one man, "but they're no good out in the fields." A pair of almost-new leather shoes was valued at 20 *fen*, while a good pair of cloth shoes such as the peasants wore was priced at 30.

One article that aroused some curiosity was an ornamental table-cloth of the kind the landlords had used in their town houses. It was a mystery to most of the villagers until the sophisticated Fu Chou-kui explained what it was for. Another ornamental item that everyone did recognize though was a silver talisman of the sort which old-fashioned landlord women presented to a daughter's son when he was thirty days old. Though there were a number of other silver articles—bracelets, lockets, and even silver *yuan*—it was mainly the cloth, clothing, and bedding that brought the total estimated value of the fruits to almost 450 *yuan*.

That evening the people's congress met to review the list of families who had reported themselves as holes and to appraise their claims from a village-wide standpoint. The next morning the joint committee, together with representatives from the people's groups, studied the list of seventy-six families who had said that they needed grain. To avoid an equalitarian approach, Lou Lin suggested that there should be three types of "grain hole"—large, medium, and small—and that decisions should be reached by comparing one family's needs with another's.

The woman team member Wu Fang said, "We should take all sorts of different factors into account, such as the yield of a family's land, the amount of its labor power, and so on."

"Better get out the account books, then," someone said, "so we can check the details."

"No need for that," someone else objected. "Everyone knows who's well off and who's not." Everyone did in fact know all that needed to be known about everyone else. The question was whether people would speak frankly, without personal or sectional prejudice.

When the name of Wang Yong-sheng's family was read, for instance, the spokesman for one of the three fermentation groups into which the meeting had divided said, after a little hesitation, "He's a small hole." The spokesman for the second group agreed. The third group gave no verdict for a long time. Apparently they had been intending to declare that he was not really a hole, but now they hesitated to contradict the other two groups. In the end their spokesman said, with no great conviction, "We agree. He's a small hole."

He had hardly finished, however, when another member of the group shouted, "He's no hole at all! He harvested a good crop of millet last year."

In a moment each of the three groups changed its first verdict and agreed that Wang Yong-sheng was no hole. People also began to mutter that the really simple-and-honest had not all reported themselves as holes.

When it came to Duan Er-de, someone said, "She's a widow. Her husband left home during the famine, and he's never been heard of since."

"Big hole, big hole," several voices called. There was no dissent.

When Wang Ze-cai's case came up, someone commented, "His wife used to be a concubine of 'Lion Yang'." This was a local bandit who had sided first with the Guomindang, then with the Japanese, and then again with the Guomindang against the Communists.

The league chairman Li Bao-yu, who was making the rounds of the three fermentation groups, overheard the remark and said, "There's no need to bring that up. A hole's a hole."

But this simple principle did not always prevail; there was a tendency for factors other than economic need to influence the verdict. For instance, it seemed to be more than the peasants could stomach to class the former heroin peddler Wang Ying-xiang as a big hole for grain. Feeling that the treatment he had received in the land adjustment was generous enough, this time they classed him as a medium hole.

In the case of Wang Fu-cheng there was a complication of a different nature. "He's too extravagant," someone said. "Look at what happened to the 12 dan of millet that was distributed to him before. It disappeared in no time."

"Yes," agreed a lean, whiskered old man, "you could move the South Hebei Bank into his home, and it still wouldn't be enough."

"Still," said a woman, "you mustn't forget that his daughter-in-law's pregnant."

"Well, let's call him a middle hole, then. It's no good making him a big one."

"But really he's a big hole, isn't he?" Lou Lin said. "So I suggest that we call him a big hole and give him some education so that he can overcome his extravagant habits."

But after more discussion the peasants decided, despite Lou Lin's advice, that it would be difficult to cure Wang Fu-cheng of his wasteful habits in so short a time. They classed him as a medium hole.

The case of Sou Wei-chuan was just the opposite. "He always goes around in ragged clothes just to make out that he's poor," people said. The three groups all agreed that he was only a small hole.

The groups disagreed about Wang Lan-fang; one said that he was a small hole, and another denied that he was a hole at all.

"He had a fine harvest last year," someone said. "Over 10 dan of husked millet. And he bought a donkey."

"We didn't make any allowance for what Old Duan spent on the funeral, so why should we count what Old Wang spent for his donkey?"

"I suppose you'd count him a hole even if he'd bought a camel."

In the end the groups agreed to count Wang Lan-fang as a small hole.

When Li Bao-yu's name was called, the league chairman protested. "I'm not a hole," he said. "I've got enough food to last me till May."

But he was given the friendly reproof, "That's not for you to decide. You just leave it to us. And remember you're a father of five now." There was a burst of laughter, for Li Bao-yu's fifth child had been born a few weeks before. Because of the size of his family and the demands of his post as a cadre, he was classed as a hole, though a small one. He would have been a larger hole except for the fact that since the adjustment there were signs of quite a boom in his trade of house building and repairing.

When the entire list of seventy-six names had been discussed, it was found that there were two big holes (both of them widows), fourteen medium holes, and twenty-six small ones. Five were labeled as doubtful pending further investigation. Twenty-nine of the self-described holes were rejected.

As the meeting broke up, the groups seemed pleased with their morning's work. Their one complaint was about the number of categories: they felt that three types of hole were not enough and that five or six would have been better.

That afternoon when they met again to discuss the applications for cloth, clothing, bedding, and the other goods that had been in the storeroom, the first question they discussed was how many different types of holes there should be. Lou Lin suggested holding the number to three, as with the grain. His recommendation was that people who needed raw cotton, cloth, clothing, and bedding should be classed as big holes, that those needing only two or three of the four items should be medium holes, and that those needing only one item should be small holes. But the majority disagreed and decided to use five categories.

The difference between three and five was not just a matter of arithmetic. The rejection of two-fifths of the applications that morning had meant that the grain was distributed where it was needed most, instead of as widely as possible. It was this very lack of equalitarianism which troubled most of the people at the meeting. The suggestion that there should be five grades was aimed at ensuring the widest distribution, tapering gradually from the most to the least needy families, with a minimum of rejections.

Lou Lin did not stick to his point. Some of the goods distributed would be changed into working capital, but many if not most would be used by their recipients as clothing and bedding. A tendency toward equalitarianism here was not of fundamental importance, as it would have been in the distribution of land. The groups finally agreed, therefore, that there should be five sizes of holes.

Apart from this change, the procedure was much the same as it had been in appraising the grain holes. But an additional factor in weighing each family's claim was the number of women it contained, for spinning, weaving, and clothes making were their job. In the first case, that of Wang Ying-su, the peasants instantly said, "Three generations of men, but no women," and the household was classified as a hole of the third size. It was not made a grade 1 hole, which was reserved for families lacking all four items, because it had enough labor power to pay widows in the mutual-aid group to make clothes. The number of children in a family was also taken into account.

People with little labor power, such as the aged, were given special consideration, and so were those with special disabilities. Old Wang Jing-yu had to keep records for the reception center, and his eyes were bad. So he was given a pair of spectacles from the fruits. And Li Chu-ying, an old, blind widow, was unhesitatingly made a big hole.

As at the morning meeting, unpopularity did not prevent a person from being accepted as a hole, but it did tend to affect the grade of the hole. For instance, it was pointed out that Wang Cheng-xiang had been an air-raid shelter. Although someone said, "We shouldn't consider that, but just give him what he needs," he was classed as the smallest type of hole without further discussion.

In general, the standard was less strict than it had been for grain, because the people whose claims would have been rejected if there had been only three grades were accepted as fifth- or even fourth-grade holes. As a result, of the 127 poor-peasant families considered, only 4 were turned down. The same number was rejected from the 28 middle-peasant applicants. Thus there were only 8 rejections out of 155 (about 5 percent), in contrast to 29 out of 76 (about 40 percent) at the morning meeting. The peasants' inclination toward equalitarianism was still strong.

Complicated calculations were necessary in order to grade holes into different sizes and take into account the number of members in each family. These were made immediately after the appraisal of the holes. The total price set upon all goods awaiting distribution was computed, and the relationship of various types of holes was established.

In the case of grain, it was decided that a big hole should count as eight points per head, a medium one as five, and a small one as three. Then all the points were added up. The next step was to find the total value of the grain (together with a small quantity of beans and other products). The price of wheat was fixed at 1.1 *fen*, millet at 1.2 *fen*, husked corn at 1.2 *fen*, corn on the cob at 0.8 *fen*, yellow beans at 1.9 *fen*. This total was divided by the total number of points and the conclusion was that big holes should receive 80 *fen's* worth of grain per head, medium holes 50 *fen's* worth, and small holes 30 *fen's* worth. Each hole family was given a ticket showing what value of grain it was entitled to receive.

The following morning, April 13, the peasant-union chairman Wang Xi-tang, the village head Zhao Zhen-fang, and other officials of the village government, as well as a number of work team members, went to the granary for the distribution.

As the cadres climbed the ladder to the loft where the grain was stored, the holes assembled in the courtyard below. The crowd was a mixed one, with many people who had played widely different roles in recent village history. The wife of the former rich-peasant trader Li Feng of the Fort was there, together with her schoolteacher son, Li Wei-shu, and the wife of her other son who had fled to Tientsin with his father after the Black Lands Campaign. So were Li Sheng-chang, son of a former *bao* head and Guomindang agent; Duan Chui-de, widow of the middleman who had created the whole secret-agent frame-up; and Wang Shao-yu, a former village head who had been denounced for graft. Rubbing elbows with them were some of the old cadres and a few of the new ones.

Everyone was in high spirits, and the holes firmly clutched their tickets as well as bags, baskets, and sacks of every description. There were many jokes about one woman's enormous sack, which could hold ten times more grain than she was entitled to.

The main topic of conversation was what to choose from the various types of grain available. "I don't want any wheat," said Wang Hung-shuang. "I'm not sick." He had been a laborer for several years, during which he had not had the luxury of eating wheat more than half a dozen times.

"Yes," said a woman, "you can live without wheat but not without millet."

The widow Duan Er-de, who was one of the two big holes, expressed a preference for husked millet to unhusked, because she had no donkey to do the milling.

At last everything was ready up on the flat roof outside the loft door. The people were called up one by one, for the roof was not strong enough to hold the crowd. Only able-bodied men could carry a heavy sack of grain down the ladder, but the women and old men had no difficulty in finding helpers.

Little by little the loft emptied, the crowd in the courtyard thinned out, and the people staggered home under their loads of grain. They hurried through their midday meal so that they would be ready for the distribution of cloth and clothes in the afternoon.

The clothing was more valuable and more colorful than the grain. The twisted crab-apple tree in the middle of the temple courtyard was in full bloom, but its delicate rose-colored blossoms were out-dazzled by the brilliant garments displayed around it. Some goods were neatly piled on trestle tables, some were stacked on reed mats on the ground, and others were draped over lines propped up by forks and hoes. Cadres and members of the league committee were arranging their wares and making ready to wait on the "customers." Clerks at tables in the lower courtyard were preparing to enter the price and the name of the recipient as the holes carried away the goods they chose. Outside, the people waited for the word to come in.

To avoid a bargain-sale rush, the holes were admitted in batches of seven or eight, starting with those in grade 1 and gradually working down to grade 5. The principle for calculating how much the people in each grade were to receive had been roughly the same as with the grain. Those in grade 1 were entitled to 5 *yuan*, 77 *fen's* worth of goods per head; those in grade 2, 4 *yuan*, 67 *fen*; in grade 3,

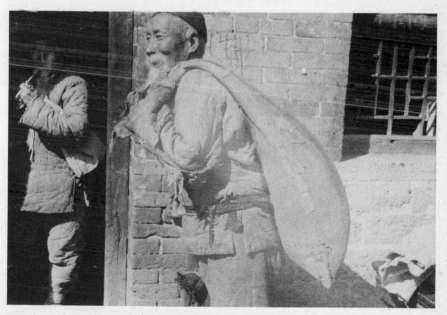

Wang Wen-sheng's father with his sack of grain.

(*above*) Distribution of the goods. Wang Yin-xiang, the ex-heroin peddler, is at the center.

(*right*) Wang Yin-xiang at the checking desk on the way out.

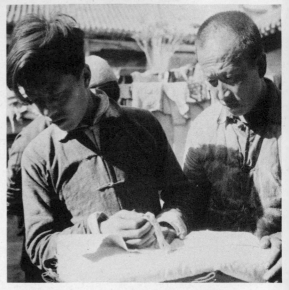

3 *yuan*, 46 *fen*; in grade 4, 2 *yuan*, 31 *fen*; and in grade 5, 1 *yuan*, 15 *fen*.

The orphan Wang Kang-yu was among the first to be admitted. As soon as the temple gate was opened for his group, he dashed in, looked intently around, and then darted to the counter piled with bolts of undyed homespun cloth. Following his married sister's instructions, he clutched the largest bolt and made off with it before the widow Duan Er-de had cautiously climbed the short flight of stone steps from the lower to the upper courtyard.

Others were equally clear on what they wanted. A woman of seventy hobbled over to a pile of silk to look for a shroud in some

The orphan boy with his bundle of clothes.

suitably subdued color, such as dark grey. She wanted material that was thin and lightweight, so that it would not hamper her movements when she had become a spirit. Garments trimmed with even the smallest piece of fur were out of the question, for to wear one would mean risking reincarnation as an animal. The committee members who were waiting on her smiled at her superstitions.

Fu Bian-de, who was acting as a clerk, picked up a bright piece of satin and facetiously offered it to a staid middle-aged woman standing nearby.

"For me?" she asked incredulously. "I wouldn't be seen in such stuff!"

His joke over, Fu tried to put the satin down, but the fine silk threads clung to his work-roughened hands and he couldn't detach it. "Mothers!" he cursed in embarrassment. "This Old Moneybags' stuff sticks to your hands."

Except for shrouds, which quite a few people were looking for, most of the peasants preferred homespun to silk and satin. Good-quality machine-made cloth came second. One burly man was preparing to give a piece of this a wrench to test its strength, as he would have done with homespun, when the team member Wu Fang warned him that it could not stand the strain. Not until all the homespun had gone did people begin to take the factory cloth, and then only with the aim of exchanging or selling it.

An old woman, heartlessly nicknamed old Gourd-face because of her toothless, protruding jaw, sorted through every pile of cloth and clothing but was unable to find anything to suit her. Instead of leaving with the rest of her group of eight, she stayed and stayed.

"What are you looking for, auntie?" Wu Fang asked sympathetically.

"I'm looking for my own stuff," the old woman replied.

"You're not from a landlord family, are you?" Wu Fang asked in surprise.

"No, but I was an air-raid shelter. And I put some of my own stuff in with the Old Moneybags' things, drat it, and mine was taken

Old Gourd-face with her sack of grain.

away along with the rest. Now I can't find it anywhere." She searched for most of the afternoon and finally discovered what she was looking for—a padded jacket of dark grey drill.

Some of the articles that she brushed aside were of a less practical nature. One was a large flag inscribed with characters meaning "Clear the Road." It had belonged to a local landlord who was an official of the Manchu empire, and runners had carried it ahead of his sedan chair wherever he traveled. There was also a "thousand-name umbrella" that had been presented to a famous local doctor. Made of brilliant crimson satin, it was inscribed in black ink with the gracefully brushed names of his patients. The imperial official's flag found a ready buyer, for the material was strong and it was just the size for wrapping up bundles. But no one wanted the doctor's umbrella, or the banners inscribed with such words as "Buddha's Heart" that had once been used in wedding processions.

A pile of books also failed to attract attention. Li Bao-en hopefully pointed it out to the young teacher Li Wei-shu, who went over the books one by one and then, shaking his head, tied them up again. They were volumes of the classics, which he had once admired, but now his reading centered on agrarian reform and the border-region government's new educational policy.

Li Wei-shu was often asked to read the price tags on the various articles, for the amateur salespeople, though they waited on customers enthusiastically, were scarcely literate. Those who could read and write with ease were keeping the accounts, which was a very businesslike operation. As each villager paused in the temple gateway on the way out, a clerk examined the tag on every article, added up the total, and checked it against the ticket which showed how much the person was entitled to. Many of the peasants could not keep track of the total value of the goods they had chosen, and they thought they had better be on the safe side by taking too much rather than too little. So the clerks' assistants were kept busy carrying back armfuls of stuff to the counters, while the clerks muttered, "These women! Always picking out more than they're entitled to."

When the person's bundle finally tallied more or less with his ticket (slight discrepancies either way were made up in cash), he moved on to the next clerk, who entered his name in an account book together with each article and its price.

The widow Duan Er-de, for example, was in grade 1 and could take 5 *yuan*, 77 *fen's* worth of goods. She had the following items entered against her name:

Item no.

| 1033 | Black felt *kang* mat | 40 *fen* |
|---|---|---|
| 900 | Woollen bag | 60 *fen* |
| 908 | Set of bedding (new) | 90 *fen* |
| 24 | Silk mixed with cotton cloth (big red flower design), 7 feet at 14 *fen* a foot | 98 *fen* |
| 974 | 4 *jin* of black cloth at 50 *fen* a *jin* | 2.00 *fen* |
| 975 | 2.2 *jin* of black cloth at 45 *fen* a *jin* | 96 *fen* |
| | Total | 5.84 *yuan* |
| | Balance due | 7 *fen* |

The league chairman Li Bao-yu was in grade 3 and was therefore entitled to 3 *yuan*, 46 *fen's* worth of fruits. It was easy to see from his list that he had a big family of young children to provide for. His list ran:

Item no.

| 860 | Piece of black cloth | 10 *fen* |
|---|---|---|
| 825 | Bundle of odds and ends | 20 *fen* |
| 961 | 2 *jin* of blue cloth at 35 *fen* a *jin* | 70 *fen* |
| 168 | 3-piece child's suit (fine red cloth) | 20 *fen* |
| 722 | Small pair of trousers (fine red cloth) | 5 *fen* |
| 97 | 2-piece child's dress | 8 *fen* |
| 816 | Child's pinafore | 8 *fen* |
| 635 | Interlined jacket of print cloth | 10 *fen* |
| 439 | Piece of white cloth for wrapping | 7 *fen* |
| 757 | Child's light-blue check jacket | 5 *fen* |
| 785 | Vegetable-green trousers | 5 *fen* |
| 693 | Red striped trousers | 15 *fen* |
| 252 | Interlined trousers, pink check | 45 *fen* |
| 251 | Pair of trousers (fine blue cloth) | 30 *fen* |
| 535 | Small interlined black coat | 10 *fen* |
| 744 | Towel | 4 *fen* |
| 859 | Piece of black cloth | 10 *fen* |
| | Total | 3.27 *yuan* |
| | Change | 19 *fen* |

In order to avoid congestion in the temple courtyard, only one member of each hole family was allowed inside to select goods. So as each person, laden with his bundle, emerged from the temple gateway, he was pounced on by the impatient members of his household.

The mother of the soldier Wang Shuang-lin was waylaid by her daughter-in-law, who insisted on having the bundle opened up so that she could go over everything on the spot. "What's this—not a single piece of silk?" she asked.

"What do we want silk for?" the old woman protested.

"For your shroud, of course," her daughter-in-law replied. "You haven't got a thing to wear when you die."

"I'm not going to die yet awhile," the old woman snorted as she piled the stuff together again. But she was obviously pleased by the younger woman's concern that she should have a fitting burial.

Next morning the work team met with the village cadres and with representatives of the different sections to discuss complaints about the distribution. There had been one or two, it was reported, from villagers who considered themselves holes but who had been turned down, or who thought that they should have received both grain and clothing but had been given only one or the other. A few had also complained that some people received fruits when they really did not need anything, and that others had been given a lot when they deserved only a little.

One representative had overheard someone say, "Wang Yi must have been allowed more than he really needed. Half the stuff he picked out was for his daughter-in-law." Evidently the old man had been trying to patch things up with his short-tempered daughter-in-law, even though it had meant giving her a large share of his fruits.

"And quite a few middle peasants got something, though a lot of poor peasants went without," one of the representatives said.

"Yes," laughed the village vice-head Wang Wen-sheng, half in jest, half in earnest, "the middle peasants got away with plenty. But whenever there's work to do on this committee and that, it's we poor peasants who have to do it. They get off scot free."

"There's no reason why the middle peasants shouldn't have received something," said the branch secretary Wang Shao-zhen. "Some poor peasants are better off than some middle peasants. It's only that they haven't had time to change their class since they fanshenned."

This explanation was accepted as valid, and there were no further complaints.

"Taking things all in all," Lou Lin said, "only three or four out of the 420-odd families in the village are really dissatisfied So I think we can say that the distribution has been carried out successfully." There was a murmur of agreement.

"But there is one complaint I heard that I should like to mention," Lou Lin continued. "I heard some people saying that it wasn't right to let all the big holes go in first and have the pick of everything, so that the small holes who went in last had to be satisfied with what was left. They said that some people from each grade should have been included in every batch of eight who were let into the temple."

"That's what I think," whispered one of the representatives to his neighbor. "It wasn't fair."

"In my opinion," Lou Lin went on, "it was correct to give the first choice to those who were in the greatest need. It will help them get on their feet and produce more. The other method would simply have been aiming at absolute equality."

Over 400 *yuan's* worth of goods had been distributed the previous afternoon, but there was still another 40 *yuan's* worth which had been set aside. This was to be a gift to the thirty-six middle-peasant families who had given up some of their land and housing to help fill the holes. It consisted of lengths of gaily patterned cloth of the sort that well-to-do middle peasants loved to dress their children in.

It was decided that the most convenient method of distribution would be to divide up all the cloth into six piles of equal value. When this had been done, the thirty-six families formed themselves into six groups of six families each and set about sharing the piles. One group was so filled with the ideal of equalitarianism which was forever cropping up in Ten Mile Inn that they decided to take each piece of cloth and divide it into six equal strips. The result was that each family received a bunch of tiny scraps, none of them big enough to make a garment.

In the distribution as a whole, over 450 *yuan's* worth of cloth and a considerable amount of grain had been given out. These allotments satisfied the needs of the poorest for food and clothing, provided them with goods which could be sold or exchanged for working capital, and equally important, boosted their morale. And all this had been accomplished without encroaching on the property of the middle peasants.

# —31—

# The Village Summary

April 14

By April 14, 1948, seven weeks to the day from the time it started, the adjustment campaign had essentially come to an end. One last meeting of the whole village was held to sum up the experiences of those seven weeks so that lessons could be drawn from them.

In preparation, the team met with the new village cadres to discuss what points should be taken up and how they should be presented. The basic issue emerged in an exchange of ideas between Lou Lin and the chairmen of the league and the union—Li Bao-yu and Wang Xi-tang.

"We should let the people express their opinions about the way the fruits have been distributed," said Li Bao-yu. "That's the demand of the masses."

"That's one of their demands," said Lou Lin. "We should explain to them that there wasn't a great deal to distribute and that even if there had been, some people would still have been dissatisfied.

"But the masses have another demand—to get on with production. That's the main road, and we should lead them along it. The other is just a blind alley."

"Yes," agreed Wang Xi-tang. "The main thing is to make everyone enthusiastic about production, whether or not they are satisfied with the distribution of the fruits."

Li Bao-yu admitted that this was the correct approach, and it was arranged that he, as chairman of the "backbone" organization, the poor-peasant league, should make the opening speech at the village meeting.

But when he stood up that night, beneath the portrait of Mao Ze-dong which glistened in the light of a kerosene lamp borrowed for this final meeting, he seemed disturbed.

"During the past forty or fifty days," he began, "we have set up the poor-peasant league and formed the new peasant union. And we've held the big unity meeting to establish the people's congress. Through these organizations we adjusted landholdings, and now we've just finished distributing some houses and property to the holes. But," he paused, then went on hesitantly, "we're afraid the filling of the holes hasn't been satisfactory, because the holes were many and the goods were few. The holes and the goods weren't appraised by a meeting of the entire village, like this one. It was done by the appraisers . . ."

Li Bao-yu had been faltering over the last few words. Now he came to a stop. He seemed to realize that he was heading up the blind alley and emphasizing the defects of the distribution instead of its achievements. It was clear that although Li Bao-yu had outwardly agreed with Lou Lin and Wang Xi-tang at the preparation meeting that morning, inwardly he had not been convinced. He himself still had the illusion which was harbored by the more backward of the peasants that a completely equal distribution would have been fairer. But though he had not been able to shake it off, he knew it was an illusion.

In this confused and contradictory state of mind, he became tongue-tied. All he could do was to laugh nervously and throw an appealing look to Wang Xi-tang at his side.

The peasant-union chairman rose and took over. He was in his element, master of himself and of the situation.

"It's true that there wasn't a lot of property to hand out, but on the whole the distribution brought satisfaction. It was the same with the houses. Our housing situation is not good, and some of the houses distributed were not very well built. But what is it we chiefly need? Shelter against cold and rain. The main thing is to repair the roofs so that they don't leak.

"Even though there wasn't very much of anything, we've managed to overcome our problems with the help of the middle peasants who offered some of their land and housing. We have food and shelter, and our hearts are at rest. In the last year or two there have been a handful of people who lived on the struggles. But in future they and everyone else will live on the fruits of their own toil.

"In all this we've received a lot of help from the work team. Before they came, we weren't clear about the Agrarian Law. Now we've distributed everything and made the adjustment according to the law. Now every family has its share; every carrot has its hole.

"If there are a few who are still dissatisfied with the distribution, we'll try and convince them. Having our minds at rest is necessary for success in production. Or if these few have real grounds for dissatisfaction, then we still have something in reserve to solve their problems.

"The main thing is that we have enough to get along on. We can be sure that we'll never again suffer from hunger. We all remember what it was like during the famine years, when we ate wild plants and a family of five lived on an ounce of millet a day. In those days we thought that a grain of corn was as precious as life itself. But we survived even those years.

"Today the only things we have to do are work hard, produce, do a good job of tilling the land we have, and live well in the houses we have. We should be thrifty, because it's no good wearing fine clothes all year and then playing hide-and-seek when bill-paying time comes. In the past, some of the old middle peasants were worried that they might be struggled against. But this adjustment has been made once and for all. There's no need to worry.

"It's many years since we had such a beautiful spring as this, with just the right amount of rain and a fine, gentle wind. So want can become a thing of the past if we work well for ourselves and for the soldiers' families. Our labor is the guarantee of our prosperity."

Wang Xi-tang's speech led the people's thoughts out of the blind alley up which Li Bao-yu had started them and directed them along the main road of production. Leng Bing then rose to give a systematic summary of the campaign.

"I shall take up four points," Leng said. "First, the adjustment; second, the relationship between the Communist Party and the masses; third, production; and fourth, democracy.

"We have made an adjustment of land and housing—a once-and-for-all adjustment. In case some people are still not clear on this point, I want to tell you definitely that there will be no more land-reform movements. The land reform has been completed in Ten Mile Inn.

"Some of you had the idea that land reform was going to make everyone absolutely equal—that everything was going to be leveled off the way we level off the grain in a peck measure. These people have been saying that things are still not leveled off, because the old middle peasants still have an average yield higher than the rest. The equalitarians think we have left things like this just for the time being, so that we can get on with production, and that in the autumn we'll start another movement. They've heard that two or three years are necessary to complete the land-reform movement, and since our movement in Ten Mile Inn has taken only fifty days, they can't believe that it's finished.

"As a member of the work team and on behalf of the Communist Party, I say that all such doubts should be swept away. The *People's Daily* has made clear that this is really the final land-reform movement, and that it is not to be compared with the movements we've had before.

"In past movements, some people were struggled against who should not have been. But now no one is considered a struggle object any longer. Only one landlord is left in the village, but he has already been struggled against. It's just because he hasn't yet labored long enough that he's not already a member of the laboring people's camp. Since he didn't have enough to live on, he's been given help exactly like the rest of the holes.

"From this it is clear that our purpose is to put an end to feudal exploitation, not simply to struggle for the sake of struggling. As to the middle peasants who were wrongly struggled against, we should offer them our apologies besides the compensation we have already given them. The responsibility for the wrong struggles does not rest on the village cadres but on higher levels of the Party. At that time the directive defining the different classes was not available, and even some leading comrades were not clear about how to classify.

"The idea of leveling everyone off and making everything even is not correct. In the past, inequality was due to exploitation. But whatever inequality exists now is not the result of exploitation. It is only an inequality in comparison with the middle peasants. If they have more land than others, this is a result of their own labor, and it's only right that they should have a higher yield than others. It would be wrong to take anything from them. The middle peasants don't hire long-term laborers; they belong to the same family as the poor-and-hired. That's why it would have been wrong to compel them to give up any of their surplus land. Some of you may think that because things aren't exactly equal, we still have holes. But since we have no landlords and rich peasants, we can fill no more holes with struggle fruits. The Communist Party does not permit such a thing. Chairman Mao does not permit it.

"As to finishing the land reform, it's quite true that it will take two or three years. But that's for the whole of the Liberated Areas, not for Ten Mile Inn.

"Here in the ninth district of Wu An, we've already been at work for nearly four months with teams of fifty or sixty people, and we still haven't finished the adjustment. And there are eleven districts in Wu An. So we don't have the time to come back to Ten Mile Inn and start all over again.

"On the whole, the adjustment in the village has been fair. But it's still up to you to make your criticisms. I know that there are one or two families who haven't been properly treated, and steps are being taken by the village government to straighten this out. But generally speaking, thanks to the help of the middle-peasant families, there are no holes left in Ten Mile Inn. Everyone is up to the standard of a middle peasant. And even the one remaining landlord will have changed his class within a year. Now your task is to organize production and make yourselves more prosperous."

Before Leng Bing went on to his second point—the relationship of the Party and the masses—the branch secretary Wang Shao-zhen spoke briefly on how the Party members themselves felt about this issue.

"During the reorganization of the Party ranks," said Wang Shao-zhen, "we Communists examined our conduct and criticized ourselves. We came to realize that we had made a lot of mistakes. We're grateful to all of you for having given us your criticism, and we pledge that we will never resent it. We feel very happy about the education we've received. I think that if I had had it a couple of years sooner, I wouldn't have made so many mistakes. At this time I want to offer you our thanks and pledge that in future we'll be good Communists, good and honest laborers for the people."

Leng Bing resumed his summary. "The question of the relationship between the Party and the masses is a very important one. The Party members have improved themselves a great deal since their education began.

"In the past some of them made mistakes, it's true. But we have to draw a distinction between mistakes that were their own and mistakes that were the responsibility of the higher ranks of the Party. For example, some middle peasants were wrongly struggled against. But we can't lay the blame on the Party cadres of Ten Mile Inn. It wasn't till January this year that we received the document with the definitions of the different classes.

"On the other hand, the Party members are responsible for their own bad work style, their mistreatment of the people, their immorality, and so on. But even when the wrongdoing is their own, we must make clear what sort of mistake is serious and what is not."

Here Leng Bing announced the punishments that had been decided on at the recent branch meeting.

Then he said, "In order to promote better relations between the Party and the masses, the Party members are urged to fulfill their pledge to be better laborers for the people.

"So from now on, we'll take note of the concrete actions of the Party members. We expect them to play an active role in production. They should be models in helping the people and in uniting the whole village. At the same time, they should be humble in their dealings with the masses.

"On the other hand, the masses should understand that while the Party members have admitted their mistakes and promised to be good laborers for the people, it is still their duty as Communists to play the part of leaders. It is the responsibility of the Communists to help the masses prosper. Everyone in the village should understand that the Communist Party itself is good and that it works for the good of the people.

"Don't think that the Party members are figures of mystery holding secret meetings. They hold meetings because they are members of an organized body. They have decided that the masses will be invited to Party meetings and encouraged to take part in discussions. Every three months the branch will ask the masses to send delegates to its meetings to make criticisms and suggestions. In that way the masses will continue helping the Party as they have been helping it during the period of reorganization and education.

"Some of you who have criticized Party members—especially those of you whose criticisms have not been just—now hesitate to have anything to do with them. I want to make it clear here and now that it doesn't matter whether what you said was true or not. The Party members should take the initiative in establishing close relations with the masses and in forgetting about incorrect criticisms. In the future, we hope, there will be no misunderstanding whatever between the Party members and the masses. As we have already said, there will be no retaliation by the Party members. Revenge is not permitted.

"It is the duty of the village branch to lead the village masses. And our Ten Mile Inn branch did lead the masses in the past; they led the fanshen movement. Nearly all the village cadres were Party members, and on the whole they did their job for the people. In the future they will still give leadership to the village.

"In the past, however, the branch decided everything. From now on, leadership should come through the work of Party members among the masses. Just now the task of the branch is to lead production. In doing this the Party members should first find out the opinions of the masses and report them to the branch. On the basis of the reports, the branch should discuss what measures ought to be taken. Once the branch has made its decisions, it should submit them to the different organizations for consideration.

"For example, Wang Xi-tang, Fu Pei-chang, and Wang Chou-he are Party members, and at the same time they are on the peasant-union committee. So they should submit the opinions of the branch to the peasant union. If the union accepts them, that's all right. But if it doesn't, the branch can't simply give orders to the peasant union or to the village government. It can lead only through the work of Party members.

"It's the same way with the village head. If he were a Party member, he could only convey the opinion of the branch to the village government committee. Under no circumstances could he force its opinions on them.

"So you can see that there's no mystery about the branch or the Party members. Their only task is to do good for the people, to think up measures which will be helpful to them. And all those who are qualified and willing to join the Party are welcome to do so. So the Party members and all the people of the village should draw together, like members of one family. And together they should all speed production to make the household prosper."

With this Leng Bing came to the third of his four points. "Our main task this year is production. And it will remain so next year and the year after that.

"Ten Mile Inn used to be a model village in production, but it did have some weaknesses. For one thing, there wasn't enough freedom about mutual aid. Joining wasn't always entirely voluntary, and once a man had joined a mutual-aid group, sometimes he wasn't able to go out on trade-and-transport when he wished.

"So some people in groups 7 and 8 have been saying, 'What's the use of all this mutual aid? I have everything I want now. I'll be able to get along all right by myself without any mutual aid.' They think they can be like the Eight Fairies in the legend, each crossing the sea with his own method—one by boat, one on a leaf, one on a cloud, and so on.

"I've heard that in other villages there are other types of confusion. Some people thought that if they produced too much they might be taken as 'mound' families and struggled against. So they thought they'd just better go along in the same old way. Some even ate a lot because they were afraid their grain would be taken away from them.

"All this shows that the mistakes made in the past have influenced their ideas. So I want to tell you straight out that all of you should do your best to produce more and make yourselves more prosperous. Mutual aid means more production.

"But mutual aid should be voluntary and reasonable. So I suggest that the thing to do now is to reorganize the mutual-aid groups and make sure that they are on a strictly voluntary basis. The old mutual-aid group heads should help the members of the different groups to organize meetings to look into the way things were done in the past, to see what was right and what was wrong. Then the members should be asked their opinions about joining up again. After examining and discussing the past, the members will come to see the advantages of mutual aid. Probably they'll want either to remain in the same group or to organize other groups. If a few individuals prefer to work by themselves in the future, that's all right. Even if one or two of the groups don't want to go on as groups, that's all right too. But generally speaking, it's much better if all the existing groups continue.

"Now I come to my fourth and last point—democracy. Ten Mile Inn has made progress through the reorganization of the ranks of the Party and through the adjustment movement. And this has all been achieved through democracy.

"But we need to remember that democracy must be based on truth, on facts. And democracy demands leadership. Now, the new cadres find it rather difficult to manage things in the village. They aren't bold enough in shouldering responsibility. I want to suggest that they should tackle things boldly, as long as they do so in accordance with the opinions of the majority of the people.

"The minority of the people should bow to the opinions of the majority. This doesn't mean that a single person should be deprived of the right to have his say. But he should not put forward his own opinion as if it were that of the whole village. He should have his say, and then he should abide by the decision of the majority. The village leaders should take into account the opinion of the majority. Under no circumstances should they insult the masses or act in any other improper way toward them.

"In making decisions, on the one hand we must see whether the views expressed are those of the minority or of the majority. On the other hand we must see whether they are right and whether they have long-range benefit. Besides this we must carry out directives from above. If the masses don't agree with a directive, the cadres should educate the masses and convince them. That is leadership. But if the directive really doesn't suit local conditions, the higher levels can be asked to modify it.

"Leadership does not consist of ordering people around. On the other hand, it doesn't mean that there should be anarchy. I've heard that in some villages the new cadres have a hard time getting people to come to meetings. They complain that they have to beat the gong until it almost breaks and then wear their legs to the bone trying to round people up. I'd like to suggest that whenever a meeting is called, those who are supposed to should attend, but that meetings should not be held when everyone is busy.

"All the people of the village should uphold the truth and not cling to prejudices. The people of Ten Mile Inn, as far as my experience goes, do stand up for the truth. They want to increase production and prosper. And I hope that the new cadres and the Party members will lead the people toward this goal.

(*left*) Members of the work team leaving Ten Mile Inn (Leng Bing, Lou Lin).

Wu Fang and He Yan-ling leaving the village.

"The village leadership should have drive; it should not tail along behind the masses. It should distinguish between what is right and what is not.

"So far as I can see, the problem in Ten Mile Inn today is not whether the masses want to be led or not, but how the new cadres and Party members are to lead. Leadership must not be relaxed; the cadres with ability and experience should help those who are new.

"Now, who should lead and who should be led? Wang Xi-tang, for example, is a Party member, and inside the Party he should follow the leadership of his group leader and of the branch secretary, Wang Shao-zhen. But when Wang Shao-zhen is invited to attend the meetings of the peasant-union committee, he should listen to the chairman of that committee, Wang Xi-tang.

"It all boils down to this: there must be both democracy and leadership. The one involves the other, and we can't get along unless we have both of them. And the leaders should neither abuse the people nor trail along behind them."

And it was on this note that the meeting ended.

# —32—

# The Team Returns to Review Its Work

May 28—

Living and working in the villages of the county's ninth district, the members of all the work teams developed close relations with the peasants which did not end when the teams left one village for another. Of course, the teams had little leisure for social life which was not directly connected with the campaign, but they ran into their peasant friends on the paths and highways and at fairs and markets. If some pressing problem arose in a village after the team members had left it, the peasants went in ones or twos to seek them out at the newspaper office in West Harmony.

When the campaign had been completed in most of the district's villages, the Central Bureau work teams held a meeting to review the results. They concluded that despite considerable progress, the new cadres in the villages were not providing firm leadership. They also decided that it was the way the work teams themselves had led the campaign which was partly responsible.

To try and correct the situation, the Central Bureau teams divided into small groups, composed of about three people, that returned to each village for four or five days. Their assignment was to assess the campaign and work with the villagers to overcome its defects.

The group sent to Ten Mile Inn consisted of the team leader Lou Lin, the woman team member Wu Fang, and her husband Li Yuan, who had previously worked with another team. They arrived in Ten Mile Inn on the afternoon of May 28, 1948, a little more than six weeks after the end of the campaign. As they made their way through the east gate of the Fort and down to the lower village, they were greeted with pleasure and surprise. Of course, one or two of the villagers began to spread the current Guomindang-inspired rumor that the campaign had not been satisfactory and was to be carried out all over again.

The rumor was soon scotched by a good deal of friendly bantering, during which the real purpose of the review was explained. After the review team had found quarters in the east-central section, they launched a series of meetings, large and small, formal and informal, with various combinations of cadres, committee members, and Party members.

The team soon learned about the things that had gone amiss since they left. The local diviner had set up business again, going into trances to discover when this or that soldier would be coming back from the front, or to protect the ripening wheat from hail. Peddlers were secretly selling incense and circulating rumors that the old ruined temple to the god of medicine at Yetao was to be restored. Gambling was going on in the north end under the noses of the village head Zhao Zhen-fang and the league chairman Li Bao-yu.

The cadres knew about these things but were doing nothing to prevent them. "Of course I realize that divining is a lot of superstition," said the village vice-head Wang Wen-sheng. "I've told my woman not to go."

"What have you said to the other women?" asked Lou Lin.

Wang Wen-sheng smiled with embarrassment. "The fact is, I haven't really spoken to them about it. I don't want to be accused of meddling in other people's affairs."

It was the same with the branch secretary Wang Shao-zhen. "I know it's wrong to be superstitious," he said. "And I argue, 'If the gods can strike me sick right now, then I'll believe in them.' But apart from that, I do nothing. I'm afraid people will get their own back if I interfere, the way some of them did during the Party education."

Cadres and committee members, Party and non-Party members alike, were all so supersensitive to public opinion, so afraid of being branded as authoritarian, that they were surrendering their leadership. One dissenting voice at a meeting was enough to hold up a decision indefinitely.

Zhao Zhen-fang said, "When my mutual-aid group was electing its leaders, the meeting went on into the night without reaching any decision. So in the end I suggested a couple of people for the job. But then some of the masses started murmuring, 'The cadres are trying to boss us again.' " In fact, only two people out of the eighty at the meeting had objected, but Zhao Zhen-fang chose to consider their grumbling an expression of mass opinion.

The cadres' passivity was related to another problem—the lack of an efficient division of labor among the members of the village government. Zhao Zhen-fang did every little routine job himself because he dared not give orders. Meanwhile other cadres asked for assistance but were unable to get it.

"Everyone comes to me with his problems, even the schoolteachers," complained the finance member Li Bao-en. "And all the storage business has been handed over to me too. Yet when the district asked our village to fill out some forms, I couldn't do it and went to Wang Fu-xin for help. But he said that he was only the village clerk, and it wasn't his business. Then I went to the finance clerk, and he said his job was to write receipts, not to fill out statistical forms for me. Although there are eight in my family, most of them are young children and we're shorthanded, especially since my eldest son joined the army. So with me being called here, there, and everywhere on village affairs, I've had to leave my hillside land unplanted. The way I feel now, I'd like to quit the job."

As the local Party members told the team, the trouble was that the village had democracy but no centralism. Unfortunately, telling the team was one thing; telling the villagers was another.

"The Party members who are ex-cadres don't lead anything anymore," said the branch secretary Wang Shao-zhen. He added with a wry smile, "And I'm one of them. If we're elected to do a job, we do it even though others shirk responsibility. And when people see us taking on thankless jobs, they say, 'The Party members really have guts. They're all right after all.'

"But except for that, we just don't know how to go about things any more. For example, I was called to attend a meeting of the village government. Since we hadn't discussed the issues in the branch beforehand, I didn't feel like saying anything. All I could have done would have been to offer my personal opinion."

In the past the Party members had not only discussed things beforehand, but forced their decisions on the people. Although the campaign had taught them that this was wrong, they had not devised a new way of working. "The trouble is," said Wang Shao-zhen, "that before, when the Party members were not publicly known, we had too much centralism. Now we have too much democracy. We're afraid of being domineering, so we've become passive."

The Party members also felt that the masses no longer respected them. In this they were mistaken; those militants who liked to make sarcastic remarks about the Party members had little support in the village. The new cadres in particular valued the past achievements of the Communists. Their complaint was that the Party members did not offer them enough guidance.

The village vice-head Wang Wen-sheng said, "The new cadres think they'd be able to plan things all right if they had closer contact with the Party members."

"During the education of the Party we were swamped by complaints," said the Communist Li Bao-en. "Yet we had worked hard for the people. I think the best thing is for the people themselves to take office for a while, and see what it's like."

The other branch members nodded in agreement, saying, "He has felt the pulse of us all."

Lou Lin and the other team members could see that they themselves had substantial responsibility for the village Party members' attitude. During the campaign they had been too fearful of pouring cold water on the masses, they had failed to shake off all influence of the poor-peasant line, and they had followed the general tendency to overestimate the impurity of the Party. Thus they had swung away from the Party's main line, partly because they had not conquered the propensity of the petty bourgeois class to be quicker to spot people's faults than their virtues. Though they had pointed out the village Communists' merits in leading the fight against Japan and against feudalism, the discussion of these virtues had been abstract compared with the team's vivid criticisms of the Party members' shortcomings.

First the members of the branch had been subjected to a period of education behind closed doors; then they had been publicly criticized —unjustly, in many cases—without being allowed to make any reply. After that they had confessed their misdeeds to the masses. Only in the last stage of the process had they been authorized to humbly refute false charges. During all this time they had been mostly isolated from the mainstream of the adjustment campaign.

Later the village Communists had been urged to play an active part in the adjustment as a means of redeeming themselves. But taking part in the adjustment, however actively, was one thing; leading it was another. And the real duty of the Communists was to lead.

Together the review team and the Party branch concluded that the campaign to extend democracy had gone to an extreme and produced ultrademocracy. What was wanted now was a means by which the branch could submit ideas to the people and have them discussed, improved upon, and implemented, if the majority agreed. In other words, centralized democracy was needed not only in the Party branch but in every organization of the village. It was the Party branch, however, which had to set an example of democratic centralism and help the other organizations to master it.

# —33—

# Preparing for the Future

"The headquarters of the Sixth Military District of Taihang is organizing a guard unit. The ninth district of Wu An is asked to mobilize five men for it. One of these men should be from Ten Mile Inn."

When this announcement reached the village, there was a hot discussion about how the new soldier should be recruited. The suggestion of the village head Zhao Zheng-fang was, "Let's just call a meeting tomorrow morning and elect someone."

The others laughed. "What! Elect a volunteer?"

Zhao sheepishly withdrew his proposal. The fact that the village cadres and Communists laughed this ultrademocratic notion down showed that the review team's discussions with them had borne fruit.

The next lesson in democracy was provided by an election campaign for the district people's congress. This congress would deal with such matters as the fairer allocation of taxes and rear service, the expansion of production, and the election of new district cadres. Ultrademocracy too would be one of the principal topics.

In Ten Mile Inn the candidates and the congressional agenda were first discussed in the village sections and then taken up at a village assembly, which also elected the delegates to the congress. Every stage of this election campaign was related to the existence of ultrademocracy in Ten Mile Inn. The need for being simple and honest was given less attention than it had been during the election of village cadres, and more emphasis was put on the candidates' resourcefulness and ability to serve the people. At the same time it was made clear that gambling, superstition, theft, laxity in attending meetings, and other such characteristics that harmed public well-being were not suitable in a candidate.

The problem of ultrademocracy was brought into the open and discussed throughout the village, and measures were proposed to eliminate it. Some of them showed the influence of feudalism, as when one old peasant suggested, "Let's paint spectacles on the faces of those who are caught gambling, and parade them through the streets." In his mind, spectacles were a mark of the landlord. Similar punishments proposed for other misdemeanors included forcing people to parade through the streets belled and reined like animals.

This time the Party members made a special effort to lead the people, and it was the branch secretary Wang Shao-zhen who formulated the proposals that were finally accepted. The first offense would rate a talking-to by one or more of the village leaders; the second offense would result in public criticism at a village meeting; the third would entail expulsion from the poor-peasant league or the peasant union; the fourth would be referred to the district government for punishment.

While the votes were being counted in the election, Wang Xi-tang make a speech in which he too stressed the need for an enlightened approach.

"In the village of Guzhen down the valley, someone caught a pilferer and started beating him. But the thief said, 'It's not right for you to beat me,' and the people agreed and said that he should be educated, not beaten. It's the same with us here in Ten Mile Inn. In discussing what should be done about the diviner, some of the people said by way of a joke, 'We can collect some scorpions up on the hill at the back of the Fort and put them inside her pants. Then if she doesn't wriggle her rump, we'll know she really has some power.' Others have been saying that those who undermine democracy, as she does, should be tied up and beaten.

"In a way, these ideas show that the consciousness of the people has been raised and that they don't like superstition and want to stop it. But we should do things in the proper way. We can invite the diviner to a village meeting, so that she can tell everyone publicly about these gods and ghosts that she's always talking about to the women in secret. And she can explain what they do and how they do it. Then we can reason with her; we can educate her and all the people who listen to her.

"If we asked people whether they wanted her to go into a trance, and if the majority agreed, then of course the democratic thing to do would be to let her go into a trance. But the fact is that very few people believe in her."

The discussion was carried further by the team member Li Yuan. "Some people have been blaming all our recent troubles on democracy," he said. "But it's not democracy that's at fault; it's the abuse of democracy." He explained the rights of individuals to express their opinions, and their duty to abide by majority decisions.

"There has been some misunderstanding," Li said, "about the education of the Party members and the reorganization of the Party ranks. Some people seem to think, 'In the past we struggled against the landlords, and now the Party members are going to get it.' But everything achieved in our Liberated Areas has been done under the leadership of our Communist Party headed by Chairman Mao. It's the same in this village. If it hadn't been for the Party we'd never have got rid of the Guomindang and the Japanese. And without the Party we'd never have had the Agrarian Law. It could never have been put into effect without the earlier land-reform campaigns. And who led those campaigns in Ten Mile Inn? The village Party branch!

"True, our Ten Mile Inn branch has made some mistakes. There have been some weaknesses in its working style. So it fulfilled only 80 percent of its duty instead of 100 percent. That means we have to do away with its weaknesses—but not with its leadership. That's why we had the education and reorganization—to put an end to bad working style and to produce better leadership.

"But the work team left the village in a hurry and didn't hand things over properly, so that both the Party members and the masses were confused. Now we want to make things clear: the Party branch led in the past, and it will lead in the future.

"When the village organizations discuss things and make decisions, they should take the Party branch's opinion into account. And if you think the Party's opinions are right, you should follow them. If you think they're not, you should discuss them with the branch. If necessary, the branch will refer them back to a higher level so that they can be changed or modified to suit our needs.

"Without the Party, we should never have been able to destroy feudalism. We should never have been able to fanshen. So in these next few days we want to help you strengthen the Party branch by recruiting new members into it."

Later at a meeting of the village cadres, Lou Lin said, "Every day the Communist Party is extending its leadership over more and more of the country. Soon it will lead the whole of China, and this means that we need more Party members. The more members there are, the more people there will be serving the masses as long-term laborers.

"But no one takes on new laborers at random. So the Party branch is seeking the help of the masses in recruiting new members. It has asked the poor-peasant league to recommend people whom it considers suitable."

Recruiting new Party members was something new to Ten Mile Inn. In the past when all or most of the Communists had to work underground, such a method would have been out of the question.

"Chairman Mao loves the working people," said the branch secretary Wang Shao-zhen at a meeting of the poor-peasant league, "and the Communist Party is the party of the working people. That's why we're asking your help.

"The people you suggest will be like unfired bricks. We'll go over your recommendations in the branch and see which of them are qualified to become Party members."

The review team members explained that Communists must be not only upright, honest, and painstaking, but also active. "In one village the people thought that being a good Communist was exactly the same as being a good fellow," Lou Lin said. "They recommended a certain man who got along well with practically everyone in the village. But he had also gotten along well with the Old Moneybags. If the Party branch had been composed of people like that, feudalism would never have been destroyed. Such men may be good members of the masses, but that doesn't mean that they are good Communists. A Party member is of one heart with the masses, not with the landlords. He upholds what is right and opposes what is wrong and is not afraid of offending others.

"A Party member should not only do these things himself, but get other people to do them. He should try to grasp what's in the heart of the people and plan for them.

"When this sort of man is discovered and becomes a Party member, then the people have found a good laborer."

After long discussion, the league recommended more than forty people—men and women, poor peasants, new middle peasants, and old middle peasants. As the Party branch had made clear, individuals were also free to apply for membership whether or not they were recommended by the league. In the end there were forty-seven names to be considered by the branch.

When it came to deciding who was and was not fit to be accepted into the Party, the Communists were strict. To belong to the Party which had led a hundred million peasants to fanshen was not something to be taken lightly, and the branch rejected some two-thirds of the names as unsuitable. Some were ruled out because they were selfish and could not be counted on to serve the people wholeheartedly, others because they were inclined to do favors for personal friends and seek revenge against personal enemies. But still more were rejected because of their passivity—their unwillingness to struggle for what was right when it might involve them in unpleasantness with their fellows.

Even the people who passed the branch's scrutiny were not immediately accepted. Lou Lin cautioned the Communists against lowering the high standards for membership in the Party. And he warned against taking in more new members at one time than could be absorbed and educated.

A great many of the villagers felt that in leading the people's struggle and then being subjected to the people's criticism, the Communists had borne something which few could endure. It was to be expected that some candidates might possess all the qualifications but one—the courage to be a Communist. So it was arranged that the people who seemed to be generally acceptable should be sounded out in personal talks by the members of the branch who knew them best. When this had been done, only eight of the original forty-seven remained.

One of the eight was Li Bao-yu, who had done good work and shown his ability to lead. Another had played a leading role in organizing the transport of government grain to the front. Two had at one time been wrongly branded as secret agents but had now been cleared. One was a woman, and in her case too the Communists showed that they had a broader vision than other villagers. For they regarded the facts that she was something of a gossip and had in the past been "immoral" as less important than her proved ability in arousing and organizing the women. The popular village clerk Wang Fu-xin, who had long been regarded as a potential Party member, was included on the list. So were the head and vice-head of the village, Zhao Zhen-fang and Wang Wen-sheng. Both admittedly had their faults, but the branch decided that these shortcomings could be overcome step by step as specific incidents arose.

In the case of Li Bao-yu there was prolonged discussion. Everyone agreed that he had ability and did an efficient job as chairman of the poor-peasant league, but Wang Xi-tang said, "We must do our duty to the Party and be objective. If a man's qualified, no matter who he is, we should ask him to join; if he's not, we shouldn't. Li Bao-yu does his work well, and he has the ability to lead. But he's guilty of favoritism. He should never have agreed to give Fu Gao-shen a share of the fruits. And he knew that there was gambling going on in the north end, but he did nothing to stop it because he didn't want to stir up any trouble with his neighbors. So I think he should correct his mistakes before he's admitted to the Party."

Wang Shao-zhen agreed that Li Bao-yu had his faults. "But," he said, "we must consider the over-all interests of the masses and the Party. Is it better to educate him inside the Party, or outside of it? I think we should admit him and, if necessary, gave him a longer probation period than the others."

Wang Xi-tang was dissatisfied with this proposal, and Lou Lin finally took a hand. Speaking not only as a team member but also as a Com-

munist at a Communist Party meeting, he supported the view that
Li Bao-yu should be admitted. He added some new points in Li's
favor:

"Li Bao-yu, like Wang Wen-sheng, has applied of his own accord
to become a member of the Party. This shows that his political consciousness is higher in some ways than that of others who have not
applied. Neither he nor Wang Wen-sheng has done anything seriously
wrong, and both can be more rapidly educated inside the Party than
out of it. Also it will be a great help to the work of the village to have
them as Party members."

In the end Wang Xi-tang was convinced, and the branch unanimously agreed that Li Bao-yu should be one of the group that was
invited to join the Party.

To induct the new members, the Party branch borrowed a former
landlord's courtyard. The same kerosene lamp which had lighted many
eventful meetings during the adjustment campaign was now hung on
a bough of a flowering locust tree. A Party flag with a gold hammer
and sickle against a red background was draped at the back of the
porch that served as a speaker's platform. A portrait of Mao was
tacked to the door. Besides the members of the branch and those
about to join it, the committees of the poor-peasant league, the peasant
union, and the village government, together with the people's congress
representatives, were present at the ceremony.

"When we took in new members in the past," Wang Shao-zhen told
them, "it wasn't such a solemn occasion. This is the first time that so
many new members have been accepted at one time, that so many
guests have been present, and so solemn a ceremony has been held.
This is the happiest occasion we have ever had."

Lou Lin agreed. "Welcoming new members into the Party is like
welcoming a new bride into the family or celebrating the birth of a
child," he said. "The people received fruits during the adjustment
campaign, and now the Party branch is receiving its fruits in the form
of these eight new members."

Lou Lin thanked the poor-peasant league for its recommendations
and asked, "Why is it that out of more than forty you recommended,
only eight were chosen?

"All the people you proposed are outstanding members of the
masses, but this is the first time that members have been recruited in
this fashion and we want to start with those who are most highly
qualified. The people who have not been invited to join this time will
continue to make progress, and they'll have another chance to join.

"The Party members themselves should also make steady progress,
correcting whatever faults are pointed out by the people. The Party

and the masses should help each other to advance. They should tie themselves together in a firm knot, like members of the same family."

After Lou Lin's speech, the new members and their sponsors were called on, one by one. The village clerk Wang Fu-xin, when asked to comment on his qualifications and his reasons for joining the Party, said, "I can't tell what my good points may be. I only feel sorry for not having given the people better service in the past. I used to be impatient when people came to me to do things for them, but from now on I'll serve them well.

"My motive in joining the Party is to do away with the feudal system and help the peasants and workers fanshen."

"Wang Fu-xin has a good attitude, and he has served the masses well," said his sponsor. "His shortcoming is that he doesn't like to point out people's mistakes, because he's afraid of offending them."

Speaking soberly and honestly, the other new members had their say. Li Bao-xi, the only old middle peasant among them, seemed especially moved. Li Yun-fen, the only woman, modestly relied on her sponsor to describe her ability both to get along with others and to lead them.

The village head Zhao Zhen-fang hesitated for a moment when his turn came. Then he said, "The Party loves and serves the poor, and I too want to serve them. I have a love of the Party in my heart. I am happy to join."

Wang Wen-sheng was last. "If it weren't for the Communist Party, which loves the masses, we poor people would never have been able to run the house. We could never have fanshenned. So I am happy from the bottom of my heart to join the Party."

When all of the members had spoken, they took the oath to the Party. Standing at the front of the crowd under the locust tree, they faced the red flag and the portrait of Mao Ze-dong. Zhao Zhen-fang and Wang Wen-sheng towered above Li Yun-fen, who stood at the end of the row on her tiny bound feet. Following the example of Wang Shao-zhen, they raised their right hands in the clenched-fist Communist salute. As he solemnly and haltingly read the oath phrase by phrase, they solemnly and haltingly repeated it:

"I wish to join the Chinese Communist Party, to render service to the people. I am willing to abide by the Party's constitution, to carry out its program, to pay monthly dues, to accept the leadership of the Party, to obey its rules, and to maintain its security. I shall not fear difficulty or sacrifice, but shall struggle to the end for the realization of Communism. If I should act against this oath, I am willing to submit to the discipline of the Party."

"Now we have eight new Communists," said the branch secretary Wang Shao-zhen. "We old and new Party members should unite with each other and with the masses. We should serve and lead them toward the final victory that is drawing near, when the people of the whole country will fanshen."

## About the Authors

David Crook was born in London and educated at Cheltenham College, England, and Columbia University. He fought in the British Battalion of the International Brigade during the Spanish Civil War, and first went to China in 1938 to teach. After serving with the Royal Air Force in the Far East in World War II, he studied Chinese at the School of Oriental and African Studies of the University of London.

Isabel Crook was born and raised in Chengtu, China, the daughter of Canadian missionaries. She received her B.A. and M.A. in psychology from the University of Toronto, and upon graduation returned to West China and Tibet to do extensive anthropological field work. During World War II she worked in a munitions factory in England and subsequently joined the Canadian army.

The Crooks both went to the Liberated Areas in 1947 to study land reform. They entered Peking in 1949 as staff members of the Foreign Languages training class. This training class eventually became the Foreign Languages Institute, where the Crooks now teach.